M000274312

Facing Up to Real Doctrinal Difference

How Some Thought-Motifs from Derrida Can *Nourish* The Catholic-Buddhist Encounter

"Robert Magliola demonstrates a well-rounded understanding of the three main Buddhist traditions—Theravada, Mahayana, and Vajrayana—contextualized within an encounter of the Buddhist-Christian theological dialogue. This scholarly study provides a valuable contribution to the growing interest not only in the concept of diversity-versus-commonness of Buddhism, but also helps both the layperson and the scholar to better understand the religions having the two largest monastic bases in the world."

—**Ven. Dr. Dhammadipa Sak (Fa Yao)**, abbot of Chuang Yen Monastery, Carmel, NY, and the Temple of Enlightenment, NYC, NY; Ph.D., dept. of theology and religious studies, University of Bristol, UK

"Participants in interreligious dialogue between Christianity and Buddhism often proceed from the assumption that to achieve mutual understanding they must dilute their differences and postulate a unifying truth that can comfortably accommodate the discrepancies between these two great spiritual traditions. In this book, Robert Magliola, a practicing Catholic who has long lived in Asia and practiced meditation with Asian Buddhists, takes a very different approach, one that does not try to gloss over doctrinal friction. While remaining faithful to the teachings of the Catholic Church and reliable in his accounts of Buddhist doctrine, he attempts to show how mutual respect, appreciation, and even love can coexist with honest, frank, and clear recognition of the real substantive differences between Buddhism and Christianity regarding the premises and prospects of human salvation."

—**Ven. Bhikkhu Bodhi**, Buddhist monk, scholar, and translator from the Pali canon (BPS, Wisdom P., etc.); president, Buddhist Publication Society (1988–2010); founding chair, Buddhist Global Relief

"Robert Magliola's book represents a substantial achievement. Magliola successfully employs Derrida to help Catholics to understand Buddhists, to learn deeply from them, and all the time without denying deep differences. . . . Magliola is wisely learned and writes with spiritual discernment and experience that profoundly illuminates his project. This is a significant contribution to Christian-Buddhist dialogue as well as interfaith studies more generally."

—**Dr. Gavin D'Costa**, professor of Catholic theology, University of

Bristol, UK; advisor to the Roman Catholic Church in England and Wales; visiting professor at Gregorian University (1998); widely published specialist in systematic theology, theology of religions, and aspects of philosophical theology related to religious pluralism.

"Robert Magliola defends Vatican II, and the Magisterium since then, that have opened the door, with cautions, to this kind of dialogical encounter with its similarities and differences. Magliola's examples from his own work in dialogue and joint practice in Asia demonstrate how the journey through this door into the frontier of difference, to which Pope Francis is calling the Church today, can edify Catholics in underdeveloped aspects of their own faith life."

—**Dr. Donald W. Mitchell**, professor of philosophy emeritus (Asian Philosophy), Purdue University; consultant to the USCCB (interfaith relations); editor, *Claritas* (Focolare International); advisory board, *Dilatato Corde* (DIM/MID); Board of Editors, *Buddhist-Christian Studies*; author of *Buddhism: Introducing the Buddhist Experience*

"This book will be a key tool in grassroots Buddhist-Christian relations. The use of Derrida may be unfamiliar to most but his thoughts mixed with those of Robert Magliola offer an insight into the spiritual bonds that can overcome mistrust, anxiety and fear of the other. As more and more Christians encounter Buddhists and vice versa such instruments as this book will become keenly valuable."

—**Rev. James Loughran**, S.A., director, Graymoor Ecumenical and Interreligious Institute (NY); editor, *Ecumenical Trends*; faculty, Centro Pro Unione summer course (Rome, Italy)

"This book is a serious-minded attempt, well-secured and deep-reaching, to open up new paths for Christian theological thought and [also] for 'dialogic meditation'. It offers a new and at-the-essence approach to the dialogue between Buddhism and theological Christianity, based not on symmetry but on asymmetry, not on samenesses but on 'founding and irreducible' differences between the two systems. Methodologically rigorous, and linked to authoritative sources of Sacred Scripture and Tradition, this work—without obfuscating anything—occupies the Catholic 'orthodox' space on the interreligious terrain."

—**Fra Matteo Nicolini-Zani**, Catholic monk of the monastic community of Bose, Magnano, Italy; Sinologist; author; coordinator of the Italian commission of the Monastic Interreligious Dialogue (DIM/MID); member of the board of directors of DIM/MID

"The renowned deconstructionist philosopher Jacques Derrida may be a *bête-noire* for many Catholic theologians. However, Buddhist scholar and Catholic theologian Robert Magliola makes the surprising yet convincing claim that an adaptation of some of Derrida's strategies makes it possible for Christians to affirm the positive role of other—in this case, Buddhist—spiritual practices and teachings in God's plan of salvation while fully espousing their faith in Jesus Christ as the universal Savior. This enlightening book will be an immensely valuable resource for those who recognize the spiritual wisdom of other religious traditions and want to understand how it is possible to avail themselves of those riches without bracketing or abandoning their Christian commitment."

—**Rev. William Skudlarek**, O.S.B., St. John's abbey (USA.) and presently at its priory in Japan, Trinity Benedictine abbey, Fujimi; *consultore*, Pontifical council for interreligious dialogue (Vatican); secretary general, Monastic Interreligious Dialogue (Rome); associate editor, *Dilatato Corde*

PRAISE FOR PREVIOUS BOOKS

From **Jacques Derrida**'s letter of Juiy 6, 1997, to Robert Magliola, regarding Magliola's book *On Deconstructing Life-Worlds* (1997):

"What a magnificent book! . . . Your profundity, your boldness, and your independence amaze and impress me."

For Magliola's *Derrida on the Mend* (1984):

"The reader will find, as I do, this enterprise not only original and bold, but plausible and extraordinarily illuminating."

—**Paul Ricoeur**, professor of philosophy, University of Paris; distinguished professor of philosophy and theology, University of Chicago

"A brilliant and dynamic cross-cultural analysis. In the section on Madhyamika Buddhism he has drawn from a range of Buddhist scholarship to translate with remarkable clarity the spirit of devoidness as articulated by the Indian Buddhist Nagarjuna."

—**Frederick J. Streng**, professor of the history of religions (Oriental/ Occidental), graduate center for religious studies, Southern Methodist University; Buddhologist; translator of Nagarjuna's *Mūlamadhyamaka-kārikā*

Robert Magliola

FACING UP
TO REAL DOCTRINAL
DIFFERENCE

How Some Thought-Motifs
From Derrida Can *Nourish*
The Catholic-Buddhist
Encounter

Angelico Press

First published
by Angelico Press, 2014
© Robert Magliola, 2014

For information, address:
Angelico Press
4709 Briar Knoll Dr.
Kettering, OH 45429
angelicopress.com

pb 978-1-62138-079-5
cloth 978-1-62138-080-1
ebook 978-1-62138-081-8

Cover design: Michael Schrauzer

Dedication

—To Our Lady of Mount Carmel, my dear Patroness, in the reflection of whose eyes I adore her Son whom she eternally contemplates.

—To Fr. William Skudlarek, OSB, *beatus vir* whom St. Algulfo of Lérins sent to help me. Without Fr. William's encouragement and example, "instant in season, out of season" (2 Tm 4:2), this work would not have come to completion.

****

—To the beloved Buddhist monastics in Taiwan, Thailand, Great Britain, Italy, and the United States who have taught me and abundantly edified me; and to Buddhists everywhere.

—To my fellow Catholics, to all Christians, and to people of good will everywhere.

—To His Eminence Jean-Louis Cardinal Tauran, president of the Pontifical Council for Interreligious Dialogue, who, with openness and acumen, animates the Church's encounter with Buddhism and the other religions in today's troubled world.

—To His Eminence Gianfranco Cardinal Ravasi, president of the Pontifical Council for Culture, who has dialogued with many a secular deconstructionist over the course of the years, and who—through the Church's new "Courtyard of the Gentiles"—animates the Church's encounter with the nonreligious in today's troubled world.

CONTENTS

Acknowledgments (Academic)

(The originals for all references and data supplied below are in dossier and can be confirmed; full documentation and corroborating contact information are available upon request)

—I thank Rev. James Loughran, SA, director of the Graymoor Ecumenical and Interreligious Institute, New York City, for examining and evaluating my exposition of Roman Catholic theology in this text and concluding that "the Catholic theology in your manuscript is excellent and precise. Your reliance on the various levels of magisterial teaching and instruments of the Catholic Church is to be commended."

—I thank Prof. Justin T. McDaniel, Buddhologist at the University of Pennsylvania, for reviewing my exposition of Buddhism in this text. He wrote to me that my exposition of Buddhism was "well-written and clear," that my project was "intriguing," and that he "really enjoyed it." He had only two objections to my exposition, the first regarding differences between the widespread practical uses of Buddhist chant and Buddhism's doctrinal declarations about chant's "ultimate" purpose; and the second regarding my deployment of the word "normative" in a Buddhist context, since the term can take on different senses dependent upon the academic sub-specialty being applied. In the present text, I have changed the pertaining content accordingly. Moreover, I have added notes explaining both Prof. McDaniel's original objections and how the relevant passages have been corrected.

—I thank Ven. Dr. Dhammadipa (Fa Yao), PhD in Theology and Religious Studies, University of Bristol, UK; Abbot of Chuang Yen Monastery and of the Temple of Enlightenment, New York, for reviewing and approving the expositions of Buddhism in this text. He was so kind as to advise me to amend two points regarding the rebirth of a "Stream Enterer" and of a "Once Returner," and to add one note regarding the "Realm of the Gods." I have made these changes accordingly, and they appear in the present text.

—I thank Ven. Bhikkhu Bodhi (former president of the Buddhist Publication Society, Sri Lanka; scholar and voluminous translator into English from the Pali Canon [BPS, Wisdom Press, etc.]; and founding chair of Buddhist Global Relief) for reviewing and approving the expositions of Buddhism in my Book-manuscript. He was so kind as to advise me, furthermore, of one doctrinal provision that I have added, now, in the present text.

—My deep gratitude to Dr. Donald W. Mitchell (Buddhologist and Catholic dialogist; consultant to the US Conference of Catholic Bishops; professor emeritus of Asian philosophy at Purdue University; and a founding father of Focolare in the United States), who has kindly reviewed the Buddhology, theology, and philosophy of my manuscript and—having read all of it—has heartily recommended its publication.

—My deep gratitude to Rev. Anthony J. Kelly, CSsR (professor of theology at Australian Catholic University; *Consultore*, International Theological Commission, Rome; former president of the Australian Catholic Theological Association), and Fra Matteo Nicolini-Zani (Monastery of Bose, Italy; sinologist, author, and coordinator of Monastic Interreligious Dialogue in Italy), who—despite their busy schedules—have reviewed the theological and interreligious components of my manuscript in their entirety and warmly approved of them.

—My deep gratitude to Dr. Gavin D'Costa (professor of Catholic theology, University of Bristol, UK), who has reviewed several sequences of my manuscript dealing with the interface of Derridean thought-motifs and Catholic theology. He has written to me that, while no specialist at all in Derrida, he can affirm from the Catholic side that my deployment of Derridean thought is not detrimental to authentic Catholic theology but, on the contrary, clearly makes a contribution to it.

—My deep gratitude to Rev. Francis X. Clooney, SJ (director of the Center for the Study of World Religions, Harvard University), and Rev. Michael Barnes, SJ (director of the De Nobili [interreligious] Centre, London, and professor at Heythrop College, University of London), for kindly permitting me to consult with them regarding strategy and format, and for their encouragement.

Acknowledgments (Personal)

My gratefulness to Claudia Kovach, my friend in the Faith for more than forty years, and to her dear husband and children: Claudia's unflinching support has helped me mightily toward the Lord down through the years . . . in my desolation and my consolation, in my sad times and my good.

My tribute to my beloved children—Lorinda-marie, elder daughter; Jon-carlo, son; Clara-marie, younger daughter—for their conscientious care; to my beloved grandchildren; and to Tsung-yu, my sacramentally bonded wife: they are flesh of my flesh and bone of my bones.

I memorialize my dear, dear parents, Florinda and Ugo Magliola, immigrants to the United States of America who, thoroughly and purely, emptied themselves out for my sake.

My appreciation goes out to so many others . . .
To name but a few ("What's in a name? . . ."):

In America: My Carmelite brethren; the Franciscan Friars at St. Francis of Assisi Church (New York City); the Ling Jiou Shan Temple/Center (Flushing); Community of Sant'Egidio (New York City); Downtown (Manhattan) Meditation Community (New York City); Executive Committee of the Delta Epsilon Sigma National Catholic Scholastic Honor Society; Chou Fang-yu; Jim Hartz; Hollie Hirst; Fr. Michael Holleran; Tao Jiang; Emmy Kang; Janet Saylor; and Tu Chung-min. (And thanks to my cousin Lorraine for bearing with me.)

In Taiwan: Master Hsin Tao; Dharma Teacher Guang Guo; Kao T'ien-en; Lin Yaofu; Chang Shui-mu; Chang Shuei-may; Huang Ru-ying; Yvette Huang; Liang Sun-chieh; Liao Ping-chun; Tso Yi-hsuan; and Yang Szu-yun.

In the Philippines: Fr. Norberto Castillo, OP, and Bro. Jaime M. Rivera, SJ.

In Japan: [Fr.] Joseph S. O'Leary, my friend: "Like two facing mirrors—in between, no reflection" (*Biyan Lu*).

In Thailand: Ven. Dr. Pithoon Vidhuro; Sr. Mallika Wannachaiwong;

Sr. Sriprai Krathong; Kirti Bunchua; Mano Mettanando Laohavanich; Veerachart Nimanmong; Warayuth Sriwarakuel; and Samusa Nakasingh.

In Italy: Comunità "Vangelo e Zen" (Desio); Fr. Francis V. Tiso; Suore di Santa Elisabetta (Rome); Marcello Ghilardi; and Pierfrancesco Marsiaj.

And of course I offer my sincere and indeed heartfelt thanks to my editor at Angelico Press, John Riess. I am so glad to report that he is to be counted among those precious few editors (and their ranks are rapidly thinning) who are personally very well-read in the academic literature bearing on the topic at hand (namely, Buddhist thought and Catholic thought). Thus working with him has been a particular delight.

Preface

Pope Francis, in his address to the staff of the Pontifical Gregorian University on April 10, 2014, advises that "the theologian who is content with his complete and closed thought is a mediocre 'theologian'. The good theologian and philosopher has an open thought, that is, incomplete, always open to the *maius* [the "more"] of God and of the truth, always developing."[1] Jacques Derrida, though he lived and moved in a life-world at a very distant remove from that of Pope Francis, pointed out again and again that writers *should* know that texts never really "close" and come to a perfect rest within themselves. Though I hope my thought is incomplete in Pope Francis's sense, and I agree—broadly speaking—with Derrida that all texts per se are radically incomplete, this present book, in its intention to focus on its declared project with clarity and thoroughness, necessarily leaves some concomitant but less pertinent concerns (relatively) unattended or "incomplete."

Thus, primary references—the Buddhist and the Catholic scriptures and authoritative statements from the Church's Magisterium and from Buddhist Sages, Masters, and other teachers established and received by the majority ("mainstream") Buddhist traditions[2]—are carefully cited and documented. Important secondary references (encyclopedias/dictionaries/compendia of Buddhism, and of Catholic theology; key works like St. Thomas Aquinas's *Summa*; etc.) are frequently called upon. Tertiary references (books, anthologies, articles, papers, etc.) commenting on primary and secondary sources, and on the Buddhist-Catholic encounter, are cited

---

1. See the ZENIT website: http://www.zenit.org/en/articles/francis-address-to-gregorian-university (translated from the Italian original).

2. In relation to Buddhists, and to Catholics, the problematic of "authoritative statements" is attended with care at several points in this book.

1

carefully but very selectively, because the sheer quantity of these is so massive. (Please permit me to note that some of my website references may be subject to "link rot" after a period of time. To circumvent this, I have tried to cite "permalinks" or DOIs when I could find them; in case of "link rot," I suggest that the reader use the name of the website to find the new URL for the site in question.)

A whole section of this book is devoted to expositions of Buddhist exclusivism and inclusivism and of Catholic inclusivism (the Church's official position at this point). Several sections treat "joint" Buddhist-Catholic meditation sessions. Discussion of tertiary literature involving the wider debate among Buddhists, Christians, and other religionists (on exclusivism, inclusivism, pluralism, and the more recently proposed alternatives) is beyond the scope of this book—any comprehensive treatment would require a book of many volumes, and a selective treatment would deflect this present book from its chosen trajectory.

In the Catholic world, there are, of course, numerous secondary and tertiary theological sources, and many articles/books on the Buddhist-Catholic encounter, that are published in non-English languages—French, German, Italian, and Spanish[3] in particular; most of these works are not available in English translation. Foreign-language sources lacking an English translation are not normally referenced in this book, simply because the majority of this book's readership is expected to be monolingual. I have, however, at several points indicated where the interested reader can pursue such other-than-English-language sources.

Finally, I want here to explain in advance why, early in the Introduction ahead, I append five successive notes that list—perhaps to an extent that may appear unseemly and disproportionate for such a format—some representative work of mine in Buddhist-Catholic relations (publications, conference papers, dialogue experiences, etc.); in Derrida's deconstruction and Buddhist philosophy (publications, lectures, teaching, etc.); in Buddhist studies (publications, lectures, conference papers); in Buddhist meditation (sustained

---

3. I very advisedly put these four languages in strictly *alphabetical* order, here!

meditative training under Buddhist monks and nuns); and in Catholic religious studies, Catholic theology, Western-form discursive meditation, and Catholic *contemplatio* (publications, lectures, teaching, formation in meditation/*contemplatio*). At first blush (*sic*), these five notes may very well seem to compose a laughably ostentatious "mini CV," but in fact they are motivated by quite the opposite scenario. Buddhology, European philosophy (called "Continental philosophy" in American universities), and Catholic theology each defines itself as a highly developed and jealously guarded autonomous discipline: academic Buddhologists, "Continental philosophers," and Catholic theologians—especially in the United States—seldom intercommunicate on a scholarly level and know very little about one another's scholarship. "Professional" interfaith dialogists tend to be much more interdisciplinary, true, but they often identify with Religious Studies and tend to be very cliquish. As for meditative practitioners, be they Buddhist or Catholic, most of them know very little about "Derridean deconstruction" and—along with mainstream Buddhologists and Catholic theologians—hold it worthy of either suspicion or downright disdain. Given this situation, for those readers who do not know of my work, I have sensed myself obliged (and rightly so) to *establish my credentials*, or at least to give a substantial indication of them.

The above-described problematic, that of a qualified interdisciplinarian addressing specialists who ignore or even eschew one another, has imposed upon me, for most of my academic life, a sense of precarious *in-betweenness*. I am very encouraged, though, by the particular phrasing that Cardinal Gianfranco Ravasi chose to use during the course of an interview reported recently on the website of the *Cortile dei Gentili* (the Pontifical Council for Culture's "Courtyard of the Gentiles"[4]). I think his words can conclude this

---

4. The "Courtyard of the Gentiles" was initiated in 2009, at the suggestion of Pope Benedict XVI, as a "space" (in its several senses: geographic sites, the World Wide Web, etc.) where the Church could dialogue, in a spirit of mutual respect, with those who are not religious but affirm the value of encounter with the "other." In the historical Jewish Temple, what came to be called the Courtyard of the Gentiles

preface. He said that he knew "how to *continue* walking across quicksand"—"*io so di continuare a camminare tra le sabbie mobili.*"[5]

---

was the outermost enclosed space, the space where non-Jews were permitted. Non-Jews came to this courtyard for several purposes, one of which was to converse in friendly fashion with learned Jews about the existence and nature of God, and other religious topics. The Church understands itself to be the "wild olive shoot" grafted into the "cultivated olive tree" of the Jews (Rom 11:17, 24). Thus, inspired by the kind of dialogue that took place in the outermost courtyard of the Jewish Temple, the Church's Pontifical Council for Culture intends its dialogue to mirror the friendly atmosphere of the original Courtyard of the Gentiles.

5. See the website www.cortiledeigentili.com > "L'Angolo del Cardinal Ravasi" ["Cardinal Ravasi's Corner"] > article of April 24, 2014 (interview by Antonio Gnoli, reprinted from *La Repubblica*).

Introduction:
Origins and Objectives of This Work

[Ippolito] Desideri[1] was fascinated by that [Buddhist] theoretical construction concerning the contingency of the phenomenal world which he found perfectly acceptable from a Christian viewpoint,[2] just as he was convinced by the Tibetans' inclination for "virtuous works" and such evident devotion that it represented "a reproach to Christians who did not yet do as much for the True God they worshipped" (MITN VI, DR.2, _02); so he could not fail to admire a religion organized according to "the rules of well-ordered reason, . . . to be admired [because] not only does it urge the avoidance of vice, . . . instilling the need for triumph over all passions, but moreover it arouses love and respect for virtue and even more surprisingly, guides Man to a humanly sublime and heroic perfection" (MITN VI, DR.3, 292).
—Enzo G. Bargiacchi, citing passages from the papers of
Fr. Ippolito Desideri, SJ (1684–1733), Jesuit missionary to Tibet[3]

1. Ippolito Desideri was an Italian Jesuit who is considered by many to be the first Western Tibetologist; he studied in the Gelukpa monastery of Sera, became fluent in spoken and written Tibetan, and produced precise accounts of Tibetan geography, flora and fauna, cultural practice, and contemporary political events (during what happened to be a very crucial time in Tibetan political history). He pioneered meaningful interreligious dialogue between Buddhism and Catholicism, and his Tibetan, Latin, and Italian works are now—centuries after his death—publicly available and causing quite an academic stir.

2. Desideri was a highly trained and meticulous theologian. He agreed with Buddhism that the human being is not intrinsically self-founding or autonomous but is *caused* and thus contingent. Needless to say, he disagreed—as a Catholic would—with Buddhism's rejection of a First Cause.

3. Enzo G. Barciacchi, *A Bridge across Two Cultures—Ippolito Desideri, SJ* (1684–1733): *A Brief Biography*, trans. Alisa Wood (Florence, Italy: IGM, 2008), p. 36, accessible online at http://www.ippolito-desideri.net/BioDesideri/Bio.Des.ingl.pdf; Barciacchi's Italian version is likewise accessible, at http://www.ippolito-desideri.net/Bio.Desideri/Sint.Bio.It.bibl.pdf. Following upon Barciacchi's biography came Trent Pomplun's likewise carefully researched *Jesuit on the Roof of the World* (Oxford UP, 2009), a study I highly recommend. Desideri was so impressed by the argumentative skill of Gelukpa scholasticism that he applied all his energy to mastering its logic and then wielding this logic in favor of his own rebuttal. His polemic is sometimes marked by a harshness uncharacteristic of so temperate a man, but

Since the time you came, O White-headed Lama, . . .
from distant regions to noble Lhasa, not only
have you done, with steadfast heart, as much good
as you can in relation to the various peoples, be they
Chinese, Mongol, or Tibetan, . . . but you have done
nothing bad at all, not even to the root of a single hair.
// Since accomplishing so much has caused you many
a hardship, please accept on my part the purest
of prayers. Though we are not familiar with [your]
religion, we grant trust and respect to all religions,
our [religion] and your [religion]; in the past we have
not ever disapproved, nor do we do so now. // Since
you are a good and pure-hearted lama, of great
virtue and guileless ["without trickery or imposture"],
we shall reciprocate [your letters].[4]
—Pho-lha-nas, Regent of the Realm (Tibet), to
Fr. Orazio da Pennabilli, OFMCap. (1680–1745),
Capuchin missionary to Tibet, during this friar's
journeying in Nepal (ca. 1732)[5]

---

this must be understood in historical context: the Capuchins back home, eager for the Church to oust the Jesuits completely from Tibet, were looking for any "evidence" to taint the doctrinal loyalty of the Jesuit missionaries. In fact, Desideri was officially "recalled"—in a missive from Rome that, in 1721, reached him in Lhasa—and the Jesuit devoted the remainder of his days to scholarly endeavor in Rome, where he edited his writings and wrote up accounts of his Asian mission. (Subsequent to my writing of the first half of this monograph, a monumental translation into English of Desideri's long personal account of his Tibetan mission has appeared, and I hasten here to insert the reference: *Mission to Tibet: The Extraordinary Eighteenth-Century Account of Fr. Ippolito Desideri, SJ*, trans. Michael Sweet, ed. Leonard Zwilling [Wisdom Pub., 2010, 832 pp.].)

4. This English rendering of the Regent's official communication is mine, and comes from the Italian translation. Both the original Tibetan and the Italian translation can be found online at http://www.oraziodellapenna.com, at its link entitled "Lettera di Pho-lha-nas a fra' Orazio in occasione di un viaggio in Nepal del 1 settembre 1732." (accessed June 9, 2011). Taking care not to alter the sense and tone of the letter, I have elided several segments of the letter where indicated, for brevity's sake.

5. Orazio Olivieri della Penna was an Italian Capuchin friar who, along with Ippolito Desideri, studied very successfully at the Gelukpa monastery of Sera. Orazio Olivieri too was an indefatigable missionary known for both his holiness and his scholarly brilliance. He produced the first full-fledged Western dictionary

Introduction: Origins and Objectives of This Work

ON THE VATICAN website one can access a very important document from the Pontifical Council for Interreligious Dialogue entitled *Dialogue and Proclamation*.[6] The document declares, "While keeping their identity intact, Christians must be prepared to learn

of the Tibetan language (ca. 33,000 word entries), and translated such classic Tibetan works as the *Skyabs-su-'gro-ba* and Tsongkhapa's *Lam-rim chenmo*. The competition between Jesuits and Capuchins originated in Europe, not the mission fields, and there is no reason to think that Olivieri and Desideri were unsupportive of each other during the relatively short time they both were in Tibet. The Jesuit left Tibet in 1721, and after that the Capuchin friar, with his confreres, stayed on—aside from a return trip to Rome and back—until 1745. In terms of academic scholarship, the Capuchin friar made his mark primarily as a linguist and translator, and the Jesuit made his as a theologian, dialogist, and (proto-) cultural anthropologist. When the Capuchins began to make Tibetan converts, the Buddhist monastic establishment felt threatened, and the converts were publicly flogged. The situation became intense, and Olivieri's Buddhist friends were unable to rescue his mission. He and his confreres left Tibet in 1745, and he died in Nepal shortly thereafter. But as Enzo Barciacchi says at the end of his *Bridge Across Two Cultures*, "the story continues." It continues but is transformed. When the 14th Dalai Lama came to Italy in 1994, he visited Pennabilli, Olivieri's birthplace, and expressed the transformation this way: "Arriving here I must say that I have experienced a strong emotion, a new emotion, something I have not experienced before, a [remarkably] intense experience. On the one hand, the events of 250 years ago have come to mind; on the other hand, I am also reminded how so much has changed from that period, from those times, to today" (my translation from the Italian version: http://www.montefeltro.net/pennabilli/tibet.htm, p. 3).

6. *Dialogue and Proclamation: Reflection and Orientations on Interreligious Dialogue and the Proclamation of the Gospel of Jesus Christ*, Pontifical Council for Interreligious Dialogue, Vatican City, 1991. To access online, use the search engine featured on the Vatican's main page, at http://www.vatican.va. Subsequent publications of the pontifical council can also be found there, including the recent *Il Dialogo Interreligioso nell'Insegnamento Ufficiale della Chiesa Cattolica* (1963–2013) / *Interreligious Dialogue in the Official Teaching of the Catholic Church* (1963–2013), presented by Cardinal Jean-Louis Tauran, president of the pontifical council; Rev. Miguel Angel Ayuso Guixot, MCCJ, secretary of said council; and Bishop Francesco Gioia, OFMCap., editor of the work, at a press conference of the Holy See Press Office on November 12, 2013. An excellent collection of scholarly essays by Catholics who specialize in encounter with another religion (or other religions) can be found in *The Catholic Church and the World Religions: A Theological and Phenomenological Account*, ed. Gavin D'Costa (T&T Clark International, 2011). Chapters 1 and 5 in particular provide good general background for the subject matter of this

and to receive from and through others the positive values of their traditions" (#49).[7] Earlier in the same document, where the "forms of dialogue" are described, the third form is "the dialogue of theological exchange, where specialists seek to deepen their understanding of their respective religious heritages, and to appreciate each other's spiritual values," and the fourth form is "the dialogue of religious experience, where persons, rooted in their own religious traditions, share their spiritual riches, for instance with regard to prayer and contemplation, faith and ways of searching for God or the Absolute" (#42).[8] The *instrumentum laboris* of the Synod of Bishops, Special Assembly for Asia (1998), also accessible via the official Vatican website, goes so far as to report that most responses from the Asian bishops "agree that Catholic truth can be served by a borrowing of concepts and ideas which are particularly Asian, all the while remaining faithful to the Catholic faith as presented in Sacred Scripture and the Church's Tradition" (#33).[9]

---

book. (On May 14, 2014, shortly before this present book was sent to press, the pontifical council—in commemoration of the fiftieth year since its founding—published *Dialogue in Truth and Charity: Pastoral Orientations for Interreligious Dialogue* [Libreria Editrice Vaticana]. A fifty-eight-page document, it is intended to provide guidelines for pastors and all the faithful who live and work with people of other religions. It features chapters on [1] official Church statements regarding the dialogue, [2] the "dynamics" of interreligious dialogue, and [3] "specific fields of interreligious relations." It adheres very closely to already published Church statements, generated over a number of years, regarding the dialogue. I have referenced, in this monograph, such key statements insofar as they pertain to the Buddhist-Catholic encounter.)

7. The paragraph continues, "Through dialogue they [Christians] may be moved to give up ingrained prejudices, to revise preconceived ideas, and even sometimes to allow the understanding of their faith to be purified."

8. The first form is "the dialogue of life, where people strive to live in an open and neighbourly spirit, sharing their joys and sorrows, their human problems and preoccupations"; the second form is "the dialogue of action, in which Christians and others collaborate for the integral development and liberation of people" (#42).

9. *Instrumentum laboris* for the Synod of Bishops, Special Assembly for Asia, "Jesus Christ the Saviour and His Mission of Love and Service in Asia: '. . . [T]hat they may have life, and have it more abundantly' (Jn 10:10)," 1998. (Available via the Vatican website.)

Introduction: Origins and Objectives of This Work

As a Catholic who has long worked in Buddhist-Christian dialogue,[10] and who has long worked and published both in French deconstruction[11] and in Buddhist studies,[12] I have noted already for a long time that (most surprisingly) a Derridean "take" on *differ-*

10. A Carmelite lay tertiary since 1982, I began my work in comparative Buddhism-Catholicism via a book chapter in a book collection from Cornell UP (1988) and a lecture at the 9th Conference of the International Association of Buddhist Studies (IABS) sponsored by the Institute for Sino-Indian Buddhist Studies, Taiwan (1989). Affiliated with the Society for Buddhist-Christian Studies (SBCS) since 1991, I gave a long presentation at its 4th International Conference (1992) and headed the delegation of Buddhist and Catholic professors from Assumption U. of Thailand's (interfaith) School of Philosophy and Religions to the 5th (1996) and 6th (2000) International Conferences of the SBCS, delivering papers and organizing pertaining panels at these conferences. In 1999, I was invited by the Federation of Asian Bishops' Conferences (FABC) and Cardinal Poupard, president of the Pontifical Council for Culture, to give a lecture (later published also in Chinese and Italian) addressing "Meditation as a Common Feature of Religions in Asia, with a Special Focus on Buddhism" at a convention jointly organized by the pontifical council, the FABC-OESC, the National Episcopal Conference of Thailand, the Graduate School of Assumption University, and Foundation Konrad-Adenauer, Archdiocesan Pastoral Centre, Bangkok, Thailand (January 31 to February 3). Other venues at which I have delivered lectures on Buddhist-Catholic dialogue include the Pontifical U. of Santo Tomàs, the Philippines (1995); the Roman Catholic Studies Group, American Academy of Religion (1998); and the Conference on Jainism and World Religions, United States (2003). At the biannual meeting of the European Network of Buddhist-Christian Studies, Liverpool, UK (2011), I gave a comparative talk on deconstructive technique in Gerard Manley Hopkins and Dogen. From 2002 to 2005, I was affiliated—as "interfaith retreatant"—with the One Center, Manhattan, New York City, branch of the Ling Jiou Mountain (Linjiushan) Wu Sheng Buddhist Monastery, Fulien Village, Kungliao, Taiwan. When the One Center moved to Oakland Gardens, Queens, New York City, I remained affiliated—as an interfaith consultant—to Ling Jiou Shan. In 2012, Ling Jiou Shan opened a temple and center in Flushing, Queens, rendering my commute easier, so I have resumed visits to that new One Center, as interfaith consultant and interfaith retreatant.

11. My philosophical work has moved from phenomenological hermeneutics (doctoral dissertation, Princeton, 1970, and my first book, 1977) to Derridean deconstruction to Madhyamaka (and some Chan/Zen) Buddhism, with the involvement, all along, of Catholic hermeneutics insofar as circumstances have enabled it. On academic leave from Purdue University, where I had been a professor since 1970, I passed a research year at the National Humanities Center (1979–1980, North Carolina); there I researched the possible intersection of Madhyamikan argumentation and French deconstruction, and from this and subsequent research came my book *Derrida on the Mend* (W. Lafayette: Purdue UP, 1984, 1986;

ence, when inculturated into a Catholic frame of reference, can satisfactorily *coordinate* two aims clearly mandated in the above citations—namely, (1) cultivation of a mind-set "prepared to learn and receive" from Buddhism and, at the same time, (2) ongoing fidelity to authoritative Church teaching (i.e., to the Magisterium). For orthodox Catholics, such a coordination of learning on the one hand and doctrinal perseverance on the other seems particularly difficult to manage when dialoguing with Buddhists, because Buddhism rejects the notion of an eternal Creator-God and affirms such teachings as serial rebirth. Catholic thinkers, it seems to me, have so far lacked a thought-structure enabling them to properly

---

rpt. 2000–2011, 2013–). First while at Purdue University, and later for many years in Taiwan and Thailand, I went on to develop the topic of Buddhism and deconstruction in many book chapters and articles, and in papers at the Society for Phenomenology and Philosophical Research, the International Association of Comparative Philosophy, the International Society for Chinese Philosophy, the International Institute of Field Being, etc. I lectured on this topic in Great Britain (King's College and Emmanuel College, Cambridge, and U. of Cardiff, Wales), France, Singapore, Taiwan, and Thailand; and I co-instructed with Frederic Jameson, Gayatri Spivak, and Wai-lim Yip at a (summer) School of Criticism (National Hsing Hua U., Taiwan, 1990). My *On Deconstructing Life-Worlds: Buddhism, Christianity, Culture* (Scholars P. of American Academy of Religion, 1997; Oxford UP, 2000–) followed, and then, in 1999, the International Association of Philosophy and Literature featured a "Close Encounter" panel on my publications. Since retirement, the philosophical side of my work has been presented primarily in writing (book chapters, articles) and occasional talks.

12. Both *Derrida on the Mend* and *On Deconstructing Life-Worlds* involve Madhyamika Buddhism, Chan, and Zen at length, but as part of a larger comparative project. I have also, all along, published in Buddhist studies per se: book chapters (Routledge P.), articles, review articles, and reviews (*Journal of Chinese Philosophy, Journal of the American Academy of Religion* [*JAAR*], "H-Buddhism" [H-Net, online Buddhist Studies Information Network], as well as journals in Taiwan [in Chinese-language translation]). I have taught courses in Buddhism at Chiao Tung U., Taiwan, and on Sogyal Rimpoche's *Tibetan Book of Living and Dying* at the Ling Jiou Shan Monastery One Center, New York City (2003 and 2005). On several occasions, I have served as an official reader in comparative Buddhist and Western philosophy for academic publishers such as the SUNY P. (1985) and Rowman and Littlefield (2007). In 2001, upon the recommendation of Robert Thurman, I was invited to be a seminar associate of the Columbia U. Seminar in Buddhist Studies, and I remained active in that forum through to 2012.

allocate Catholic and Buddhist values (including *truth*-values) in terms of dialogue.[13]

What I shall propose in this present study is that a Derridean formulation of difference, when inculturated into a Catholic frame of reference, can explain *how* it can be that Buddhism and Catholicism *radically differ* at bottom (so that each religion has its own unique "identity") yet mutually *edify* (so that Catholics can learn and receive "from and through" Buddhists, and vice versa). It may be the case, as well, that some Buddhists find themselves in an analogous predicament when facing Catholicism, and the same Derridean thought-model may be of service to them on their side of the dialogue, in this regard. Personally, during my considerable meditation training in Buddhism[14] and interaction with Chinese and Thai

13. Belief systems radically differ, and it is religiously dishonest to overlook these differences or spirit them away via some furtive sleight of hand (argumentative or otherwise). For some decades, it has not been fashionable—in interreligious circles—to accept real difference, and among those who accept real difference, there are only some who work out beneficial ways to "continue the dialogue" and in fact to learn "all the more" from the "other" precisely because of mutual difference. The relatively new discipline of "comparative theology" associated with Fr. Francis X. Clooney, SJ, successfully does this, I think—via its dialectic of shared experience—and I quite admire it. At Harvard Divinity School, the *Journal of Comparative Theology*, inspired by Fr. Clooney, provides us with some hope that a true comparative theology will continue on into the next generation of scholars/practitioners; the journal is an "online publication in which graduate students and emerging scholars share articles" that engage in comparative theology. A very good book exemplifying this new discipline, by Fr. Scott Steinkerchner, OP, is *Beyond Agreement: Interreligious Dialogue Amid Persistent Differences* (Rowman and Littlefield, 2011), long sequences of which deploy Wittgensteinian strategies to dialogue with Taoism. This book of mine develops along a different vector, however: I examine the relational mechanism whereby radical difference *enacts or "appoints"* the samenesses superjacent on its very difference so that "shared experience" comes by way of these "founding acts" of difference.

14. In 1972, an academic colleague who was a lifelong Buddhist first introduced me to the rudiments of Zen meditative practice. In Taiwan, I made several study visits to famous Chinese masters and a visiting Korean master, but still lacked the necessary formal training. In Thailand, I began formal *śamatha-vipassanā* meditation training at Wat Mahadhatu (Bangkok) in 1994, under the direction of Rev. Dr. Pithoon Vidhuro, starting with a closed and very strict Eight-Precept retreat and continuing by way of one-day meditation visits to that Wat when I was

Buddhists, my experiences have not rendered me uneasy: both my radical difference from Buddhists and my ongoing study/edification when among Buddhists have survived intact (and indeed have increased). Perhaps my youthful training in a Jesuit seminary for three and one-half years and my familiarity with Ignatian spirituality—its theological openness, its long history of encounter with Buddhism, and so on—have much to do with this constancy; as

---

in Thailand, through to 1998. Along the way, I made short (three-day) retreats, when possible, in diverse Mahayanist systems, e.g., Kagyu/Nyingma at Karme-Choling, VT (in October 1992); Soto Zen at Wainwright House, Rye, New York (in July 1993); and Gelukpa at Lam Rim Buddhist Centre, Wales, UK (in November 1994). I directed Theravada *śamatha* meditation sessions at National Changhua U. of Education, Taiwan, once a week, through the spring semester of 2000. In 1999, I met Fa-shih (Dharma Teacher) Guang Guo at an interreligious conference and made a closed week-long retreat (in June 2001) at the monastery of her Master, Dharma Master Hsin Tao (Chinese Chan and several Tibetan Vajrayana lineages), at his home monastery, Ling Jiou Mountain Wu Sheng Monastery, Taiwan. In the United States, in autumn 2001, I began meditation visits to the One Center, Ling Jiou Mountain's monastery in Manhattan, New York City, and from 2002 through summer 2005 I practiced meditation one or two days each week there, under Dharma teacher Guang Guo's supervision. On January 2, 2006, Dharma teacher Guang Guo gave me certification "to demonstrate the form and mode of Buddhist meditation to others, especially in the context of interreligious dialogue," and in relation to my "work with Catholic monastics." At the end of summer 2005, the One Center in Manhattan had closed, moving to Oakland Gardens, Queens, thus rendering my commute from New Jersey very difficult. I thus began to practice meditation regularly with the Downtown New York Meditation Community (Theravada)—at a Manhattan site located relatively close to my own residence—and continued there from 2010 to 2012. In 2012, Ling Jiou Shan opened a new One Center in Flushing, New York City, so I resumed more active affiliation with Ling Jiou Shan as both meditator and interfaith consultant. In Desio, Italy, at the Vangelo e Zen ("Gospel and Zen") institution administered by the Padri Saveriani (Xaverian Fathers, an Italian Catholic congregation specializing in overseas missions, especially to the Orient), I made a closed retreat in Lent of 2012 and a Long Retreat in spring 2013 (Soto Zen meditation, integrated into a Catholic monastic day). I received from Fr. Luciano Mazzocchi, who trained in Soto Zen in Japan for many years, an official *Attestato* ("Certification") declaring me qualified to teach meditation "as transmitted in Zen and in other Oriental forms" (in which I have been trained) to "priests, Religious, and laity of the Catholic Church," in accordance with "the spirituality of dialogue promoted by Vatican Council II." A photocopy of the *Attestato* granted to me constitutes Appendix One in this book.

does, for sure, my continuing practice as a Carmelite lay tertiary (a disciplined program of prayer and meditation each day). The foregoing have benignly influenced my academic work in Catholicism,[15] too, I think, so my writing in Catholic theology, for example, does not feel threatened by Buddhism or the "unexpected" that Buddhism always manages to send my way.

It is my plan in this work to borrow not only Derridean "differ-

---

15. Representative publications and papers of mine in Sacred Scripture: a book chapter on Isaiah 66 (Routledge, 1992); an article on Psalm 110 (Philippines, *Colloquia Manilana*, 1995); and papers at the SU of New York, Stony Brook (1987), the U. of Durham, UK (1989), and King's College, Cambridge, UK (1990). Besides the chapters pertaining to Catholic theology in *Derrida on the Mend* and *On Deconstructing Life-Worlds*, representative publications and papers of mine in theology: book chapter on poststructuralist vs. historico-critical approaches in Trinitarian theology (RVP), (Catholic U. of America, 2001), referenced at some length later in this present monograph; the long Catholic apologia for my work included in my Afterword, pp. 235–70, in J. Y. Park, ed., *Buddhisms and Deconstructions*, "with Afterword by Robert Magliola" (Rowman and Littlefield, 2006); and papers on John Paul II's *Segno di Contraddizione* (Viterbo, Italy, February 24, 1979, followed some days later by a semi-private audience with John Paul II, at the Vatican, upon official presentation of the translation of his *The Acting Person*, Analecta Husserliana); on Catholic adaptations of Husserlian and Heideggerian thought (Manila, Philippines, Pontifical U. of Santo Tomás, 1995); on liberation theology (Tacoma, Washington, SBCS, 2000); and on missiology (Rutgers U., 1996; Roman Catholic Studies Group, American Academy of Religion, Orlando, Florida, 1998). Examples of closed Catholic retreats I underwent in my later years are the following: at the Contemplative Path, Amarillo, Texas, five days, March 1994 (director Fr. Patrick Hawk, CSsR); at the Catholic Community of the Beatitudes, Denver, Colorado, eight days, February 2002 (*Communauté des Béatitudes*); and at Vangelo e Zen, Desio, Italy (Padri Saveriani), closed Lenten retreat, March 30 to April 10, 2012, and Long Retreat, February 2 to April 3, 2013. At the Graduate School of Philosophy and Religions at Assumption U., Thailand, I taught the graduate seminar in Catholic spirituality; and, among other venues, I have directed workshops and short practice sessions in "Catholic meditation using Oriental form" at the Redemptorist Retreat Center, Pattaya, Thailand (in May 1997) and at the Graduate Program in Pastoral Care and Counseling, Neumann U., Pennsylvania (in January 2006). In *Dilatato Corde*, Vol. III, No. 2 (July–December 2013), Dialogue Interreligieux Monastique / Monastic Interreligious Dialogue, http://www.dimmid.org, I have an article on Vangelo e Zen, Italy, showing Fr. Luciano Mazzocchi's Catholic theology and spirituality, including the influence of Buddhism on his thought. During 2012 and 2013, I was an official reader/reviewer in Buddhism/comparative theology/postmodernism for the *Harvard Theology Review*, Harvard University.

ence" but quite a few other Derridean thought-motifs and apply them to the Buddhist-Catholic dialogue. Foremost among these is perhaps my proposal of several applications to meditation formats in which Buddhists and Catholics join, because several Derridean thought-motifs suggest formations that safeguard, in the words of the previous pope, the "different uses proper to the various religions" and do not lend themselves to "syncretist interpretations."[16] As a Catholic trained in both the Catholic prayer tradition and Buddhist meditation, I sense that I can respectfully but responsibly offer suggestions in this regard.

Of course, I am well aware that many Catholics in particular will greet with consternation, not to mention skepticism, the proposal that any good can come from the movement called French deconstruction (which they stereotype as "just another anti-religious postmodernism"[17]), but I dare to hope that some of them will find

16. See "Message of His Holiness Benedict XVI to Bishop Domenico Sorrentino on the Occasion of the Twentieth Anniversary of the Interreligious Meeting of Prayer for Peace," translated from Italian, Libreria Editrice Vaticana, September 2, 2006. (http://www.vatican.va/holy_father/benedict_xvi/letters/2006/documents/hf _ben-xvi_let_20060902_xx-incontro-assisi_en.html.)

17. Actually, "anti-religious postmodernism" would be an incorrect generalization in its own right, since quite a few postmodernists are not irreligious at all. Derrida distinguished his work from postmodernism in any case, and did so for two reasons. First, he wanted to distance his work from the "hodge-podge" thinking characteristic of many postmodernists, and second, he shrank from the politically extreme right-wing propensies of some forms of postmodernism. *Deconstruction for Derrida is "postmodern" only in the broad sense, and when I refer to some of my work as "postmodern," I likewise mean the adjective only in the broad sense*—namely, as a variable or "floating" set of maneuvers that interrupt what purport to be "closed systems," systems professing to "come to rest" within their own intact frames. (Deconstructionists used to revel in what is the obvious pun in English— "framed systems 'frame' their disciples," "what a frame-up!" and the like, but even clever quips become stale after a while.) What interests me is that Pope Francis's favorite contemporary philosopher and cultural historian is Methol Ferré, a Uruguayan from whom he often quotes. Ferré maintains that "only the Church is truly postmodern" because only it can break "hedonistic atheism," the "modernism" of today's First World culture. And associated with such a "libertine atheism," says Ferré, is its fellow traveler, "'nebulized theism', a diffuse theism without historical incarnation." (See Sandro Magister, "The Pope and the Philosopher," March 31, 2014, at www.chiesa.espresso.repubblica.it/articolo/1350753?eng=y.)

themselves properly convinced by the applications themselves, as we develop each of them one by one. As for those irrevocably resistant to Derridean thought-motifs of any kind, I implore them to bypass the Foreword, where—insofar as it pertains to this work's project—I set forth Derrida's theory of "difference," and instead proceed directly to Parts One and Two. Part One's detailed comparisons of Buddhist and Catholic teaching can stand in their own right, as can Part Two's descriptions of interreligious encounter and of joint meditation.

Dear Buddhist readers, I think this work may be of considerable interest to you because, in order to show the salient differences and samenesses between the two religions, I necessarily explain the pertaining Catholic teachings as well. And surely, those Buddhists who wish to deepen their involvement in dialogue, or at least in joint meditation, need to better understand the beliefs (and practices) of their Catholic counterparts. My experience has been that the typical Buddhist understands Catholics even less than the typical Catholic understands Buddhists. Furthermore, many Buddhists seem to think that Catholicism consigns Buddhists to punishment in the afterlife on grounds of "false belief," whereas in fact the Catholic Church affirms that Buddhists can indeed attain heavenly beatitude. There are also many Buddhists who do not know the reasons *why* Catholics enter into dialogue. And there are many Buddhists who are *suspicious* of Buddhist-Catholic dialogue and of Catholic intent. This present work aims to address all these matters.

Ronald B. Epstein, the Buddhologist so widely known for his ongoing work at the late Ven. Master Hsuan Hua's Institute for World Religions and at the Buddhist Text Translation Society, supplies us with a most inspiring anecdote told by Master Hua himself. Believing that "it is important for people of all religions to learn from the strengths of each religious tradition," the Master undertook the following initiative:

[Master Hua] invited his good friend Paul Cardinal Yu Bin, the Catholic Cardinal of Taiwan,[18] to join him in establishing a World Religions Center at the Sagely City of Ten Thousand Buddhas and to be its first director [the Cardinal happily agreed].[19] He suggested that the Cardinal be a "Buddhist among the Catholics" and that he himself would be a "Catholic among the Buddhists." Unfortunately the Cardinal's untimely death delayed the plans for the Center, which in 1994 opened in Berkeley as the Institute of World Religions.[20]

Master Hsuan Hua and Cardinal Yu Bin lived and died steadfast in their respective faiths—the point, rather, is that Cardinal Yu Bin intended to deepen among Catholics an understanding of Buddhism and Master Hsuan Hua intended to deepen among Buddhists an understanding of Catholicism. Cardinal Yu Bin had been active at Vatican Council II (1962–1965) and no doubt was heartened by its decree *Nostra Aetate*, which says of Buddhists:

> Buddhism in its various forms testifies to the essential inadequacy of this changing world. It proposes a way of life by which men can, with confidence and trust, attain a state of perfect liberation and reach supreme illumination either through their own efforts or by the aid of divine [to be understood as "supramundane power," in this Buddhist context] help. (*Nostra Aetate*, #2)

While making clear that the Catholic Church fundamentally parts with much of the Buddhist teaching represented above (sections of my study will specify these radical differences), the declaration goes on to say of Buddhism and the other non-Christian religions:

---

18. Cardinal Yu Bin (1901–1978) was, to more accurately phrase it, the rector of Fu Jen Catholic University in Taiwan. He was born on the Chinese mainland (Kirin, now Jilin), was ordained in 1928, and appointed archbishop of Nanking in 1946.

19. According to the Institute of World Religions link of the Dharma Realm Buddhist University website, "In 1976, Paul Cardinal Yu Bin graciously consented to be the Institute's first director" (http://www.drbu.org/index.php/IWR/iwr.html, accessed April 14, 2009).

20. *Buddhist Text Society's Buddhism A to Z*, compiled by Ronald B. Epstein in collaboration with the Editorial Committee of the Buddhist Text Translation Society (Burlingame, CA: BTTS, 2003), p. 255.

The Catholic Church rejects nothing of what is true and holy in these religions. She has a high regard for the manner of life and conduct, the precepts and doctrines, which, although differing in many ways from her own teaching, nevertheless often reflect a ray of that truth which enlightens all men. (Ibid.)

The photograph[21] of Master Hsuan Hua and Cardinal Yu Bin, side by side and intently discussing plans for a new Institute of World Religions, is very precious to me. Two dear old Chinese men, both born around the turn of the last century and in the same part of the Chinese mainland (Jilin, in the northeast), tenderly and warmly sharing, in California, in the twilight of their years, a sacred ideal—there is no doubt in my mind that this remarkable convergence was "meant to be." It was meant for Buddhists and it was meant for Catholics, and somehow I think it was meant for this very work here, because I myself have—via my marital in-laws—kindred who were themselves born in the northeast of China. And it so happens that I have personally known, before, Chinese old men whose eyes water and glisten when their paths cross after a long time . . . Chinese old men who can at last gather some tinder, stoop over it, and together set ablaze a fire that can warm everyone around. I know what such a scene looks like, and I can indeed sense it in the old photograph.

If Master Hsuan Hua proposed to be, for the purposes explained above, a "Catholic among the Buddhists," he always remained also a "Buddhist for the Buddhists" and in his own right a "Buddhist for the Catholics." That is to say, he critiqued other religions, including Catholic Christianity. My experience has been that many Buddhists do not know the specific doctrinal attitudes and arguments of authoritative Buddhist masters and other Buddhist spokesmen vis-à-vis Catholicism. (There is in fact a range of attitudes and arguments, and sometimes Buddhist lay folk know the position of their own Master or tradition in this regard but not those of other Buddhist Masters or traditions.) It pleases me to report that this work has a lengthy section devoted solely to quotations and explanations

---

21. Displayed on the pertaining Dharma Realm Buddhist University website (see URL in related earlier note).

regarding a wide range of Buddhist critiques of theism in general and Christianity in particular, including Catholic Christianity.

It pleases me to invite, also, Buddhist readers who *do* know Buddhism well, so that they can verify the accuracy of my accounts and descriptions of Buddhist teachings and practices. I would like to think that I have paid meticulous attention to received Buddhist teachings and to Buddhist scholarship and its resources.

Buddhists may also take some interest in this work's discussion of Derridean deconstruction as such, since, after all, the wider academic community knows me mainly for my publications comparing Derridean deconstruction and analogous Buddhist (especially Madhyamikan) operations.

Catholic readers will find that, in accordance with the purposes of interreligious dialogue that we have cited from authoritative Vatican sources, Parts One and Two of this study will enable them to "deepen their understanding" of Buddhist teachings and practices, to "appreciate" them, and to "learn and receive" from them in an appropriate manner (that is, such that there are no concessions to "relativism"[22]). Indeed, in this regard it is revealing to point out to Catholics that my opposition (at the SBCS international meeting in

22. See John Paul II, "Inauguration of the World Day of Prayer and Peace, Assisi, Oct. 27, 1986": "The fact that we have come here does not imply any intention of seeking a religious consensus among ourselves or of negotiating our faith convictions. Neither does it mean that religions can be reconciled at the level of a common commitment in an earthly project that would surpass them all. Nor is it a concession to relativism in religious beliefs" (#4) (cited also in Benedict XVI's letter to Bishop Sorrentino, see my earlier pertaining note). The success of books on "dual belonging," such as Paul Knitter's *Without Buddha I Could Not Be a Christian* (Oneworld Pub., 2009), witnesses to the popularity nowadays of "consensus" attained by reduction of definitive religious differences to 'common-ground'. It is not that I dissent from this book's title as such: surely the Church can envisage that in some cases divine grace can mediate through Buddhism to sustain a Catholic's Catholic faith. What is objectionable, rather, is the relativism that reduces explicit Buddhist and Catholic differences to what Knitter calls "Interbeing" (pp. 22, 112), the "one, universal Spirit" (p. 129). For my review of Knitter's book, see the *Journal*

Tacoma, Washington, August 2000)[23] to a dilution and distortion of both Buddhism and Catholicism in the name of an underlying "common ground" was welcomed most enthusiastically by many—indeed I would say the majority—of Buddhist monastics, teachers, and practitioners in attendance. Buddhists who know and live their religion are zealous of their convictions too.

As to the question of "learning and receiving," the helpfulness of Buddhism has perhaps been most felt in the area of meditation. For decades already there have been, with full ecclesiastical permission, very fruitful exchanges between Catholic and Buddhist monastics.[24] In several places, this present study addresses issues involving meditation and the Buddhist-Catholic dialogue. In this regard, my own

of the American Academy of Religion, Vol. 78, No. 4 (December 2010), pp. 1215–18 (reprinted in *Dilatato Corde*, Vol. II, No. 1 [January–June 2012] on the Dialogue Interreligieux Monastique / Monastic Interreligious Dialogue website, http://www. dimmid.org). No doubt Paul Knitter is a good and kind man who wants to expedite religious encounter, but I would remind him that the Christian mystics warn that for the most important things we must learn to "wait," to "wait on God," for good things come in "God's good time." Upon coming away from a reading of Catherine Cornille's insightful *The Im-Possibility of Interreligious Dialogue* (Crossroad, 2008) and its gentle call for humility, commitment, interconnection, empathy, and hospitality in interreligious dialogue, one senses—I think—just such a "state of soul": that of a "waiting," but a "fertile waiting." Waiting, however, does not mean entropy. Religious commitment, as Cornille says, "entails assent to the truth-claims of a particular tradition and recognition of the authority of the tradition in matters of doctrine and discipline" (p. 66).

23. My presentation was entitled "Taking a Different Tack: On the Role of Difference, Not Common-Ground, in Healing and Buddhist-Christian Dialogue," Sixth International Conference on Buddhist-Christian Dialogue, sponsored by Pacific Lutheran University and the Society for Buddhist-Christian Studies, Tacoma, Washington, August 7, 2000.

24. See, for example, the very active Dialogue Interreligieux Monastique / Monastic Interreligious Dialogue (already cited in several contexts). DIM/MID is a commission of the Benedictine Confederation with formal links to both branches of the Cistercian order. It promotes dialogue "especially at the level of religious experience" and includes "dialogue partners" that include monastics, clergy, and laity from several religions. Buddhist nuns, monks, and laity constitute a sizable portion of its participating members. There are at present four continental commissions—for Europe, North America, India/Sri Lanka, and Australia. The European Commission comprises ten regional sub-commissions—for France, French-speaking Belgium, French-speaking Switzerland, Germany/Austria, Great Britain

special interest over these years has been in the adaptation of Tibetan Vajrayanist form, with its chakra sites, visualizations, etc., to Catholic meditation (by thematizing the Vajrayanist mode in a Catholic way). At the invitation of the Pontifical Council for Culture and the Federation of Asian Bishops' Conferences, I explicated and demonstrated this adaptation at its convention in Bangkok, Thailand, in February 1999.[25] As for this present study, at one point in its second annex it proposes and demonstrates the possible adaptation of a Chinese and Japanese Buddhist mode identified with Chan (Ch'an)/Zen, namely, the deployment of *gong'an* (*kung-an*).[26]

This work has two annexes. If Derridean strategies (most surprisingly) can be of service to Buddhist-Catholic dialogue, as I hope to have effectively demonstrated by the end of Part Two, it may be the case that Derridean strategies can be of service in the future to Catholic theology too. The first annex proposes some vectors along which such an aggregation can possibly proceed. After all, Catholic theology in its early history adapted Platonism and Neoplatonism,

---

and Ireland, Holland and Flemish-speaking Belgium, Hungary, the Iberian Peninsula, Italy, and Scandinavia. Several of these sub-commissions maintain their own websites with ongoing bibliographical listings of pertaining works in their own native languages. Many of the individual members of DIM/MID engage specifically in the Buddhist-Catholic encounter and participate in joint Buddhist-Catholic meditation sessions; among these, quite a few are well-known leaders and specialists in the encounter and in meditation in particular. Needless to say, I cannot list all of these members here, but the interested reader can consult the DIM/MID (and its *Dilatato Corde* online journal, Fr. Pierre de Béthune, OSB, editor in chief) to find them. Those I personally name in this book happen to be those whose paths I have happened to cross in my own life—either via reading or direct experience. Such intersections, I am quite convinced, are arranged by divine providence more than anything else.

25. See R. Magliola, pp. 71–82, in *Proceedings: The Convention on "Christian Humanism: Illuminating with the Light of the Gospel the Mosaic of Asian Cultures,"* a convention jointly organized by the Pontifical Council for Culture, the FABC-OESC, et al. (see my pertaining earlier note) (Pontifical Council for Culture, the Vatican, 1999).

26. This monograph romanizes Mandarin Chinese according to the Pinyin system, except in the case of some well-known personal or proprietary names. Especially in the case of well-known Chinese Buddhist terms, the Wade-Giles form of romanization is supplied immediately after the Pinyin, either parenthetically or after a diagonal.

although Plato affirmed such radically non-Catholic theses as metempsychosis and the Neoplatonists affirmed such non-Catholic theses as emanationism and the *Dēmiourgos*. In the case of Aristotelianism, for many centuries Catholic theology rejected or ignored what of Aristotle was textually available because of its seeming intractability—i.e., its scientific grounding in senses and phenomena seemed less friendly than Plato's "World of Ideas." Then, in the thirteenth century, because of Aquinas but for other reasons too, there came the enormous turnaround, and an adapted Aristotelianism went on to become the privileged vehicle for Catholic philosophy and theology. In view of such widely known precedents, it seems to me that the refusal of many mainstream Catholic theologians even to read Derrida is "imprudent."

The second annex returns to the Buddhist-Catholic encounter, and—again in line with *Dialogue and Proclamation*'s call to "learn and receive from" the "positive values" of other religions—it singles out, from the *instrumentum laboris* of the Synod of Asian Bishops cited above, the notion that "Catholic truth can be served by a borrowing of concepts and ideas which are particularly Asian, all the while remaining faithful to the Catholic faith."[27] The Holy Spirit so disposed events in history that the early Church grew, in numbers and influence, in a Hellenized milieu and moved westward and northward (this is not to deny that precious fractions of Christianity moved eastward or southward). Given the Hellenization of the Church, its doctrinal formulations—the divinely inspired fruit of its ongoing "developmental theology"—have come to be expressed largely within a Greco-Roman framework. As Benedict XVI in particular emphasizes, it is with this fruit that we enter into dialogue with the thought-systems of southern and eastern Asia. Though such a dialogue has been active, indeed intensely active, for quite some time already, I here suggest some further ways in which Catholic doctrines, while remaining *in full effect* in terms of their history and formulation, can be represented and inculturated in Asia. Lastly, I make some suggestions as to how "concepts and ideas" can be borrowed from southern and eastern Asia and from Buddhism

27. See #33.

in particular, so that not only Catholic Asian theology but also the theology of the universal Catholic Church can be *further* developed. As Vatican Council II very clearly declares, "The Tradition that comes from the apostles makes progress in the Church, with the help of the Holy Spirit. There is a growth in insight into the realities and words that are being passed on. . . . Thus, as the centuries go by, the Church is always advancing towards the plenitude of divine truth, until eventually the words of God are fulfilled in her."[28]

The body proper of this monograph has a short but dense theoretical Foreword and then the pith and marrow of the work, Parts One and Two. The Foreword explicates those thought-motifs that we will adopt/adapt from Derridean thought in order to pose an irreducible difference between Buddhism and Catholicism, and also to formulate the nature and vitality of the samenesses between the two religions. Derridean thought-motifs, it is very important to note, pertain—in Derrida's thought—to the mundane world[29] (and *not* to the "supramundane" considerations that Buddhism and Catholicism respectively bring into play as "ultimates"). There are three Derridean thought-motifs adopted/adapted in the Foreword: (1) pure difference (rather than some entitative ground or other holism) as "founding"; (2) time/space double-binds; and (3) purely negative reference as appointive of "samenesses." I am well aware— as previously indicated—that, in particular, philosophers exclu-

---

28. *Dogmatic Constitution on Divine Revelation* (*Dei Verbum*), #8, in Austin Flannery, OP, ed., *Vatican Council II*, Vol. 1, *The Conciliar and Post Conciliar Documents* (hereafter VAT2D), new revised edition, 1992 (Northport, NY: Costello; Dublin: Dominican P.; 3rd printing, 1996). Ahead, my long note to the subtitle "Catholicism and Other-Power" (introducing the section of the same name) supplies full publication information for authoritative Catholic sources that I cite in this present work (and supplies the abbreviations used in this monograph for pertaining references). The first part of the section itself is devoted to a detailed explanation of how the Catholic Church understands its "teaching authority" (history, modes of functioning, etc.).

29. Which is to be taken, here, in the broadest sense, that is, as that which is humanly and naturally accessible to mundane human comprehension.

sively formed in, and convinced by, the mainstream Greco-Roman philosophical tradition or its descendants and offshoots may consider Derridean thought to be "nonsensical." If those among them who have agreed to read the Foreword persist in such a conclusion, I most earnestly ask them (and I know that here I am repeating) to read the rest of this work anyway, for the sake of the other material that is proffered there, e.g., the description of the teachings of Buddhism and Catholicism respectively, especially in relation to Buddhist-Catholic relations, or the detailed "phenomenology" of joint meditation (and here I am also careful to explain the Magisterial protocols governing such sessions).

Part One focuses on the Buddhist teaching of self-power (in its diverse forms) on the one hand and the Catholic teaching of other-power (salvation as a divine gift) on the other as "irreducibly different" from each other. This irreducible difference, Part One argues, is "appointive of"—in the Derridean manner—the samenesses between the two religions. Several other key differences between Buddhism and Catholicism are also detailed here, and an account is made of the many samenesses. Part One also explicates the positive attitude of the Catholic Church toward the possible beatitude (in Catholic terms = "salvation") of someone who lives and dies as a sincere Buddhist; the same Part also explains how the diverse Buddhist traditions evaluate the possibility of eventual beatitude (in Buddhism = "liberation," "awakening") for someone who, "in this lifetime," is a practicing Catholic. As will be demonstrated in detail, Catholic "salvation" and Buddhist "awakening" (no matter what version of it) radically differ, so that the respective definitions of beatitude are radically different.

It may come as a surprise to some readers that in the modern day both authoritative Catholic teaching and the established Buddhist teachings of two of the three Buddhist grand "doctrinal traditions" are "inclusivist." In religion, the term "inclusivism" as it is understood here means that the religion in question has a doctrinal paradigm that positively accommodates, *but only in its own terms*, the practitioners of another religion (or other religions). The accommodation, depending on the religion in question (the "true religion"), allows for the possibility of ultimate beatitude for the religionists of the other religion, but not because of what is doctrinally unique to the other religion. Part One gives considerable attention to the aforesaid doctrinal provisions that Buddhism and Catholicism apply to each other.

It is imperative, in Part One and throughout this whole work, that the reader attentively and conscientiously consult all the notes, because many crucial definitions, distinctions, historical references, etc., appear only in the notes. The notes are by no means "merely citational." The nature of this work obliges its content to be dense with information of many kinds, and the insertion of all these details into the body of the text would have obstructed the narrative (and often argumentative) flow.

Part Two invokes three specific Derridean formats that help us properly configure, both in the order of doctrine and in the order of practice, the respective intentionalities of committed Catholics and committed Buddhists in relation to each other. Special but by no means exclusive attention is given to the joint meditation sessions—often of Buddhist and Catholic monastics, but of qualified laity too—that have been taking place for decades already and are increasing in numbers and influence. (Here, in a very special way, the "dialogue of religious experience" comes to the fore.) While meditation itself, particularly for some Buddhists, may be concept-free and image-free (as it can be, indeed, for some Catholics, too), there are ideological and practical considerations that structure the joint meditation of Buddhists and Catholics, and these can be conceptually and experientially described. This Part proposes that these descriptions can be fruitful and privileged sites wherein we can live in the present and await the future.

May Buddhists and Catholics who read this work be mutually transformed by their encounter.

May they find their commitments to truth and compassion—as the pertaining Latin root verb *aedificare* suggests—truly built up or "edified."

Foreword:
Pertaining Thought-Motifs
From Jacques Derrida

PEGGY KAMUF, in her Introduction to *A Derrida Reader*,[1] supplies us with examples that serve as a helpful propaedeutic to Derridean 'double-bind':

—It's like the famous graffito, "Do not read this."
—Exactly. That negative imperative phrase enacts, in the most economical fashion, the predicament of a double bind.... by reading the command, he or she ignores it; but ignoring the command (by not reading it) does not rectify things, does not equal obedience to a command that also demands to be read, that is, to

---

1. Peggy Kamuf, ed., *A Derrida Reader: Between the Blinds* (Columbia UP, 1991); citation is from pp. xiv–xv. This collection represents the early- and middle-phase Derrida, those writings that made his reputation and remain the most influential. My publications on and university teaching in Derridean deconstruction draw almost exclusively from this stage. (In Derrida's later phase, his attention shifts away from the deconstruction of epistemology itself, a philosophically more radical project, to the deconstruction of religious discourse, a more thematic and thus less radical philosophical project. John D. Caputo's *The Prayers and Tears of Jacques Derrida: Religion without Religion* [Indiana UP, 1997] depends on the late-phase Derrida but abandons the Catholic faith; my *Derrida on the Mend* and subsequent works draw mainly from the early- and middle-phase Derrida but affirm the Catholic faith—see, for example, *Derrida on the Mend*'s Part 4.) Kamuf's introductions to the selections are very helpful in their own right, and I recommend them to those unfamiliar with Derridean thought. For those who want to study the early and middle phase of Derrida's thought in more detail, a good start can be made by reading Christopher Norris's *Derrida* (London: Fontana, 1987). The endorsements on the dust jacket of my *Derrida on the Mend* (Purdue UP: 1984) are so kind as to call my exposition "extraordinarily illuminating" (Paul Ricoeur), a "great achievement" (John H. Nota, SJ), and "a brilliant and dynamic cross-cultural analysis" (Frederick J. Streng), so I think I can recommend it too with some confidence to the reader.

be acknowledged as command in order to have the force of a command. Thus, the "someone who reads" is but the stage of a certain performance positioned by this double bind. That performance is always, in one way or another, to be compared to the act of reading a dictionary entry for *reader*: before one can receive the order of the concept, one has already given an example of it. The predicament is temporal (but qualifying it in this or any other manner does not resolve it; the predicament remains whole, at this very moment) because the meaning of the act (its concept) is not given in the present of its performance, it is not one with or immanent to the act, but divides that "moment" upon itself, disperses it among the non-present modes of before and after the act. . . . . . Neither the singularity of an act nor the generality of a concept of reading or meaning can be thought of as absolutely prior to the other, as a cause or condition of possibility of the other. . . . Rather than a logical order of determining priority, this relation is one of an irreducible difference, ... Each moment or term is cut across, divided by the other. Each inscribes the other in itself and is inscribed by the other outside of itself. (pp. xiv–xv)

Here,[2] the cited graffito *functions as a metaphor*: the command's doubly bound configuration represents *the human condition in space/time*. According to the differential vectors marked out by the "Do not read this," the 'prior' (or 'outside'[3]) required by the command is necessarily inscribed into the performance (or 'inside') of reading it, of necessarily violating the command. In this scenario,

---

2. Because this Foreword is replete with quoted passages (from Kamuf, Derrida, and Bateson), many of which "embed" their author's specialized terms; and because my exegesis necessarily invokes—besides the terms from the quoted passages—other specialized terms as well, in this Foreword double quotation marks ("__") enclose both quotations and terms extracted therefrom; and single quotation marks ('__') enclose other particularized terms. Elsewhere in this work, more deference can be given to stylistic considerations, so the above-cited norms are not consistently applied.

3. Kamuf's exposition of the bind situation necessarily acts itself out spatially as well as temporally. "It is as spatial as it is temporal," a Derridean can say. That is, in spatial terms, "prior" translates into "outer" and "performance" into "inner," and all of these terms negatively double-bind each other. Derrida argues that time and space are in double-bind relation to each other, as we shall see.

the past (or outside) is inscribed into the present (or inside), and vice versa, so the present (which is *outside* of the past) is inscribed into the past's *inside*. Thus the two, 'past' and 'present', cannot "be thought of as absolutely prior to the other, as a cause or condition of possibility of the other.... Rather than a logical order of determining priority, this relation is one of irreducible difference,... Each moment or term is cut across, divided by the other."

What appears as a unitary formation—the "performance positioned by this double bind," which Kamuf, above, also calls the "predicament" that "remains whole, at this very moment," is in fact "positioned," constituted, by what is underneath the apparent wholeness, namely, it is constituted by the relation of "irreducible difference" that—without real mixing—instead inscribes each into the other. The relation of "irreducible difference" is *purely negative reference* because each 'term' (terms belong to the order of "concept") or each "moment" (moments belong to the order of 'experience') is—in mutual reinscription—absolutely "cut across, divided by the other."

Kamuf's version of double-bind, while posing the issues in a somewhat different way from Jacques Derrida (indeed, the reader may privately notice, shortly, these discrepancies), still serves to ease us into the problematic as Derrida poses it. That is, Kamuf introduces us to concatenated notions: (1) "irreducible difference," or the relations of purely negative reference, (2) the double-binds of temporality, meaning, act, and (implied) space, and (3) purely negative relations as 'appointive' of apparent unitary formations.[4] Now let us proceed to Jacques Derrida.

In Derrida's early essay "Differance" ("Différance"),[5] which did so much to establish his reputation in English-speaking countries,

---

4. In Kamuf's demonstration, the "apparent unitary formation" is the imperative command, the "performance positioned by this double bind," the very "predicament"—**"Do not read this."** That is, on its face this command appears as a holistic formation.

5. In Derrida's *Speech and Phenomena*, trans. D.B. Allison (Evanston, IL: Northwestern, 1973), pp. 129–60; orig. Fr. *Marges de Philosophie* (Éditions de Minuit, 1972), pp. 1–29.

we find a crucial passage[6] introducing his famous neologism "differance" and summarizing several important strands of his argument:

> Differance is what makes the movement of signification possible only if each element called "present," appearing on the stage of presence, is related to something other than itself, but is retaining [*gardant en lui*] the mark of the past element and is already letting itself be hollowed out [*se laissant déjà creuser*] by the mark of its relation to the future element—the trace relating no less to what is called the future than to what is called the past, and constituting [*constituant*] what is called the present by this very relation to what it is not, to what it absolutely is not; that is, not even to a past or a future considered as a modified present.[7]

The "present" (the 'phenomenon' or 'life-formation') is no more than the marks (marks have no 'body' of self-identical meaning) constituting/constituted by what the "present" *absolutely is not*. Derrida continues:

> In order for it [[the phenomenon, the life-formation][8]] to be, an interval [*un intervalle*] must separate it from what it is not; but this interval that constitutes it [*qui le constitue*] in the present must also, with one and the same stroke [*du même coup*], divide the present in itself, thus dividing, along with the present, everything that can be conceived on its basis, that is, every being—in particular, for our metaphysical language, the substance or subject. This interval, dynamically constituting and dividing itself [*se constituant, se divisant dynamiquement*], is what could be called *spacing* [*espacement*], time's becoming-spatial [*devenir-espace du*

6. Below, I use my own translation as it appears in my *Derrida on the Mend* (DOM), pp. 32–33. My translation in *Derrida on the Mend* duplicates Allison's translation but amends it where "careful exegesis has required greater literality" (see DOM, endnote 93, p. 195; and regarding my inclusion of words that Allison fails to translate, see endnote 95). In this work I repeat my translation as it appears in DOM, but discuss the meaning of the passage within a different frame of reference.

7. Original Fr. text in *Marges de Philosophie*, p. 13.

8. The words enclosed in double brackets here are my gloss. In this Foreword, parentheses within translations from Derrida duplicate Derrida's parentheses in his original French.

temps]—or space's becoming-temporal (temporalization) [*devenir-temps de l'espace (temporisation)*].[9]

The imperatives (the 'commands' or 'injunctions', we could just as well say) of (negative-) space-relations and the imperatives of (negative-) time-relations operate crosswise to each other, i.e., spatial and temporal coordinates necessarily abrogate each other.

The diachronic incessancy of (negative-) time thwarts any spatial 'fixation'; the synchronic demands of (negative-) spatial measurement thwart incessant temporal flux. Thus the time/space bind. As Derrida sometimes puts it, '*program* and *dia*gram' perpetually undo each other. (Of course, Werner Heisenberg's work in quantum physics famously uncovered a somewhat analogous indeterminacy involving the position and momentum of waves.) Derrida concludes:

> And it is this constitution [*constitution*] of the present, as an "originating" and irreducibly nonsimple [*non-simple*], and therefore, in the strict sense, non-originating, synthesis of marks [*de marques*], of retention's and protention's traces [*de traces de rétentions et de protentions*] (to reproduce here, analogically and provisionally, a phenomenological and transcendental language that will presently be revealed as inadequate) that I propose to call protowriting, prototrace, or differance [*archi-écriture, archi-trace ou différance*].[10]

The "present" (the 'phenomenon' or 'life-formation') is a "synthesis of marks" *appointed* by "protowriting, prototrace, or differance." [Etymology, to "appoint": < apointier (M.F.) < a/ + pointier < point (O.F.) < punctum (L.), "small hole."[11]] The "present"—note the

---

9. *Marges de Philosophie*, pp. 13–14.

10. Ibid., p. 14.

11. I choose in English the verb "to appoint" to distinguish the operation being described here from Hegelian *aufheben* (which Derrida shows to be residually "substantive") or any other substantialist mechanism. Derrida often "plays" in a Talmudic way with the French noun *point*, two of whose primary lexical senses are "period" (the punctuation mark) and "hole" (of a strap, etc.). To "punctuate" (*ponctuer* [Fr.] < punctus [Lat.]) by means of a "period" is to perform a *non*-substantive operation: the puncture or bodiless "hole" accomplishes the punctuation. Thus, the verb "to appoint" befits Derrida's philosophical proposal in the passages I am quoting, namely, that the "present" is accomplished by purely negative references.

word both in French and English can refer to a time-formation or a space-formation—is not a *true synthesis* as philosophy traditionally defines it, because it is not really a unitary or holistic assemblage. Thus Derrida inserts the parenthetical caveat about the inadequacy of the "phenomenological and transcendental" terminology (the same a fortiori applies, of course, to the words "originating," "proto-," "archi-," etc., which imply substantive foundation). Rather, what we call the "present" or the phenomenon is in fact "irreducibly nonsimple" because it is *constituted* ("appointed"), in this context, by pure *negative* references to the past and pure *negative* references to the future. The so-called temporal "traces" of retention/protention are, *du même coup*, pulled contrariwise by spatial "traces." (Derrida sometimes uses the word "mark" and sometimes the word "trace" to indicate that which is "there but not (entitatively) there." "Marks" or "traces" are purely relational rather than substantive because they *mark* sites only by indicating what they are *not*.)

In short, temporal negative references are caught in a double-bind with spatial negative references, so there arises (what he calls elsewhere) a non-entitative 'knot'—"time's becoming-spatial" or "space's becoming-temporal." The so-called temporal traces of retention/protention are "with one and the same stroke" pulled contrariwise by spatial traces, forming a kind of 'knot'.

These double-bound *not*s are knots that are "irreducibly non-simple," so they are "non-originating."[12] Knots 'on their face' assume the appearance of life-formations, of samenesses, of the 'here and now', but—in fact—purely negative relations 'are constitutive of' knots. What is more (less?), it is crucial for us to recognize that Derrida intends—as he necessarily must, given the logic involved—that (negative-) time/space double-bind and its non-entitative appointment of sameness is paradigmatic for the 'arising' of all 'phenomena'. Pure difference founds sameness.

In physics, Albert Einstein's theory of special relativity, reconciling Newton's laws of motion with electrodynamics, and Einstein's

---

12. "Origin" in traditional metaphysics implies self-identical sources rather than pure negative relations. The *Aufhebung* of Hegelian dialectic involves self-identical elements, their opposites, and their combination.

theory of general relativity, reconciling Newton's laws of gravity with special relativity, of course initiated radically new concepts of time, space, and matter, concepts which are being continually reworked and refined as contemporary physicists and others propose theories of quantum gravity ('string theory', and others). It is important to realize that in contrast, Derrida—while deconstructing the "phenomenological" and "transcendental" language (and concepts) of Edmund Husserl, and indeed, in a broader sense, of all Western metaphysics—remains a *philosopher* and not a scientist. That is, he is critiquing from within the experiential world of human beings, or otherwise put, he is critiquing human thinking about human mundane experience, human 'life-worlds' (so he remains "phenomenological" in the wide sense[13]). Philosophy belongs to the *sciences humaines*, that branch of study which addresses humankind, its history, culture, realizations, and behavior. Physics belongs to the *sciences naturelles*, that branch of study which addresses the biophysical domain. Nonetheless, though this is not the venue for pursuing the question, it is intriguing to note as an 'aside' that Derrida's deconstruction of time, space, and entities as Western metaphysics has historically conceived them leads to alternatives that resonate well with the 'space-time' of contemporary physics. **And, as is the case with contemporary physics, the Derridean deconstruction of metaphysical time/space does not devalue as such the appearances of the life-world. For Derrida, 'samenesses' as such, though constituted by purely negative references, remain valid and viable on their own level.**

The foregoing is already enough of Derrida for what will be, ahead, our (it is to be hoped) prudent adaptation for the purposes

---

13. In the wide sense, the phenomenological refers to that which is humanly *experienced* (as opposed, for example, to that which can only be accessed via the scientifically empirical, usually involving scientific experiment and mental abstraction; the molecular and atomic levels are good cases in point). In that Derrida concerns himself philosophically with human life-worlds, he remains a phenomenologist. Among the philosophies he deconstructs is "Husserlian phenomenology." In Husserl's technical usage, phenomenology is the description of the formal structures of phenomena that appear when one "suspends" the "natural attitude."

of Buddhist-Catholic dialogue. Here, I close this section with an analogy drawn from empirical science and pertaining to pure negative reference as it is related to sameness. The analogy comes from what will be for some readers a perhaps unexpected source, namely, cognitive psychology. As an analogy for the Derridean way of framing the question, it is quite faulty, but it may serve those who prefer to work in terms of a more 'scientific' and less 'philosophical' paradigm. Gregory Bateson, in his well-received and highly influential *Mind and Nature* (1979) and in his subsequent work, argues that perception, the appearance of phenomenon by way of stimuli, is caused precisely by *pure difference*. Bateson, the provenance of whose work is of course the empirical Anglo-Saxon tradition, supplies us with a metaphoric scenario for perception that may be applicable also to Derridean difference: the scenario of switching electricity on and off. And here I am very much beholden to W.S. Waldron, who in his "The Dependent Arising of a Cognitive Unconscious in Buddhism and Science" cites[14] this passage from Bateson:

> [T]he switch, considered as an electric circuit, *does not* exist when it is in the on position. From the point of view of the circuit, it is not different from the conducting wire which leads to it and the wire which leads away from it. It is merely "more conductor." Conversely, but similarly, when the switch is off, it does not exist from the point of view of the circuit. It is nothing, a gap between two conductors which themselves exist only as conductors when the switch is on. (Bateson, pp. 108–9[15])

My application addresses in particular how Derridean 'sameness', a sameness appointed by pure difference, can be demonstrated according to the above scenario. I would suggest here that 'sameness'

---

14. In *Contemporary Buddhism*, Vol. 3, No. 2 (2002), p. 144. Waldron on the Buddhist side draws from both the Pali canonical tradition and from the Yogacaric tradition, whereas on the Buddhist side in my own publications I have used Madhyamaka; difference functions as constitutive in all these Buddhist traditions, though there is considerable variation among them as to how difference is constitutive.

15. Pagination here is according to the edition of Bateson's book in my library, *Mind and Nature: A Necessary Unity* (New York: E. P. Dutton, 1979, 1st edition).

is analogous not to the switch (which is either "more conductor" or a "nothing") but to *switch-function*: (1) the switch-function is appointed, constituted, by the pure difference between 'on' and 'off'; (2) the switch-function remains the same whether it is engaged as 'on' or 'off' (though it must be always engaged as one or the other); and (3) the switch-function is not a common-ground for both 'on' and 'off' because the switch-function is always (purely) exhausted in either one of these two alternatives ('on' or 'off'). One can develop this reading further, and say that the switch-function as such is to change or switch the switch-material from conductor to nonconductor status and back. This switch-function remains the 'same' but is constituted by the pure difference between 'on' (conductor status of the material) and 'off' (nonconductor status of the material). If the electric circuit were always on, or always off, there would be no switch-function as such. (If a switch-function were to be exercised only once, the switch-function would have ceased immediately after its exercise.) It is not as if the switch-function is a common-ground to 'off' and 'on', since the function is always purely and absolutely engaged as either 'off' or 'on', and 'off' (purely) *is-not* 'on' and vice versa. (This 'sameness' is akin to what has been called—elsewhere in the Derridean literature—"sameness without self-identity.")

Having given an account of Derridean 'purely negative reference' and how 'purely negative reference' appoints 'samenesses', this work—after the brief interpolation below—proceeds to Part One.

"The doctrine of the Stagirite [Aristotle] is the opposite of the teaching of the Church: [witness his] affirmation of the eternity of the world, the concept of God as 'engine' and of the soul as the 'form' of the material body, and the reality of essences." Nonetheless, the Church comes to "adapt Aristotelian teaching to Christian thought," developing an impressive and long-lasting philosophical expression of the Christian faith.
—S. Auroux and Y. Weil, *Dictionnaire des auteurs et des thèmes de la philosophie*[16]

16. Hachette, 1978, p. 271 (trans. mine, here).

PART ONE

Buddhist and Catholic Doctrines: Samenesses and Irreducible Difference

The Pertaining Buddhist and Catholic Doctrines Compared

Overview

Here at the outset, let me clarify that this work aims to address Buddhism and Catholicism as they presently stand. The Buddhist *Dhamma/Dharma* (in the sense, here, of "teaching") is represented by the expositions of contemporary Buddhist Masters and other authoritative guides established and received by the majority Buddhist traditions. The official teachings of (Roman[1]) Catholic Christianity are represented by the formal declarations of the Magisterium, or "teaching authority,"[2] of (Roman) Catholicism. Great pains will be taken, ahead, to supply direct quotations and other references from the pertaining proper sources,[3] Buddhist[4] or Catholic.

---

1. The adjective "Roman" has been attached to "Catholicism" in the English language since the sixteenth century because the Church of England considers itself the "Anglo-Catholic Church" and wishes, obviously, to be distinguished from what it calls the "Roman Catholic Church." In this present work, when I use the word "Catholicism" or "Catholic," I mean the Church that Anglicans call "Roman Catholic."

2. As already noted, the Magisterium (Lat. *magisterium*, "office of a teacher") is explained ahead.

3. The vast preponderance of Roman Catholics in the world—if they could be surveyed as to how Catholics differ from other Christians—would agree that Catholics take the pope and the episcopacy (and so on down the line of command) as officially representing the Church's teaching. In other words, the vast majority would accede to the Church's public "power structure." They accede to what Jean-François Lyotard would (semi-)pejoratively call the Church's "grand narrative."

35

Though there need not be only one, the irreducible difference between Buddhism and Catholic Christianity, as I see it, is that Buddhism is ultimately a "self-help" (or "self-power" or "self-effort") religion and Catholic Christianity is ultimately an "other-help" (or "other-power") religion.[5] That is, Buddhism asserts that human beings can and must ultimately earn[6] their supra-mundane beatitude, and Catholics assert that human beings can only receive

Buddhism is not as centralized as Catholicism, and the roles of authority in the various Buddhist traditions differ from those in Catholicism. The vast preponderance of Buddhists in the world "look to" or heed well-known monastic figures or other practitioners who are respected as trustworthy spiritual guides (and sometimes as helpers and heroes/heroines).

4. Prof. Justin McDaniel (PhD, Harvard), the Buddhologist at the University of Pennsylvania who was so kind as to verify my exposition of Buddhism in this book, requested that I remove from the text any reference to "norm" or "the normative" in my presentation of Buddhist teaching and practice; these requested adjustments have been implemented in their entirety. In the contemporary academy—especially in sociology, cultural studies, and cultural anthropology—the meaning of the term "norm" and its linguistic derivatives of course pertains to the *median* "real practices or beliefs" of a group, rather than those systematically encoded in official teaching. My first draft often understood the word in its prescriptive or regulative sense, a meaning it retains in much formal Buddhology and Catholic theology. Indeed, given my formation in European Continental philosophy and my teaching career in post-structuralism, the paradigm-shift that Michel Foucault and Jean-François Lyotard largely helped to engender is very familiar to me (though I much prefer deconstruction to postmodernism, and Derrida avoided the term "postmodernism" in relation to his own work). Regarding my initial draft, it was unmindful of me to have assumed that my use of the prescriptive/regulative sense of the term "norm" and its linguistic derivatives was clear from context alone.

5. This does not mean that "self-power" and "other-power" do not themselves reduce further, but rather that "samenesses" between Buddhism and Catholicism reduce to this difference—that is, this difference irreducibly differentiates the two religions from each other. ("Self-power" and "other-power" can each reduce further: for example, "other-power" in this religious context is constituted by the pure negative references between Calvinist, Catholic, Islamic, and other forms of religious "other-power.")

6. When I say that according to Buddhism human beings can and must *ultimately* earn their supra-mundane beatitude, I do *not* mean that in Buddhism the prospect of supreme "awakening" is—in the normal course of affairs—independent of necessary help, be it from the teachings of the historical Buddha and from teachers of his Path (as in Theravada) or from, as well and most of all, from Buddhas and Bodhisattvas (as in Mahayana and Vajrayana). What I *am* saying is that

supra-mundane beatitude as a gratuitous gift from Another-power with whom they freely cooperate.

We can demonstrate this irreducible difference by way of so obvious (and frequently treated) a case of sameness as communal religious chant, a practice of both religions.

(Think, on the Buddhist side, of the rhythmic Pali chant of Theravada monks, the guttural chant of Tibetan monastics, the soaring chant of Chinese Mahayana monks and nuns, the staccato chant of Japanese or Korean Mahayanists, etc., and of Western [Latin] Gregorian or Eastern [Greek, Syriac, etc.] chant on the Catholic side.) Chant as "communal religious song" is formally characterized by tonal, metrical, and oftentimes verbal repetition. This formal structure, coupled with religious intention, contributes—in both religions—to (1) concentration, focus (or, conversely put, curtailment of distraction), and (2) what we can call the psychological engagement of the "more-than-discursive" or "other-than-(merely) discursive." These "samenesses" analogically correlate to what we called, in the preceding theoretical section, "phenomena" or "life-formations." That is, the samenesses of Buddhist and Catholic chant are "syntheses of marks" that are constituted by more primordial differences. The "samenesses" that appear are "real" at their level of synthesis,[7] and they are spiritually *fertile* samenesses that can encourage mutual understanding and support, and mutual "help-for-the-world" (jointly administered "social services," joint opposition to war and injustice, etc.).

When we seek for a "ground-in-common," a "self-identical foundation," that establishes the samenesses of Buddhist and Catholic chant, whatever we may find proves to be a synthesis of marks in turn, until we meet the most "founding" (in Derrida's differential sense) irreducible differences, and the most "founding" irreducible difference turns out to be, even here, precisely that between Bud-

according to Buddhism individuals must take the *last* step into liberation themselves, either by following through with the teachings (as in Theravada) or by purely/completely recognizing that they themselves are the Buddha (as in Mahayana and Vajrayana). These issues, and their many variants, will be analyzed in depth as this book proceeds.

7. In this context, some would say they are "relatively" real.

dhist "self-power" and Catholic "other-power." In official Buddhist teaching, Buddhist chant, in the *ultimate* sense, is directed toward a liberation understood to be independent of any "Creator-God"[8] (the notion of an absolute Creator-God is regarded as a mere "fabrication"). Catholic chant, instead, is ultimately directed toward Another, a Creator-God who is the salvific source.

Liberation for a Theravadin, as this monograph will soon show in enough detail, is achieved by the individual's *own effort*. The Theravadin is guided by the teachings of Siddhattha Gotama (P.; Skt. Siddhartha Gautama), whose chronology, roughly speaking, ranges from sometime in the sixth century through to sometime in the fifth century BCE, depending on the criteria used.[9] Siddhattha Gotama is called "Buddha" because he attained *sammā-sambodhi* (P. "full and perfect awakening") and practiced each *pāramī* (P. "perfection") in such wise that he could uniquely and supremely lead others to liberation. For a period of forty-five years before his death at the age of eighty, he disseminated the Dhamma (P. *dhamma*; Skt. *dharma*), i.e., the Teachings, which—if steadfastly

8. Across the three major Buddhist traditions, this is the authoritative teaching on the *ultimate* purpose of chant. In his "Buddhism in Thailand: Negotiating the Modern Age" (in Steven Berkwitz, ed., *Buddhisms in World Cultures: Comparative Perspectives*, ABC-CLIO/Greenwood, 2006, pp. 101–28), Justin McDaniel distinguishes the "idealistic" form of a "rational, canonical Buddhism" (p. 107) from what he has found to be very frequently the case in Thailand—that Buddhist practice, including chant, is deployed to afford protection from threatening spirits and to win favors from deities, Buddhas, and Bodhisattas. Clearly, McDaniel researches what is "normative" in what is called the socio-cultural sense—see my earlier related note. From the viewpoint of official and scriptural Buddhism, the apotropaic and invocatory uses of chant (even when these, new or old, derive from a mix of popular Buddhism and shamanism) *are* indeed acceptable and—especially in Mahayana and Vajrayana—are sometimes highly recommended; nonetheless, they belong to levels of practice that fall short of chant's *ultimate* purpose.

9. Given that Indian and Western calendars are difficult to correlate, and that Indian sources did not systematically record dates, the chronology of the Buddha's life is difficult to establish with accuracy, ranging from 624–544 BCE in parts of Southeast Asia to 448–368 BCE in much of East Asia. Dates based on Western scholarship are 566–466 or 563–463 BCE, though according to Keown's dictionary, the current consensus among Western scholars is that he died between 410 and 400 BCE. See "Date of the Buddha" in Damien Keown, ed., *A Dictionary of Buddhism* (Oxford and New York: Oxford UP, 2003).

followed—guide others, usually over a long series of rebirths, to *bodhi* (P. and Skt. "awakening"). Thus the Buddha was simply a human being, but one who over many lifetimes underwent spiritual transformation by sheer self-reliance and eventually—as Siddhattha Gotama—became fully awakened. Theravadins assert that there can be only one Buddha in any given "Buddha-era."

"The Four Noble Truths" on which the Teaching of Gotama Buddha is based are said to be strictly analytic, with the fourth of these truths expounding an "Eightfold Path" of self-reliant practices. The Four Noble Truths are that life is unsatisfying and painfully flawed (P. *dukkha*; Skt. *duḥkha*); that this condition is due to ignorant desire or craving; that desire/craving can come to a cessation so that one is liberated; and that the Eightfold Path is the means to achieve this *bodhi*. The eight self-reliant practices are (1) right view, (2) right intention, (3) right speech, (4) right action, (5) right living, (6) right effort, (7) right mindfulness, and (8) right meditative concentration.

According to doctrinal Theravada, the universe is not a deeply structured holism, nor is it created or sustained by a transcendent force of any kind. The liberated does not "become one with" or "merge with" a universe or any holism. Technically, for a Theravadin, the ownness of effort is precisely what "self-power" means. At the moment of "liberation without remainder,"[10] the "liberated" is absolutely unconditioned or "nibbanic" (rendering moot the passively moded word "liberated," of course). The nibbanic (English adjective from the noun "Nibbāna" assimilated from Pali *nibbāna*) cannot—even at some sublime level—be identified with the empirical world.

For a Mahayanist or Vajrayanist (though the doctrinal "workings-out" between and within these two traditions often differ very much), liberation is also achieved, in the final analysis, by one's

---

10. In Theravada, an *arahant* (Skt. *arhat*) is "one who has attained 'awakening' or enlightenment." "*Nibbāna*-without-remainder" is that of an *arahant* whose psycho-physical factors and thus whose individuality is halted for all time. "*Nibbāna*-with-remainder" is that of an *arahant* who still bears the effects of karma, though new karma can no longer be produced.

own effort, though a more directly interventionist help from others, and much transfer of merit (what Buddhists in their terms call "other-help"), can vastly *abet* one's *own* effort. This "other-help" in Mahayana and Vajrayana, much of it coming from Buddhas and Bodhisattvas, is assimilated (i.e., "becomes or is recognized as one's own") by the "self-power" of the individual. Such is the case even in what Buddhists specifically call "other-help" schools, such as Pure Land Buddhism (Japanese *Jōdo Shinshū* and its spin-offs may be the only conspicuous exceptions). Thus, Mahayana and Vajrayana, though largely differing from Theravada on how self-power is structured, do firmly keep self-power *in the determining position*.

In Mahayana and Vajrayana, there are many sutras (Buddhist scriptures: a *sūtra* is a "discourse of Buddha," *sutta* in Pali), while in Theravada there are just those in the Pali Canon. The majority of Mahayanists and Vajrayanists also affirm many ahistorical Celestial Buddhas who function synchronically in paradises or Pure Lands of their own, whereas Theravadins only affirm that there were six Buddhas prior to Siddhattha Gotama Buddha (unique to the current Buddha-age but now nibbanic, though his living Teaching abides for a finite period of time), with more Buddhas to come but only in the future, each with his own Buddha-age, in temporal succession.

Mahayanists and Vajrayanists understand a "Bodhisattva" to be a being in a state of very advanced "awakening" (or "enlightenment," as *bodhi* is often rendered) who—out of an overwhelming compassion—aims to bring those who are mired in the cycle-of-birth-and-death to enlightenment. Mahayana, literally "Great Vehicle," and Vajrayana, literally "Diamond Vehicle," both call themselves "Big Vehicle" traditions because of their Bodhisattvic drive to liberate all sentient beings. Indeed, among Mahayanist and Vajrayanist common folk, a Bodhisattva is primarily perceived as a heroic Supernal Being who delays her/his entry into Nirvana until all sentient beings have been guided into *bodhi* and can thus likewise enter Nirvana. In this sense, "*universal salvation*" is a key teaching of most Big Vehicle schools.

The many Big Vehicle schools differ as to why a Bodhisattva is not a Buddha: some affirm that a Bodhisattva is on the way to Buddhahood but has further perfection yet to achieve; some, proceeding on different doctrinal assumptions, maintain that a Bodhisattva delays Buddhahood in order to liberate other beings; and, depending on school, there are diverse other explanations as well. In Theravada, instead, "Bodhisattva" (in Theravada's Pali, *bodhisatta*) is the word by which Siddhattha Gotama in his discourses referred to himself in his previous lives and in his current life before he attained full Buddhahood. The standard use of the word *bodhisatta* thus applies only to the one on the way to becoming a Buddha, and not to others on the path to awakening. According to the Pali Canon, a *bodhisatta* still suffers from such human afflictions as sickness, sorrow, and delusion because he is not yet a Buddha.

In the majority traditions of either Mahayana or Vajrayana, at the moment of liberation the "liberated" fully realizes that s/he is *not* distinct from the unfathomable, the "unconditioned" that is *empty* of all determinations. But unlike Theravada, the majority Mahayana and Vajrayana as they stand at the present time (and this has been the case for many centuries) affirm the *trikāya* ("three-mode"; Skt. literally "three-body") doctrine whereby the unfathomable, the "unconditioned" (the definition of which we have just now recounted), is the first of *three* bodies (though the first is identical with them all). The Buddha is understood to manifest in three modes or "bodies": (1) the *dharmakāya* or "Truth-Body," which is the "unconditioned," the ultimate reality and truth; (2) the *saṃbhogakāya* or "Enjoyment-Body," which is the celestial and sublime form that teaches, surrounded by hosts of Bodhisattvas (and other supernatural beings), in the Pure Land of the Buddha; and (3) the *nirmāṇakāya* or "Emanation-Body," which constitutes the *projections*[11] of the Buddha into the worlds of suffering, the cycles-of-birth-and-death, in order to teach and guide. (Note, therefore, that much Big Vehicle Buddhism considers Siddhartha Gautama Buddha—whom it often calls Sakyamuni [Skt. *Śakyamuni*, "the Sakyan sage"]—to be a *nirmāṇakāya*-projection and not a mere human being who has after many rebirths earned nirvanic realization.)

---

11. Such "projections" seem to be understood in what Christian theologians would call a "Docetist" formulation.

Another benchmark difference between Theravada and the majority of present-day Big Vehicle schools is that the latter affirm in one way or another (again depending on school) that—in Reality—*nirvāṇa* and *saṃsāra* are *identical*.[12] As we shall indicate later in somewhat more detail (see the section entitled "Buddhism and Same-Power"), this ontological identification seems to have developed out of a more epistemological formulation, namely, that life can be regarded in two ways: according to *saṃvṛti-satya* ("world-ensconced" or "concealing" or "relative" truth) and according to *paramārtha-satya* ("supreme truth"). Though the history of this Buddhist problematic is complicated and much controverted to this day, the mixing of the epistemological and ontological seems to have started early on, so what came to be called the Teaching of the Two Truths refers simultaneously to the knowing and the known.

Nowadays, it is usually through the theme of "emptiness" that the Mahayana or Vajrayana layperson meets (the historical consequences of) the above Teaching. *Śūnyatā* ("emptiness") is the purely "unconditioned" and thus noncharacterizable, but nonetheless *śūnyatā* is *enabling*. The empirical world continues on in its mundanity and concreteness (indeed, to be *appreciated* in all its particularity) but is purely *śūnya* or "empty." Indeed, it is said that only a Buddha's awareness, because it is both omniscient and enabling, can fully *realize* and *accomplish* this subtle Teaching, though Bodhisattvas and other relatively enlightened beings can intuit it in proportion to their degree of enlightenment.

It should be clear at this point that in Big Vehicle Buddhism the definition of self-power undergoes a massive shift from that which we see in Theravada. The *trikāya* doctrine, because it deems the purely *"unconditioned"* to be the first "body" of the *Buddha*, transforms the Ultimate into the *Buddha* himself. There are several other important strands of Buddhist development that diversely contribute to this outcome. The *tathāgata-garbha* (Skt. "embryonic Bud-

---

12. This formulation is variously addressed, and at length, by Buddhist philosophers: in Western terms one could say that some read it epistemologically and some read it ontologically. The problematic of *śūnyatā* is treated in more detail, ahead, in the section entitled "Buddhism and Same Power."

dha") tradition, for example, affirms a *buddha-dhātu* ("Buddha-nature") which is the inherent Buddhahood of all sentient beings, and some Chinese and Japanese schools extend Buddha-nature to all things whatsoever. In several important Big Vehicle schools, the *tathāgata-garbha* is explicitly understood as "intrinsically luminous mind" (which is the Mind of the Buddha, or the "Buddha-mind" of all sentient beings). Especially in Tibetan Buddhism, this Buddha-mind is often understood as "clear light" or "luminous space" in order to emphasize that Buddha-mind is purely unconditioned but beatific and enabling. From its side, all the while, the Two Truths doctrine, by rendering *identical* the purely "unconditioned" Ultimate (viz., "emptiness") *and* the empirical or relative self (along with the latter's whole samsaric world), has been engineering much of this massive shift.

The combined effect of these sometimes convergent and sometimes divergent factors builds toward what is, in terms of our overall thesis, a crucial general conclusion: according to the majority traditions of Big Vehicle Buddhism, each and every one is *not* in Reality *distinct* from the "purely unconditioned" (whether the "purely unconditioned" is identified with the Buddha-body or Buddha-nature or emptiness, or any of various other formulations, depending on tradition and school). Therefore, the process of liberation can be recounted (at least in abstract conceptual terms) as a Self-reflexive "acting-out." Since, strictly speaking, nothing is "outside" of *dharmakāya* or *śūnyatā* or the *buddha-dhātu*, etc., self-power is really an exercise in Self-power. Thus, what this present work is proposing is again confirmed, though this time by a more circuitous route. Theravadin self-power and Mahayanist/Vajrayanist Self-power are both "self-power" in the wider or generic sense, that is, "self-power" understood to mean "power helping itself."

I am very well aware, however, that there is a lurking danger in my deployment of the term "Self-power," here, to describe how the "unconditioned" functions in Mahayana and Vajrayana. The term "Self-power" can quite easily suggest—especially to theists—that *śūnyatā*, *dharmakāya*, "Buddha-nature" (or whatever the formulation of the "unconditioned") is a Personality or perhaps an Absolute in the sense of an entitative substratum. While in the history of

Buddhism some Buddhist schools have accused other Buddhist schools of a masked retreat (back into the Divine Substantialism that Sakyamuni Buddha rejected), almost all Buddhist schools would firmly repudiate any such characterization of their teaching. Lest I give any impression that the "unconditioned" in Buddhism is God-like (in a Vedantic sense, for example), I shall use, in lieu of what I mean by self-power, the term "Same-power" (which seems better able to fend off misreadings). In sum, Theravada affirms "self-power," Mahayana and Vajrayana affirm "Same-power" (which is how "self-power" operates in Mahayana and Vajrayana), and Catholicism affirms "Other-power."

Catholicism's (irreducible) difference from Buddhism is that other-power is, in the final analysis, in the determining position. (Because Catholicism's "other-power" is "God," depending on context I shall be sometimes calling it "Other-power.") Other-power is in the determining position whether we address the status of the individual in this life or in heavenly beatitude. God "freely" *initiates* the "prevenient grace" that with the individual's freely willed consent enables the process of "sanctification" to continue. Without grace, a person cannot achieve ultimate beatitude. (Note, however, that Catholicism holds that those whom God "in His[13] unfathomable wisdom" chooses *not* to send the invitation to explicit Christian belief can still achieve salvation if they "strive to lead a good

---

13. To the uninformed, the use of the masculine possessive pronoun (and also the masculine pronoun) in reference to God can be misleading insofar as it can be misread to mean that God is gendered. Thus, the official Catholic Catechism is at great pains to remind us that "God is neither man nor woman" and "transcends human fatherhood and motherhood" (see #239 in *Catechism of the Catholic Church: With Modifications from the Editio Typica* [hereafter CCC], 2nd edition, New York and London: Doubleday, 1997). But because Jesus Christ called God by the name "Father" and taught His followers to do so, the Church knows that there are necessarily reasons for this. "Jesus revealed that God is Father in an unheard-of sense" (CCC #240), identifying God's "Fatherhood" with the First Trinitarian Person's "generating" of the Second Trinitarian Person. This is not at all to deny that "God's parental tenderness can also be expressed by the image of motherhood" (#239); indeed, Scripture, the saints, and the consistent Catholic tradition repeatedly do so.

life";[14] note too, however, that it is still God's grace, earned by Christ's death and resurrection, that is understood to enable, though latently, their striving and ultimate salvation.) For *everyone*, Christ's unique and historical redemptive act is *absolutely* required, and His grace must be individually imparted for the individual's salvation to occur.

God creates, sustains, and is present in all creation but is *distinct from* creation. God is present in human beings in a special way because they are made par excellence "in the divine image" (that is, they have intellect and free will), and God is "supra-naturally" present via grace in those who are in union with the "divine life"; even so, God remains ultimately *distinct from* human beings. This is the case even after death, when an individual who has died "in grace" is in heavenly beatitude. In the "Beatific Vision," the human person intuitively (i.e., without the mediation of ideas or images) "sees" God and shares in the divine (Trinitarian) life, but still is *not identical* with God. (Here note the following, however: as always in Catholicism, doctrinal formulations and even the words of Holy Scripture themselves are regarded only as clues—precious clues, but clues nonetheless. That is, they are true "insofar as they can go,"[15] but they reveal only to the extent that the human mind, even the human mind enlightened by grace, can understand. Regrettably, this point is often overlooked.)

---

14. See *Dogmatic Constitution on the Church* (*Lumen Gentium*), #16, in VAT2D. I am using the broadest language found in the Church documents, so as to include Buddhists and other non-theists. Ahead, my long footnote to the subtitle "Catholicism and Other-Power" (introducing the section of the same name) supplies the bibliographical information needed to demonstrate authoritative Catholic teaching.

15. The words of Sacred Scripture are precious because they represent privileged clues that God chose to give as Revelation. "Revelation" is a technical term within Catholicism, referring both to the ways by which God self-discloses to humanity, and to the content of such revelation. Some of these ways/content are accessible via natural human reason and some are not. Those that could never be known without God's extraordinary intervention into history are designated as "supernatural Revelation." The content of supernatural Revelation is called the *depositum fidei* ("deposit of faith") and is understood to have been fully transmitted in its foundational form by Jesus Christ during his historical mission.

There are many other pure differences between Buddhism and Catholic Christianity, though perhaps—in the Derridean sense—less "founding" than the difference between Buddhist "self-power" and Catholic "other-power" (terms taken here in what I have called their wider or generic senses). Buddhists affirm a cycle of temporal rebirths of karmic effects, and Catholics affirm one temporal birth/death for each individual. Buddhism's rebirth is not of a "soul" per se but of karmic effects that have an affinity for one another, and these through a series of links (Skt. *nidāna*) can generate a "sentient being" both "like and unlike"[16] the preceding sentient being that died and caused the pertaining karmic effects to be reborn. There can be countless thousands upon thousands of rebirths (*kamma* [Pali] or *karma* [Skt.], literally "action," = "law of cause and effect"), and liberation is achieved by a gradual or sudden elimination of the attachments that keep the *karma* going.

Both Buddhism and Catholicism affirm that individual wrongdoing incurs for the perpetrator negative consequences from which s/he must be first purified if s/he is to achieve eventual beatitude. However, in Buddhism it is karmic retribution, sometimes over many lifetimes, that can effect this purification, whereas in Catholicism properly repented sins are forgiven but some disfigurement of the soul remains and must be purified either in this life or in the purgatorial state after death.

The Sangharaja of Thai Buddhism, His Holiness Somdet Phra Nyanasamvara (1913–2013), has said in an interview[17] that in terms of social behavior, no Buddhist doctrine marks off a Buddhist from a Christian more than that of *kamma*, since it couples a calm acceptance of past and present misery with a strong motive to reform for

---

16. The scriptural reference is to *The Questions of King Milinda* (*Milinda-pañha*), II, 2, 1. The relevant passage can be readily found on the Buddhanet website at http://www.buddhanet.net/ pdf-file/milinda.pdf (accessed December 23, 2009), trans. Bhikkhu Pesala (new revised edition, 2001; Penang, Malaysia: Inward Path).

17. Privately recounted to me by my colleague, Dr. Kirti Bunchua (director of the [interfaith] Graduate School of Philosophy and Religions, Assumption U. of Thailand), after his personal interview with the Sangharaja sometime in autumn 1994.

a better future; whereas, in his opinion, Christians in a miserable physical or psychological plight are more tempted to question the God they believe in, especially if they consider the misery to be undeserved. Actually, I think it only fair to point out that I have personally known, on the Buddhist side, quite a few Buddhists who have racked their consciences with self-questioning because they cannot, at least in this present life, know what bad deed in a previous life occasioned their present (acute) suffering, since clearly they do not perceive the latter commensurate with any harm they have done in this life. In fact, Buddhism and Catholicism have their respective counsels/remedies in the face of what can be called these "existential protests." While agonizing and understandable indeed, and I have in my own life so agonized many a time, it seems to me these protests derive in the main from ("merely") psycho-emotional repugnance . . . either that or, in a few cases, from something much more consequential, namely, doubt in the pertaining doctrinal system itself. From my point of view, Catholicism is particularly advantaged among the major Christian denominations because it emphasizes that suffering in life can be a call to share in Christ's redemptive mission[18] and thus on these grounds a blessing in its own right.

The Sangharaja's appraisal directs us to another (but associated) pure difference: Buddhism affirms that perfect justice prevails as the subtext of the mundane world, and Catholicism affirms that both because of the "Fall" of the first parents of the human race and individual human "sin" (the freely willed choice of evil), a real and thoroughgoing injustice[19] often prevails in the mundane world. The difference, broadly speaking, between Buddhism and Catholicism on this point is best encapsulated here in terms of a concrete example (though, as always, one must keep in mind that examples necessarily speak *in grosso modo*). If, let us say, a rich politician who is a

18. This teaching is explained ahead, at the end of this monograph's section entitled "Catholicism and One Life-Span Only."

19. Justice/injustice here is not meant in the theological sense of "justification," which is a technical term in theology meaning the graced state conferred upon a person through Baptism.

thief steals from his subordinate, in Buddhist terms he has committed an injustice and as such should be punished according to the civil law. He also on the subtextual level has violated the second Precept,[20] "Not to take what has not been given," and thus has generated bad *kamma/karma* for himself, and he will suffer a perfectly "just" karmic retribution in this rebirth or a subsequent rebirth. But most classical Buddhist ethicists would also insist that on the subtextual level it is also the case that the subordinate, though he is a victim on the surface level, deserves his victimhood—indeed, it is a karmic retribution, maybe for a violation of the very same second Precept in his present rebirth or before.[21]

Catholicism would concur that the politician has violated civil justice and also transgressed a morally binding precept (the Seventh Commandment), but it certainly would not dare to conclude that the subordinate is on a subtextual level suffering from divine retribution for individual sin (according to Catholicism, suffering may be divine punishment or purification for individual sin or imperfection but the Church should steadfastly and humbly prescind from any such presumption in an individual case).

One of our conclusions here can be, then, that *both* Buddhism and Catholicism, when they are being true to themselves, *promote* material and spiritual assistance to the needy, and thus they can (and do) cooperate in many socio-cultural and even religious projects. But this is not to gainsay in the least that these very "samenesses" are established by more profoundly different teachings on suffering-and-justice.

While by no means coextensive among Buddhist denominations, as are the root teachings of self-power and the law of karma, two other teachings—(1) "universal liberation" and (2) vegetarianism (as an application of the "non-harming of sentient beings")—do characterize very significant representations of the Buddhist reli-

20. The Five Precepts incumbent on all Buddhists are (1) do not kill or injure living beings, (2) do not take what has not been given, (3) avoid misconduct in sensual matters, (4) abstain from false speech, and (5) abstain from all intoxicants.

21. There are technical exceptions: for example, the subordinate may be a Bodhisattva agreeing to be the victim of theft in order to somehow help someone toward liberation.

gion. The doctrine of "universal liberation," identified with the dominant traditions within Mahayana and Vajrayana Buddhism, asserts that *all* sentient beings will eventually be liberated. The great Vajrayanist traditions of Tibet, Mongolia, etc., and, in the Far East, the Chinese Huayan, Tiantai, and Chan schools so formative of contemporary Mahayana Buddhism in China, Japan, and Korea, assert this universal liberation, as do the Pure Land schools. The doctrine of universal liberation is not treated at length in this Section One ("The Pertaining Buddhist and Catholic Doctrines Compared") but is implied in those Big Vehicle teachings that are addressed in more detail. Its far-reaching significance emerges clearly in Section Two ("Buddhism and Catholicism Appraising Each Other"), where there is a discussion of the locus assigned to Catholics in Mahayanist/Vajrayanist doctrinal paradigms. In contrast with Big Vehicle Buddhism, Catholic Christianity affirms that "eternal damnation" is possible (though it is important to add that in Catholicism God predestines no one to hell: ultimately, the individual's own freely chosen hatred and selfishness drive him/her to the hell-state).

Vegetarianism as a form of *ahiṃsā* (nonharming) is extremely important in Chinese Buddhism, though less so in South Asian, Japanese, Korean, and Tibetan Buddhism. (Thus I limit what this monograph says about it to the following). Pali scriptures and Mahayana scriptures differ as to whether Buddha ate meat when it was presented to him. A Theravadin monk is prohibited from eating meat if he sees, hears, or suspects that an animal has been slaughtered specifically on his behalf, lest he be complicit in the violation of the first Precept ("not to injure or kill"). Mahayanists, among other reasons, encourage vegetarianism in order to cultivate Bodhisattvic compassion. Chinese Mahayanist monks and nuns strictly abstain from meat, usually because all sentient beings are understood to be embryonic Buddhas (that is, Buddhas-to-be). Indeed, there are Mahayana sutras and other authoritative writings that condemn meat-and-fish eaters to the hells. Most Chinese Buddhist laypeople abstain at least periodically from meat-eating, and devout practitioners abstain completely. In contrast, Catholicism requires—as a form of penance—abstention from meat on certain days in the Church calendar, but does not otherwise discourage meat-eating. In the past, some of its more austere religious communities of monks and nuns have practiced vegetarianism, and some of these still retain a modified vegetarianism; the primary rationale for the practice is usually ascetical, rather than the Mahayana Buddhist's "respect for other sentient beings."

We proceed now to the more developed comparisons of Buddhist teachings and Catholic teachings that are contrary to each other. The respective teachings are documented by pertaining authoritative sources. If readers want to pursue any concept or term or reference on their own, in more detail, the following suggestions may be helpful. For the benefit of this monograph's monolingual readers, I have limited these to sources available in English. For research in Buddhism, one may begin by consulting three recent dictionaries/encyclopedias of Buddhism, their editors and contributors all highly regarded in Buddhist studies: *Encyclopedia of Buddhism*, ed. Robert E. Buswell (New York: Macmillan Reference Books, 2003); *The Encyclopedia of Buddhism*, eds. Damien Keown and Charles S. Prebish (London: Routledge/Curson, 2004); and *The Princeton Dictionary of Buddhism*, by Robert E. Buswell and Donald S. Lopez (Princeton, NJ: Princeton UP, 2013). There are several other distinguished Buddhist dictionaries and encyclopedias in English of this same comprehensive type. For either more specialized or more concise treatments, there are now many other Buddhist dictionaries so-designated, and many Internet resources readily available. These all supply bibliographies for further work. The Buddhist scriptures are vast, but there are quite a few single-volume readers that collect selections, in English translation, arranged thematically and/or historically (and some include significant canonical but non-scriptural sources as well). Two relatively recent ones are *Buddhist Scriptures*, ed. Donald S. Lopez Jr. (Penguin Classics, 2004), and *Original Buddhist Sources: A Reader*, ed. Carl Olson (Rutgers UP, 2005). Catholics in particular may be interested to know that one of the most successful contemporary introductions to Buddhism, now in its second edition, is written by an established Buddhologist who is a Catholic and a member of the Focolare Movement: Donald W. Mitchell, *Buddhism: Introducing the Buddhist Experience* (Oxford UP-USA, 2nd ed., 2007). For a collection of classical Buddhist philosophical texts, ranging from the beginnings of formal Buddhist philosophical thought through to the twentieth century, I highly recommend *Buddhist Philosophy: Essential Readings*, eds. William Edelglass and Jay Garfield (Oxford UP, 2009). It organizes its translations, accompanied by expert explanatory essays, in sections entitled "Metaphysics and Ontology," "Philosophy of Language and Hermeneutics," "Epistemology," "Philosophy of Mind and the Person," and "Ethics."

Catholicism is more centralized than Buddhism, so its official teachings can be located more easily. The complete publishing information for Vatican Council II, collections of the declarations of previous Ecumenical (or "General") councils and papal encyclicals, and the recent *Catechism of the Catholic Church* (revised ed., 1997) can be found below, with further affiliated material, in the lengthy footnote to the section in this monograph entitled "Catholicism and Other-Power"; several footnotes below it, the publishing information for biblical references used in this monograph is supplied (along with pertaining abbreviations). For concepts, terms, historical references, etc., I also suggest the *New Catholic Encyclopedia* and its *Supplements*, 2nd ed., 15 vols. (Catholic University of America and the Gale Group, 2003), and the still classic *Sacramentum Mundi: An Encyclopedia of Theology*, Karl Rahner, SJ, et al., 6 vols. (London: Burns and Oates, 1968–1970). Many readers still find the "old" *Catholic Encyclopedia* (Encyclopedia Press, 1914) useful in many respects; it remains readily available in most libraries and is online at www.newadvent.org/cathen. There are also, in English, several Catholic dictionaries and many Internet resources. Of the many twentieth-century Catholic theologians who perform brilliantly and whose work is sound, I would recommend, here, Henri de Lubac, SJ, and Hans Urs von Balthasar. The publications of both are voluminous. In the case of de Lubac, my favorite remains what is considered by many his jewel, a relatively early work of his (1953) that is entitled in its English translation *The Splendor of the Church*, trans. Michael Mason (Ignatius Press, 1999; orig. Eng. edition, Sheed and Ward, 1956). Balthasar has written a comprehensive account of de Lubac's body of work, entitled *The Theology of Henri de Lubac: An Overview*, trans. Joseph Fessio, SJ, and Michael Waldstein (Ignatius Press, 1991; orig. Ger. edition, 1976). In the case of the very prolific Balthasar, I think it is best to start with a collection of selected texts. I recommend *The von Balthasar Reader*, eds. Medard Kehl and Werner Loser (Crossroad, 1997). A short but very good summary of Balthasar's theological approach can be found in Angelo (now Cardinal) Scola, *Hans Urs von Balthasar: A Theological Style* (Wm B. Eerdmans, 1995; orig. It. edition, 1991).

Buddhism and Self-Power

Let us now establish each of the above differences in more detail, beginning with what I see as the founding difference, namely, Buddhism's self-power and Catholicism's other-power. Indeed, the Buddha Sakyamuni's insistence on radical self-reliance and his denial of the existence of a Supreme God (understood to mean an eternal and personal God who creates the universes and everything in and of them) are key features of his teaching. "Therefore, O Ananda, be ye lamps[22] unto yourselves, rely on yourselves, and do not rely on external help" is the famous "parting admonition" uttered by the Buddha in his "Farewell Discourse,"[23] and in the canonical *Book of Gradual Sayings* the Buddha asserts that "nothing was created by a Supreme Creator."[24] This emphasis on self-power carries through in one form or another to the present day and characterizes the doctrine of all three Buddhist traditions, Theravada, Mahayana, and Vajrayana. Herewith a few contemporary examples from prominent Buddhist teachers:

22. Or "islands." The word in the original text is ambiguous. See Ven. Mettanando Bhikkhu, "Applied Buddhist Philosophy in Academic Research," chapter VII, endnote 5, in Warayuth Sriwarakuel, Manuel B. Dy, et al., eds., *Cultural Traditions and Contemporary Challenges in Southeast Asia: Thai Philosophical Studies* (Washington, DC: Council for Research in Values and Philosophy [CRVP], Catholic U. of America, 2005; 2009).

23. Ven. Mettanando Bhikkhu, ibid., points out that there are several versions of the "parting admonition," such as that in the *Mahāparinibbānasutta*, 2, 33; and that in the *Aggaññasutta*. One of the readily available Internet sources is http://www.accesstoinsight.org/tipitaka/dn/dn.16.1-6.vaji.html.

24. *Aṅguttara Nikāya Suttapiṭaka*, Pali Text Society, AN 1, 173. The *Aṅguttara Nikāya* is very extensive, with several thousand suttas in eleven books. Online, see http://www.accesstoinsight.org/tipitaka/an/index.html#an9.

There can be no first cause, because each cause becomes an effect and each effect a cause.[25]... *Nibbāna*, the goal in Buddhism, corresponds to salvation, except that the former is not attained through the agency of another or outside being, but solely through one's own efforts.[26]
—Ven. Dr. H. Saddhatissa (Theravada)

But the Buddha teaches that we have to effect our salvation by our own effort and mental purity.[27]
—Ven. Dr. K. Sri Dhammananda (Theravada)

On the surface, taking refuge [in the Buddha, Dharma, Sangha, what is called the Triple Gem] appears to mean believing in or relying on the protection of an external power; but on a more profound level, such faith and reliance are only helpful conditions that propel one's body and mind to realize one's wishes for protection and blessing.[28]
—Ven. Yin-shun (Mahayana)

We should not think of the Buddha as some entity outside of ourselves. When we prostrate, we should not seek the Buddha's help.... So why do we prostrate? Because the world would not know how to practice without Dharma [the Buddha's Teaching],

---

25. The doctrine of "dependent arising" affirms that all phenomena arise in dependence on causes and conditions themselves dependent on causes and conditions "from beginningless time," so that phenomena do not have intrinsic being. To understand Buddhism, it is crucial for non-Buddhists to understand that what has been called traditionally in the West the "cosmological argument from existence" to "uncaused cause" is in Buddhist eyes itself a fallacy: in short, a Buddhist would maintain that if everything always has cause(s), it does not make sense to argue that there can be a first cause. *How* "dependent causality" is to be properly understood becomes, in Buddhism, one of the main themes of philosophical inquiry, and several important differences arise. Madhyamaka Buddhism argued that the law of dependent causality itself makes sense only if it is equivalent to *śūnyatā*, or emptiness. In turn, Theravada in particular tends to regard some Mahayanist formulations of emptiness as a cryptic return to the heretical notion of "uncaused cause."

26. *An Introduction to Buddhism* (London: London Buddhist Vihara, 1976), pp. 23, 26.

27. *Buddhism as a Religion* (Kuala Lumpur, Malaysia: Buddhist Maha Vihara, 1994), p. 19.

28. *The Way to Buddhahood: Instructions from a Modern Chinese Master* (Boston: Wisdom P., 1998), p. 28.

and the Dharma was given to us by the Buddha. Therefore, we prostrate out of gratitude. . . . The Buddha does exist, but there is nothing we can get from him.[29]
—Master Sheng-yen (Chan School, Mahayana)

Your savior doesn't come from outside; it comes from inside. You can love; you do have the capacity to appreciate the other person, to feel grateful.[30]
—Ven. Thich Nhat Hanh (Vietnamese, Mahayana)

It has nothing to do with authority. It is your responsibility to take care of yourself. That's the discipline. That's mine, too.[31]
—Hakuyu Taizan Maezumi Roshi (Soto Zen)

The Pure Land schools and/or practices of Mahayana and Vajra-yana seem to come closest to dependence on other-power. A Pure Land (Skt. literally "Blissful Land," *sukhāvathī*) is generally understood to be a supernal world generated by a *saṃbhogakāya*, a Buddha's "Enjoyment-Body" that is the fruit of aeons of religious practice. (Perhaps the most widely preached is the Western Paradise of Amitabha Buddha.) By abetting the rebirth of his devotees into his Pure Land, a Buddha fulfills his vows, taken upon his commitment to the Bodhisattvic way aeons earlier (when he was not yet a Buddha), to lead to Buddhahood all those who invoke him (once he shall have attained Buddhahood himself). What is crucial to my case, however, is that standard Pure Land doctrine stipulates that the Pure Land is not ultimate beatitude, not full Buddhahood, but rather a condition where Buddhist practice, especially meditation, is uncommonly easy (with direct instruction from the Buddha, and absence of temptation or distraction). In short, practitioners must still ultimately liberate themselves. The Buddha's other-power is to facilitate self-power. The only conspicuous exception I can find is one of Japan's Pure Land schools, Shinran's *Jōdo Shinshū* (True Pure

29. *Ch'an Magazine*, summer 2001 (Elmhurst, NY: Dharma Drum, 2001).

30. Thich Nhat Hanh, *Anger: Wisdom for Cooling the Flames* (New York: Riverhead Books, 2001), p. 111.

31. "Life is the Best Treasure" (transcription of *shosan*, 1988 summer *ango*), *The Ten Directions* (fall–winter 1998), p. 13.

Land school), in which self-power is considered an affront to (and by its very nature a blockage of) the absolute saving other-power of Amitabha.

Herewith some contemporary examples of Pure Land teachers taking care to establish that the Pure Land enables a practitioner's self-power:

> Your life is eternal and you will become a Buddha after you complete your study under Amitabha Buddha.[32]
> —Upasaka Li Ping Nan (Chinese, Pure Land)

> [T]he Buddha is our teacher and not a god.... Praying to the Buddhas, Bodhisattvas or spirits simply does not do it.[33]
> —Ven. Master Chin Kung (Chinese, Pure Land)

> This Western Pure Land was created by Buddha Amitabha as an ideal place of cultivation [meditation, etc., in order to progress to Buddhahood] as those who are born there are no longer subject to reincarnation within the six realms [hells, hungry ghosts, animals, humans, asuras, and the heavens of the gods].[34]
> —Ven. Master Chin Kung (Chinese, Pure Land)

> In the case of *Dewachen* [Tibetan representation of *sukhāvathī*], you get there but that does not mean you become enlightened. What happens is that you will not revert to cyclic existence; rather, you will have, instead, all the positive and auspicious conditions for the accumulation of merit and primordial wisdom. You will be able to abandon all non-virtue there and practice to tame and train your mind until such point you are ripe for enlightenment.[35]
> —His Holiness the Drikung Kyabgön, Chetsang Rinpoche (Tibetan, Drikung Kagyu tradition)

---

32. *A Buddhist Goal That Can Be Achieved in One's Present Life* (Taichung, Taiwan: Taichung Buddhist Lotus Association, 2000), p. 14.

33. *The Collected Works of Ven. Master Chin Kung* (Kuala Lumpur, Malaysia: Amitabha Buddhist Society, 1999), pp. 84–85.

34. Ibid., p. 299.

35. "Amitabha Buddha and the Pureland of Dewachen," trans. Michael Lewis (San Francisco Ratna Shri Sangha), pp. 3–4, from http://www.purifymind.com/AmitabhaDewachen.htm (accessed August 16, 2004).

Catholicism and Other-Power[36]

If this section is to cite authoritative Catholic sources so as to substantiate Catholicism's belief in Other-power, some description of how the official "teaching authority" (the Magisterium) functions is in order.[37] In the (Roman) Catholic Church, official teaching authority is vested in bishops who are validly ordained in what is taken to be a historically direct line of descent from Christ's Twelve

36. Unless otherwise noted, all references to Vatican Council II documents are cited from the volume identified above, Austin Flannery, OP, ed., *Vatican Council II*, Vol. 1, *The Conciliar and Post Conciliar Documents* (VAT2D), new revised edition, 1992, 3rd printing, 1996 (Northport, NY: Costello; Dublin: Dominican P.). References to other documents representing the generalized "teaching office" of the Catholic Church (declarations and decrees of past councils; papal encyclicals; documents of Vatican congregations; etc.) are to the following collection: Jacques Dupuis, SJ, et al., eds., *The Christian Faith in the Doctrinal Documents of the Catholic Church* (CF), 7th revised and enlarged edition (Bangalore, India: Theological Pub. in India, 2001; in the United States, New York: Alba House). It is to be noted that in Dupuis, above, references to the Latin collection, H. Denzinger and A. Schönmetzer, *Enchiridion Symbolorum, Definitionum et Declarationum de rebus fidei et morum* (hereafter DS), are to the 36th edition, Freiburn im Breisgau, 1976. In most cases, references I have not readily found in Dupuis, above, or which I had already researched and belong to a pre–Vatican Council II era are instead to J. Clarkson, SJ, J. Edwards, SJ, W. Kelly, SJ, and J. Welch, SJ, trans. and eds., *The Church Teaches: Documents of the Church in English Translation* (hereafter CT) (B. Herder, 1955; reprint, Rockford, IL: TAN, 1973). It is to be noted that in CT, correlations are to the 24th edition, and "in the case of more recent documents" (i.e., "recent" as of 1955) to the 28th and 29th editions of the *Enchiridion*, H. Denzinger, ed. (hereafter DZ).

When my source is CT, any correlations to DZ are to those represented in CT. (Let me advise the reader here that after my preparation of doctrinal references in this present book, Ignatius Press published, in 2012, a new bilingual Latin/English version of the *Enchiridion Symbolorum*, updating its collection of source-texts through to the end of 2008: *Enchiridion Symbolorum: A Compendium of Creeds, Definitions, and Declarations of the Catholic Church*, eds. H. Denzinger and Peter Hunermann; most but not all numerical references are consistent with DS. The arrival of this updated and readily available version makes access to source-material very convenient.) References to the universal catechism of the Catholic Church are, as already specified above, to *Catechism of the Catholic Church: With Modifications from the Editio Typica* (CCC), 2nd edition revised in accordance with the official Latin text promulgated by Pope John Paul II (New York and London: Doubleday, 1997).

37. See *Lumen Gentium*, ch. 3.

Apostles[38] and who are united with one another and with the bishop of Rome (since it is historically understood that St. Peter became the bishop of Rome and was martyred there). That St. Peter was, and consequently that the bishop of Rome is, in a unique way "holder of the keys of the Church" is established scripturally by Mt 16:18–19:

> And I tell you, you are Peter [Aramaic *Kēphā*, "Rock"[39]], and on this rock [Aramaic *kēphā*, "rock"] I will build my church, and the powers of death [literally "gates of Hades"] shall not prevail against it. I will give you the keys of the kingdom of heaven, and whatever you bind on earth shall be bound in heaven, and whatever you loose on earth shall be loosed in heaven.[40] (R/I)

Catholicism also invokes many other scriptural passages and arguments to demonstrate this "Petrine supremacy" (see, for example, Jn 21:15FF.). Of course, other Christian denominations contest, in one

38. Among the long-received scriptural sites for this teaching authority are Mt 18:18; 28:16–20, but Catholicism involves many other scriptural sites too in order to establish this Apostolic authority. See *Lumen Gentium*, ch. 3.

39. Scholars have reconstructed Christ's original Aramaic, which I supply in parentheses in this passage (Christ spoke Aramaic; Matthew's Gospel, as it has come down to us, is written in Greek).

40. From *The R.S.V. Interlinear Greek-English New Testament: The Nestle Greek Text with a Literal English Translation* (hereafter R/I) by Rev. Alfred Marshall, DLitt, with a foreword by Rev. Preb. J.B. Phillips, MA, accompanied by marginal text of the Revised Standard Version (Grand Rapids, MI: Zondervan, 1970). Because this source alternates Greek text and a literal English translation, line by line, it in general permits more proximity to how the original scriptural text communicates (also, such an arrangement constrains at least somewhat the possible resort to grossly partisan readings on the part of translators). The corresponding RSV translation on the sidebar of each page allows for convenient comparison with the interlinear text on the same page. Thus, unless indicated otherwise, New Testament translations cited in this present monograph are from either the RSV text or the interlinear text conjointly displayed in the above volume. Of course, the above volume's Nestle Greek Text, though a standard in the field, is already replete with editorial selection, in that it represents editorial preferences drawn from a much wider range of Greek variants and diverse codices. Also, the grammar and vocabulary of the Greek even in Nestle's text permit "literal" English translations differing from Marshall's "literal" translation. (And many times the disputation can be about what the "literal" meaning is, or whether the "literal" meaning is even the intended meaning.) Given these factors, I sometimes cite *The Jerusalem Bible* (hereafter JB),

form or another, some or most or all of Catholicism's official interpretation of its teaching authority. The venerable communion of Churches commonly called "Eastern Orthodoxy," for example, broke with the Western Church in the eleventh century largely over the issue of the Petrine Supremacy, the Roman version of which it rejected. Eastern Orthodoxy has retained the attribute "Catholic" as one of its appellations and considers itself properly "Catholic." Let me remind the reader, however, and especially the Christian but non-Catholic reader, that one of my main aims in this monograph is to represent Buddhism to non-Buddhists (and particularly to my fellow Catholics) and to represent, as here, Roman Catholicism to Buddhists. This monograph is *not* intended to address intra-Christian dispute.

The bishops and the Roman Pontiff (Lat. *pontifex*, "bridge builder") together constitute what is called the Apostolic assembly or "college" (Lat. *collegium*). The *elaboration* of how the Magisterium functions has developed, evolved, and been refined over many centuries, and it is crucial to attend to the *degree of authority* involved in the declaration of any given "teaching."[41] Let us first address, however, the origins of the teaching authority as the Catholic Church perceives them.

Christ gives the Apostles this mandate: "Go therefore and make

---

Alexander Jones, gen. ed. (Garden City, NY: Doubleday, 1966); sometimes *The Holy Bible: Revised Standard Version*, 2nd Catholic edition (hereafter IB) (San Francisco, CA: Ignatius P., 2006); and sometimes *The New American Bible* (with New Testament 1986 revision and Psalms 1991 revision), as it appears in *The Catholic Study Bible: The New American Bible*, 2nd edition (hereafter S/A), D. Senior and J. J. Collins, eds. (New York: Oxford UP, 2006). This present monograph also uses the above-named translations for its Old Testament references. Nowadays, I think that scholarly exegetes, be they non-Catholic or Catholic, try in all sincerity to be philologically accurate, but the biblical text is often so ambiguous that very real exegetical differences continue unabated. In these cases, this present monograph—true to its purpose of representing, on the Christian side, the viewpoint of the Catholic Church—draws from Catholic biblical exegesis.

41. Some aspects of this question, and its subtlety, are treated in the helpful chapter by Francis Sullivan, SJ, "Evaluation and Interpretation of the Documents," in Michael A. Hayes and Liam Gearon, eds., *Contemporary Catholic Theology: A Reader* (London and New York: Continuum, 1999), pp. 335–48, especially pp. 341–42.

disciples of all nations, baptizing them in the name of the Father and of the Son and of the Holy Spirit, teaching them to observe all that I have commanded you; and behold, I am with you always, to the close of the age [Gk. *sunteleias tou aiōnos*, "completion of the age," understood to mean until the "end of the world" when Christ will manifest Himself in His "Second Coming"]" (Mt 28:19–20). In Jn 17:17, Jesus Christ prays to God the Father for the ones the Father "has given" him: "Sanctify them in the truth; thy word is truth." Christ promises that after His death, resurrection, and ascension, He will send the Holy Spirit down upon the Church: "When the Advocate [Gk. *paraclētos*] comes whom I will send you from the Father, the Spirit of truth that proceeds from the Father, he will testify [= bear witness] to me" (Jn 15:26 S/A). And Acts 2:1–4 tells us that at Pentecost the Holy Spirit did indeed descend on the disciples as Christ had foretold. Later, in 2 Pt 1:12, Peter tells the brethren, "You . . . are established in the truth you have" (S/A).

Nonetheless, in the face of these assurances that Christ will be a continuous presence in the Church, that the Holy Spirit will abide in and inspire the Church, and that Christians will persevere in the truth, the fact of the matter is that the Scriptures are replete with a multitude of ambiguities and lacunae, and indeed many scriptural passages can be interpreted in contradictory ways. What is more, the Christian community existed before any written record thereof, and what later came to be called the New Testament was assembled not without considerable controversy and dispute. This is why the Catholic Church maintains that from the beginning it is the Holy Spirit that guided the successors of the Apostles, and that this "Apostolic college" even in its embryonic early form was already sorting through such a tangle of potential perplexities and making divinely inspired decisions. Catholicism can amass much historical evidence in this regard, and it can also note that Christian groups that reject the notion of Apostolic Succession have been and are at odds with one another even on the most consequential questions of faith and morals.

In particular, it has been my experience that societies with a predominantly "post-Reformation Christian" history miscalculate what the (Roman) Catholic Church takes to be the Church's relation to the

New Testament. According to Catholicism, God's inspiration of the New Testament texts *worked in and through* the Church community that produced them. The New Testament was brought forth by God in and through the bosom of the Church, Christ's "Spouse." Scripture is divinely inspired because its authors were divinely inspired, and not the other way around (see CCC #106, 108–9). (Catholicism holds the same, *mutatis mutandis*, for the Old Testament: the Old Testament is divinely inspired because its authors were divinely inspired.) Also, it is very important to note that Catholicism, while affirming the inerrancy of Scripture, "is not a 'religion of the book'" but the "religion of the 'Word' of God," namely, the "Word" who is the living Christ, the Son of God (see CCC #108). The inerrancy of Scripture does not mean that God dictated its text word for word but rather that God worked through the biblical authors and their unique styles and limitations, so that the truths that God intended to reveal do stand accurately in the biblical text. Precisely because biblical exegesis must take into account the diverse factors of historical conditioning, the religious and literary genres available to the biblical authors, and so on, Catholicism argues that the Magisterium is absolutely necessary. How otherwise could one filter out, especially in the case of abstruse biblical passages, those teachings that are eternal truth, and distinguish them from those that are, for example, empirically limited or—as is sometimes the case—divinely intended but only for a limited span of time?

In this monograph, authoritative Catholic teaching on faith ("articles of faith" to be accepted as true) and authoritative Catholic teaching on morals (moral laws that are "binding," i.e., obligatory) are substantiated by reference to the following: (1) scriptural texts that the Church invokes in support of a pertaining teaching on faith or morals; (2) declarations of ecumenical councils (official declarations, on faith or morals, of the college of bishops; these must be ratified by the pope, and they usually include many embedded scriptural passages as well as citations to the early Church Fathers,[42]

42. The term "Church Fathers" (or "patristic writers") refers to great Christian writers who passed on and clarified Christian teaching from about the second through the eighth century.

etc.); (3) papal encyclicals (an official papal letter, often in the form of a long address, usually directed to the bishops of a region or the whole world; encyclicals often include many embedded scriptural texts, etc.); and (4) the *Catechism of the Catholic Church* (an official exposition of Church teaching, promulgated by John Paul II in 1992 and republished in 1997; its most noteworthy precedent is the *Catechism of the Council of Trent*, promulgated in 1566 to promote reform and as a response to the tracts of Luther and Calvin). The *Catechism of the Catholic Church* officially belongs to what is called the "ordinary Magisterium of the Church" (see below) because it was prepared and revised by the worldwide body of bishops and then solemnly promulgated by the pope as a "sure and authentic" reflection of what the Church teaches on faith and morals.

Two modes of infallibility are said to belong to the "extraordinary Magisterium," namely, solemn definitions of a valid ecumenical council and solemn papal declarations when they are delivered *ex cathedra* ("from the chair" of Peter).[43] The preponderance of a Council's assertions are not infallible. Nor are papal definitions and judgments infallible unless they are declared to be such (and there are remarkably few instances of these). When, however, a conciliar or papal definition/judgment is infallible, a Catholic must give "the assent of faith" (sacred assent).[44]

The non-infallible teachings and judgments of either a valid ecumenical council or the pope when carrying out his official functions belong to the "ordinary Magisterium" (CCC #892). Such definitions/judgments are, in the words of the Congregation for the Doctrine of the Faith, "not irreformable"[45] (i.e., they are subject to change, or may indeed prove to be wrong). Catholicism affirms a "developmental theology": the "deposit of faith"—the deposit of divinely revealed truths—is taken to be "fixed," i.e., confined to the Scriptures and the oral Tradition of the Apostles, but the Church's

---

43. *Lumen Gentium*, #22.
44. *Lumen Gentium*, #25.
45. Instruction *"Donum Veritatis"* on the *Ecclesiastical Vocation of the Theologian* (Congregation for the Doctrine of the Faith, May 24, 1990), #24.

understanding of this fixed data continues to mature and evolve until the end of time.

To the "ordinary Magisterium," the Catholic owes the "religious submission of intellect and will" (CCC #892). Regarding official papal actions, papal encyclicals[46] belong to this class, as does the *Catechism of the Catholic Church* promulgated by John Paul II. Among Catholic theologians—conservative, liberal, and otherwise—there is a considerable range of opinion as to the degree of certainty attributable to the declarations of the ordinary Magisterium. Some conservatives tend, at least on the practical level, to almost equate the ordinary and extraordinary Magisterium. Some liberals, apart from outright dissenters, tend to treat declarations of the ordinary Magisterium as nothing more than today's "marching orders."

That Catholicism maintains that Jesus Christ is the Other-Power necessary for the "salvation" of any and every human being can be shown from the following sources. Given that the supply of such sources is, as one would expect, enormous, I have presented some commonly cited ones from Scripture, Vatican Council II, and the *Catechism of the Catholic Church*. The reader will note that the Church documents are replete with scriptural references.

In the Gospel of Matthew (Mt 28:18), the New Testament, Jesus Christ proclaims, "All authority in Heaven and Earth has been given to me" [by God the Father], and in the Gospel of John (Jn 3:5) he declares, "Truly, truly, I say to you, unless one is born of water and the Spirit [taken by Catholicism to be the sacrament of Baptism], he cannot enter the kingdom of God." Some authoritative Church articulations of these teachings are:

> No one is freed from sin by himself or by his own efforts, no one is raised above himself or completely delivered from his own weak-

---

46. Nowadays, an "Apostolic constitution" is understood to have priority over an "encyclical."

ness, solitude, or slavery; all have need of Christ who is the model, master, liberator, saviour, and giver of life.
—Vatican Council II, *Ad gentes divinitus*, from #8

The reason for missionary activity lies in the will of God, "who wishes all men to be saved and to come to the knowledge of the truth. For there is one God and one Mediator between God and men, himself a man, Jesus Christ, who gave himself as a ransom for all" (1 Tm 2:4–5), "neither is there salvation in any other" (Acts 4:12).
—Vatican Council II, *Ad gentes divinitus*, from #7.

Basing itself on Scripture and Tradition, the Council teaches that the Church, a pilgrim now on earth, is necessary for salvation: the one Christ is the mediator and the way of salvation; he is present to us in his body which is the Church. He himself explicitly asserted the necessity of faith and Baptism (cf. Mk 16:16; Jn 3:5), and thereby affirmed at the same time the necessity of the Church which men enter through Baptism as through a door.... Even though incorporated into the Church, one who does not however persevere in charity is not saved. He remains indeed in the bosom of the Church, but "in body" not "in heart." All children of the Church should nevertheless remember that their exalted condition results, not from their own merits, but from the grace of Christ. If they fail to respond in thought, word and deed to that grace, not only shall they not be saved, but they shall be the more severely judged. [text references Lk 12:48 and also Mt 5:19–20, 7:21–22, 25:41–46; Jas 2:14]
—Vatican Council II, *Lumen Gentium*, from #14 (affirming the necessity of "his body which is the Church")

The account of the Fall in Genesis 3 uses figurative language, but affirms a primeval event, a deed that took place at the beginning of the history of man. Revelation gives us the certainty of faith that the whole of human history is marked by the original fault freely committed by our first parents.
—*Catechism of the Catholic Church*, #390 (repeats the mainstream Christian teaching regarding Original Sin [the sin of disobedience prompted by the prideful intent to usurp the relation between God and humankind])

This sacrament [Baptism] is also called "the washing of regeneration and renewal by the Holy Spirit" [Ti 3:5], for it signifies and actually brings about the birth of water and the Spirit without which no one "can enter the kingdom of God."

"This bath is called *enlightenment*, because those who receive this [catechetical] instruction are enlightened in their understanding. . . ."[47] Having received in Baptism the Word, "the true light that enlightens every man," the person baptized has been "enlightened," he becomes a "son of light," indeed, he becomes "light" himself. [text references Jn 1:9; 1 Thes 5:5; Heb 10:32; Eph 5:8]
—*Catechism of the Catholic Church*, from #1215 and #1216.

The doctrine of original sin is, so to speak, the "reverse side" of the Good News that Jesus is the Savior of all men, that all need salvation, and that salvation is offered to all through Christ. The Church, which has the mind of Christ [see 1 Cor 2:16], knows very well that we cannot tamper with the revelation of original sin without undermining the mystery of Christ.
—*Catechism of the Catholic Church*, #389

For more citations regarding Other-Power, and Christ as this only and necessary Other-Power, see Vatican Council II, *Dei verbum*, #4–7, and *Gaudium et spes*, #1, 45.

Buddhism and Same-Power

In Mahayana and Vajrayana Buddhism (and we continue to talk of these as they prevail today), the progressive "awakening" of the practitioner is understood to be the developing realization that self-power is really Same-power, i.e., the realization that the empirical (or "relative" or "conventional") self is really the "same" as the Buddha, the Buddha-as-the-purely-Unconditioned, the Buddha-as-Pure-Emptiness (*śūnyatā*). (It is to the point, here again, to keep in mind that the majority Big Vehicle traditions affirm that [what we are calling] "Same-power" is *not* to be confounded with an

---

47. The text is here quoting from St. Justin's *Apol*.1, 61, 12. St. Justin was born ca. 100 and martyred 165 CE.

animating Soul because Pure Emptiness, when properly understood, precludes reification and is truly empty of all determinations.)

Both Mahayana and Vajrayana today represent various developments of Nagarjuna's[48] revolutionary version (second century CE) of how *nirvāṇa* and *saṃsāra* relate to each other. In his famous *Mūlamadhyamakakārikā*, he says, "There is not the slightest difference / Between cyclic existence (*saṃsāra*) and *nirvāṇa*. // There is not the slightest difference / Between *nirvāṇa* and cyclic existence."[49] The mundane is at once absolute emptiness (and the converse).[50] The prevailing formulations take this to mean that the Buddha-as-Pure-Emptiness is at once the mundane world (and everything and everyone "in" it). Mahayana and Vajrayana both have produced many diverse conceptualizations and nomenclatures that aim to reflect this Reality[51] of the unconditioned/conditioned, the Absolute/Relative (or conversely, the Relative/Absolute), but conceptual or phenomenological descriptions—while they can function as true clues, true directives to the Reality—cannot measure up to the Reality. Big Vehicle Buddhism emphatically asserts that only perfect Realization (full "awakening") can recognize itself-and-everything to be the Reality.

48. Nagarjuna (ca. 150–250 CE), one of the most influential Indian philosophers and a key figure in the development of Mahayana, wrote, among other works, the pivotal treatise *Mūlamadhyamakakārikā* (*Fundamental Verses on the Middle Way*). The *Mūlamadhyamakakārikā* (hereafter MKK) presents the "Two Truths" (*saṃvṛti-satya*, relative or mundane truth, and *paramārtha-satya*, absolute or ultimate truth) in such a way that they are truly identical, though only the enlightened person can recognize (and live) this identity. The enlightened individual can function—at will—according to *saṃsāra* (cyclic existence) yet see *saṃsāra* as *śūnyatā* (emptiness) and thus as nirvanic. In enlightenment, *saṃsāra* is *nirvāṇa*, *nirvāṇa* is *saṃsāra*, and there is no difference between them.

49. MKK XXV:19, in Jay L. Garfield, trans. and commentary, *The Fundamental Wisdom of the Middle Way: Nagarjuna's* Mūlamadhyamakakārikā (Oxford and New York: Oxford UP, 1995), p. 331.

50. There has been much theoretical debate over whether Nagarjuna intends the "Two Truths" to be taken epistemologically or ontologically. Regardless of what one holds in this regard, the argument I shall be making in this section still applies.

51. "Reality" is a word with a distinctly Western philosophical history. I use it here as shorthand to signify the meaning "what is really the case," though again, words cannot capture what enlightenment truly is.

The majority Mahayana and Vajrayana traditions today subscribe in one way or another to the *trikāya* ("three body") doctrine that we have already introduced. This doctrine asserts that Buddhahood functions in three "bodies" or modes or dimensions. The first is *dharmakāya*, the formless "Truth-Body" that is identical with absolute undifferentiated Reality or emptiness. The second is *sambhog-akāya*, the "Enjoyment-Body" that is a differential manifestation of Buddhahood (so there are many Buddhas, each dwelling in his/her/its[52] own celestial and blissful Pure Land and preaching to a multitude of beings who have earned, in one way or another, their right to be there). The third is *nirmāṇakāya* or the "Emanation-Body," the projection of a Buddha who, motivated by boundless compassion, assumes form so as to teach sentient beings in the lower worlds.

In terms of our argument about Same-power, the *dharmakāya* or Truth-Body is most pertinent because it is understood to be the "ultimate enabling" of all things. This teaching derives in part from Nagarjuna's declaration: "when emptiness works, everything works."[53] Often, depending on tradition and school, this "empty but enabling" is represented by metaphors that evoke what we call in Western parlance the "positive," such as "fundamental nature of mind," the "Ground Luminosity" or "Pure Light," even "Cosmic Body." (Some Chinese Buddhists even speak of the Truth-Body as the "Big I" and the individuated relative self as the "little I.") On the basis of what are called the ten *tathāgata-garbha* sutras, the "embryonic Buddha" tradition conceives of the "ultimate" in very "positive" terms, so that it can even be described as a "real and eternally existing essence that is primordially replete with all the qualities of a Buddha."[54] As for Chinese Chan, Japanese Zen, and Korean Son,

---

52. Buddhas transcend gender but can manifest as gendered or even non-gendered.

53. From MKK XXIV:14, in Frederick J. Streng, trans. of Nagarjuna's *Fundamentals of the Middle Way*, in the appendix to Streng, *Emptiness* (Nashville, TN: Abingdon P., 1967), p. 213. Stanza XXIV:14 in its entirety reads, "When emptiness (*śūnyatā*) 'works', then everything in existence 'works'. If emptiness does *not* 'work', then all existence does *not* 'work.'"

54. See concise description of "*tathāgata-garbha*" in Keown, *Dictionary of Buddhism*, p. 296.

they are perhaps best known for the teaching that any individual's "original nature" *is* already the Truth-Body, so that enlightenment is no more than the uncovering of "original nature" clouded over by ignorance. According to this way of thinking, liberation does not involve the "striving after an objective"; rather, it is the discovery of what one already is.

The crucial point, however, is that in mainstream Mahayana and Vajrayana—whatever the doctrinal conceptualization or nomenclature—there is always what we are calling Same-power in the sense that there is no "ultimate enabling" that is "outside" of this Reality (and indeed, there is no sentient being or no thing whatsoever "outside" of it). Indeed, it is on these very grounds that Theravada Buddhists, since they affirm self-power but not Same-power, sometimes accuse Mahayana and Vajrayana of surreptitiously restoring the notion of a great Soul that Sakyamuni Buddha's doctrine of *anātman* (no-soul and no-Soul) rejected. (It should be clear, already, that this present monograph intends to avoid partisanship in such intra-Buddhist debate.)

At this juncture, the *pure difference* between Same-power and Catholicism easily comes into focus. In Mahayana and Vajrayana, each and everyone (in/as *dharmakāya* or whatever/however the ultimate enabling force is called/conceived, depending on formulation) is *not* distinct from the "ultimate enabling," the "purely unconditioned." Each and everyone *is* absolute Same-power. In Catholicism, on the other hand, God the Absolute is the First Cause of everything else and is understood to be present in all creation by divine "essence, presence, and power"[55] but to be *distinct* in intrinsic nature and thus to transcend creation. Even the individual in beatitude (experiencing the Beatific Vision), though *sharing* in God's "life," remains in the final analysis still forever a creature, still forever *distinct* from God.

---

55. God is the First Cause of every creature, so—in the parlance of classical theology—every creature's being and action are *contingent* and transparent to the divine omniscience. See, for a succinct account in these terms, Etienne Gilson, *Thomism*, trans. by L.K. Shook and A. Maurer of Gilson's *Le Thomisme*, 6th edition, 1965 (Toronto: Pontifical Institute of Medieval Studies, 2002), p. 104.

What we are calling "Same-power" is clearly represented in the following selection of authoritative statements from leading Mahayana and Vajrayana masters:

> Sunyata, the nature of emptiness, is the ultimate reality of all objects, material and phenomenal. . . . Sunyata is the negation of a permanent self and of independent existence.[56]
> —H.H. the 14th Dalai Lama (Gelukpa tradition, Tibetan Buddhism)

> The Buddhas and the lights of wisdom are in no sense separate from you, but your own wisdom energy. To realize that is an experience of non-duality, and to enter into it is liberation.[57]
> —Sogyal Rinpoche (Dzogchen lineage, Tibetan Buddhism)

> In reality, the real and the false are the same (in nature); the living and the Buddhas are not a dualism; and birth-death and Nirvana as well as enlightenment (*bodhi*) and distress (*kleśa*) all belong to our self-mind and self-nature and should not be either grasped or rejected. This mind is pure and clean and fundamentally is Buddha.[58]
> —Ven. Master Hsu Yun (Chan, Chinese Buddhism)

> Don't know mind cuts through thinking. It is before thinking. Before thinking there is no doctor, no patient; also no God, no Buddha, no "I," no words—nothing at all. Then you and the universe become one. We call this nothing-mind, or primary point. Some people say this is God, or universal energy, or bliss, or extinction. But these are only teaching words. Nothing-mind is before words.[59]
> —Zen (Son) Master Seung Sahn (Son, Korean Buddhism)

---

56. In H.H. the 14th Dalai Lama, "A Brief Introduction to Tibetan Buddhism," in the Dalai Lama and Ven. Chan Master Sheng-yen, *Meeting of the Minds* (Elmhurst, NY: Dharma Drum, 1999), p. 12.

57. *The Tibetan Book of Living and Dying* (New York: HarperSanFrancisco, HarperCollins P., 1999), p. 312.

58. *Ch'an and Zen Teaching*, Series One, ed. and trans. K'uan Yu Lu [Charles Luk] (Berkeley, CA: Shambhala, 1970), p. 28.

59. Cited in Mu Soeng, *Thousand Peaks: Korean Zen—Tradition and Teachers* (Cumberland, RI: Primary Point Press, 1991), p. 222.

What Buddha found out—this is the key—is that my life is the life of everything else, all together. . . . Buddha guaranteed us, when he attained realization, that all of us, all sentient beings, have the same wisdom and virtue the Buddha Tathagata has.[60]
—Hakuyu Taizan Maezumi, Roshi (Soto Zen, Japanese Buddhism)

Catholicism and the Creator/Created Distinction

God is the immanent cause and sustainer of creation but transcends creation and so is distinct from it. Here is a sampling of pertaining Church texts in this regard:

Since he is one unique spiritual substance, entirely simple and unchangeable,[61] he must be declared really and essentially distinct from the world, perfectly happy in himself and by his very nature, and inexpressibly exalted over all things that exist or can be conceived other than himself.
—Vatican Council I (CT #355, DZ 1782)

We believe that God needs no pre-existent thing or any help in order to create, nor is creation any sort of necessary emanation from the divine substance.
—*Catechism of the Catholic Church,* #296

God is infinitely greater than all his works. . . . But because he is the free and sovereign Creator, the first cause of all that exists, God is present to his creatures' inmost being: "In him we live and move and have our being" (Acts 17:28). In the words of St. Augustine, God is "higher than my highest and more inward than my innermost self."
—*Catechism of the Catholic Church,* #300[62]

Besides presence by way of immanence, God can be said to be present in a special way in human beings. The human powers of intellect and free will are unique reflections of the nature of God:

60. In *The Ten Directions* (fall–winter 1988), p. 13.
61. This is somewhat analogous to what Buddhist philosophy calls the "unconditioned."
62. See also CCC #2007.

So God created man in his own image, in the image of God he created him; male and female he created them.
—Gn 1:27 (IB)

Man, as sharing in the light of the divine mind, rightly affirms that
by his intellect he surpasses the world of mere things.
—Vatican Council II, *Gaudium et Spes*, #15

For God willed that man should "be left in the hand of his own
counsel" [see Ecclus. 15:14] so that he might of his own accord seek
his creator and freely attain his full and blessed perfection by
cleaving to him.
—Ibid., #17

According to Catholic teaching, there is another order as well of
God's presence. It is conditional[63] but also the most sublime and
crucial. It is God's presence by way of "sanctifying *grace*." However,
even a person "in the state [condition] of grace" remains distinct
from God in this life and afterward remains distinct from God
when in celestial beatitude. The distinction is not that between subject and object, since the graced human being in this life and in
celestial beatitude relates to God in a "union" that is "mysterious"
(that is, transcends the capacity of the human mind, in this world,
to understand). The New Testament refers to union with God both
in terms of "face to face" relationship (1 Cor 13:12) and in terms of a
partaking in the "divine nature" (2 Pet 1:4). Herewith some authoritative Church assertions in regard to "the order of grace":

The grace of Christ is the gratuitous gift that God makes to us of
his own life ["I am the vine, you are the branches," Jn 15:5], infused
by the Holy Spirit into our soul to heal it of sin and to sanctify it. It
is the sanctifying or deifying grace received in Baptism [and then
sustained and increased throughout life by love and the other virtues, all of which are nourished by an ongoing sacramental life[64]].
—*Catechism of the Catholic Church*, #1999

63. It is "conditional" in that this order of God's presence inheres in the individual unless s/he commits a very serious ("mortal," i.e., deadly) sin against the moral
law, that is, against what is good.
64. "Sacrament" will be defined ahead (there are seven sacraments in Catholicism).

> The merit of man before God in the Christian life arises from the fact that God has freely chosen to associate man with the work of his grace. The fatherly action of God is first on his own initiative, and then follows man's free acting through his collaboration, so that the merit of good works is to be attributed in the first place to the grace of God, and then to the faithful.
> —*Catechism of the Catholic Church*, #2008

Contrary to the teachings of some non-Catholic Christian churches, Catholicism is careful to preserve man's freedom during this operation:

> God's free initiative demands man's free response.... The soul only enters freely into the communion of love.
> —*Catechism of the Catholic Church*, #2002

> Moved by the Holy Spirit and by charity, we can then merit for ourselves and for others the graces needed for our sanctification, for the increase of grace and charity, and for the attainment of eternal life.
> —*Catechism of the Catholic Church*, #2010

> Filial adoption, in making us partakers by grace in the divine nature, can bestow true merit on us as a result of God's gratuitous justice.
> —*Catechism of the Catholic Church*, #2009

Of course, the very notion of a person's freedom even in this "order of grace" requires distinction between God and humans, as does the notion of "filial adoption." Indeed, in recent times the distinction between God and the graced soul was once again explicitly addressed by Pius XII:

> But if they [theologians] do not want to deviate from true doctrine and from the legitimate teaching authority of the Church, they must accept the following general and indisputable principle: to reject every explanation of this mystical union [of God and the graced soul] according to which the faithful would in any way so pass beyond the sphere of creatures and sacrilegiously encroach upon the divine, that even a single attribute of the eternal Godhead could be predicated of them as their own.
> —*Mystici Corporis* (1943) (see CT #321, DZ 2290)

According to Catholic teaching, persons who die in a "state of grace"—unless they are already holy enough to enjoy the Beatific Vision—pass through a period of purification (the state or condition of "purgatory") and then, perfected to the extent permitted by their individual capacity, proceed to this Vision. It is to be noted, in the authoritative declarations which follow below, that the Church—while insisting that the Beatific Vision is not a subject-object relation—still takes great care to preserve the distinction between God and the persons in beatitude (the "Blessed"). The heavenly beatitude of the Blessed obviates concept and image; the Blessed, through unmediated intuition, directly know and love the Triune God:

> ... [T]hese souls have seen and see the divine essence with an intuitive vision and even face to face, without the mediation of any creature by way of object vision; rather the divine essence immediately manifests itself to them, plainly, clearly and openly, and in this vision they enjoy the divine essence.
> —Constitution *Benedictus Deus*, Benedict XII (1336) (CF #2305, DS 1000)

> God himself will be the goal of our desires; we shall contemplate him without end, love him without surfeit, praise him without weariness.
> —*Catechism of the Catholic Church*, #2550 (here quoting St. Augustine)

> Thus when our wise predecessor of happy memory, Leo XIII, was treating of the divine Paraclete [Gk. "the Advocate," God the Holy Spirit] within us, he appropriately turned his gaze to that beatific vision wherein one day in heaven this mystical union will find its perfect consummation. "This wonderful union," he wrote, "which is properly called indwelling [...] differs only by reason of our condition or state from that in which God embraces and beatifies the citizens of heaven." In that vision it will be granted to the eyes of the mind, its powers augmented by supernatural light, to contemplate the Father, the Son and the Holy Spirit, for all eternity to witness closely the processions of the divine Persons, and to enjoy a beatitude very similar to that with which the most holy and undivided Trinity is blessed.
> —*Mystici Corporis*, Pius XII (CF #1997, DS 3815)

The rapture of the Beatific Vision is not truly conceivable, much less truly representable, in human terms, but perhaps its best metaphoric *trace* appears in the gorgeously ecstatic climax to Dante's *Divina Commedia* (*Paradiso*, canto xxxiii: 49–145). Here, the Beatific Vision is of God the Living and Eternal Light in whom the beatified souls are transfixed: "Whoever sees that Light is soon made such / that it would be impossible for him / to set that Light aside for other sight; // because the good, the object of the will, / is fully gathered in that Light; outside / that Light, what there is perfect is defective" (100–105).[65] The Light is "simple" (= unconditioned), so "It is always what It was before" (111). Nonetheless, the perceiver discerns a Threeness at one with the Oneness: in the "exalted Light, three circles / appeared to me; they had three different colors, / but all of them were of the same dimension; / one circle seemed reflected by the second, / as rainbow is by rainbow, and the third / seemed fire breathed equally by those two circles" (115–20).

In its endnote to the aforesaid description, the Mandelbaum translation notes, "The description of the three circles discerned within the single Light is theologically impeccable: all three are equal, the second reflects the first (the Son proceeds from all eternity from the Father), and the third (the Holy Spirit) is the fire of Love that is breathed from both ('that Love which / One and the Other breathe eternally [x: 1–2]')."[66] In terms of our present discussion, it is crucial to point out that Dante carefully arranges his language so that the souls in heaven gaze upon this Tri-unity from *within* the Light. The speaker penetrates *into* the Light: ". . . I united my gaze with the Infinite Goodness ["*col valore infinito*," literally, "with the Infinite Worth"]. // O abounding grace whereby I presumed to fix my look *through* the Eternal Light so far that all my sight was spent therein" (80–84). The famous Dante scholar and translator Charles S. Singleton glosses this passage as follows: God is

---

65. Dante Alighieri, *The Divine Comedy: Paradiso*, "verse translation" and intro., Allen Mandelbaum, endnotes by A. Oldcorn and D. Feldman, with Giuseppe Di Scipio (New York: Bantam, 1986), p. 301. The quotations that follow below are also from this translation.

66. Ibid., p. 428.

thus named "the Infinite Worth as the journey in gazing attains to Him through the light of glory by which He sees Himself."[67] The Beatific Vision is neither a subject-object relation nor an absolute identification with the Tri-unity.

Dante's *Paradiso*, canto xxxiii, also gives us the opportunity here to note the role of Mary, Christ's mother, both as intercessor and as emblem of/for all graced souls. The first thirty-nine lines of the canto are a rendering of St. Bernard's famous prayer to Mary, and right afterward (40–45) Dante describes Mary's response: "The eyes that are revered and loved by God, / now fixed upon the supplicant, showed us / how welcome such devotions are to her; // then her eyes turned to the Eternal Light . . . ." Here, Dante encapsulates precisely how Mary plays a key role in the evangelization of humanity. Mary looks into the Dante-figure's eyes and then gently directs his glance upward to the Eternal Light. Catholic Christianity takes Mary to be the perfect model of discipleship, and one of the Church's favorite scriptural sites is the Miracle at Cana, where Mary channels the petitions of the guests and instructs them, "Do whatever he tells you" (Jn 2:5).[68] Thus Mary is identified with the Church and called the Mother of the Church (CCC #507, 963–75).

67. Charles S. Singleton, *Paradiso*, Part II, *Commentary* (Princeton, NJ: Princeton UP, 2nd prt. 1977; 1st Princeton/Bollingen pbk. prt. 1982), p. 575.

68. At the marriage feast of Cana, Mary notes that the wedding party is running out of wine. She alerts Jesus her son, who replies, "O woman, what have you to do with me? [literally, what to me and to you?] My hour has not yet come." But Mary promptly goes on to instruct the servants, "Do whatever he tells you." Jesus tells them "to fill the jars with water" and then to "draw some out and take it to the steward of the feast." They do so, and it is discovered that Christ at Mary's behest has performed his first miracle, changing the water into wine, very precious wine. This is the first miracle Jesus performs, and it inaugurates his public ministry. Thus it turns out that Mary teaches us ("servants") to do "whatever he tells us" and to have confidence. And that Jesus moves up the time of his first miracle and the beginning of his public preaching teaches us the intercessory influence of Mary over her son. Indeed, in this regard, some great saints even tell us that the address "Woman," literally meaning "Lady," a formal title of respect in Aramaic, also alludes mystically to the "woman clothed with the sun, with the moon under her feet, and on her head a crown of twelve stars," of the Book of Revelation (Rv 12:1). In this passage from Revelation, the last book of the New Testament, the Woman clothed with the sun symbolizes both Mary and the Church of which she is the Queen.

Mary's "Immaculate Conception" (when conceived in the womb of her mother, she was without the Original Sin marking all other human births) and her Assumption into heaven (after death, she was bodily "assumed" or "taken up" into heaven) both function to exemplify, in a more sublime valence, what is and shall be true for *all* graced human beings. That is, unless or until the graced soul is defiled by sin, Baptism makes the individual soul "immaculate," and on the Last Day (Christ's "Second Coming" at the end of the world), all persons-in-grace will bodily "ascend" (we are but the "kernel" of what we shall be, says 1 Cor 15:37; and "we are God's children now; it does not yet appear what we shall be, but we know that when he [Christ] appears we shall be like him, for we shall see him as he is," says 1 Jn 3:2).

Because she is a mere creature yet carried and nourished the Incarnate God in her womb, Dante—quoting St. Bernard quoting an ancient Marian trope—addresses Mary as "daughter of your own son" ("figlia del tuo figlio," *Paradiso*, xxxiii: 1). The configuration of Mary and the Divine Child in her womb bodily acts out a rhetorical figure, "the complicity of the container and the contained." The configuration acts out, in a more literal way, what is spiritually the case for each and every graced soul (including Mary's graced soul). Grace effects a mysterious union with God that is a kind of "complicity": though not divine, the graced soul "partakes of the divine nature." And a person-in-grace, insofar as Christ in a special way can work through such an individual, spiritually and bodily *enables* Christ to touch others and the whole world. In sum, Dante recognizes that the imagistic trope "figlia del tuo figlio" is a Marian catechism-in-brief: Mary as privileged representative of the human race physically nourishes the God who, Incarnate, has a human body from her very flesh, and in turn, via the gift of grace, the Incarnate God spiritually nourishes the human race (including Mary).

The "complicity of the container and the contained," as a figure, also supplies us, here, with an ideal opportunity to describe the sacrament of the Eucharist, which for Catholics is a most sacred *mysterium*—indeed, the very "source and summit of the Christian life" (CCC #1324). On the eve of Passover, at His Last Supper before His death, Jesus transformed the traditional bread and wine into the

"Eucharist," His Holy Sacrifice, His "Real Presence." He commanded that this Holy and Divine Liturgy (Gk. "public work"; in Christianity, public participation in the "work of God"; in the Latin rite, more colloquially called the *Missa* or "Mass") be *perpetuated* throughout the world until His Second Coming, when it will culminate in the "heavenly banquet" (a metaphoric term, of course). At Mass, the participants can receive the Eucharist during the Communion part of the service, and it is precisely here that the aforesaid "figure" applies. When ingesting the consecrated "bread" (and "wine"), the "communicants" (those "receiving Communion") receive into their very persons the Presence of their Creator. This divine Presence, like the "appearances" of the bread (and wine) themselves, is assimilated into the communicant, where the Presence remains as "grace."[69] Complicity of the container and the contained.

Besides the Eucharist, there are six other sacraments in Catholicism. Because the Church regards "matter" as such, that is, the material world, to be beautiful and participatory in Christ's redemption of all things, each of the sacraments requires an "outward sign" properly symbolizing the invisible grace that it supplies. Each of the sacraments is understood to have been instituted by Christ Himself: He efficaciously works through them to confer the grace that they outwardly signify (thus the sacrament of Baptism, because it is the sacrament of regeneration, includes ablution in water; the sacrament of Anointing of the Sick, because it is the sacrament of healing, includes oil; and so on). All told, there are three sacraments of "initiation" (Baptism, Confirmation, the Eucharist), two of "healing" (Penance and Anointing of the Sick), and two of "singular mission" (Holy Orders and Matrimony) (see CCC: Part Two).

Buddhism and Rebirth

In Buddhist teaching, "non-ego" or "non-soul" (Skt. *anātman*; P. *anattā*) is one of the three attributes ("marks") of phenomena. The other two marks are *anitya/anicca* ("impermanence") and *duḥkha/dukkha* (variously rendered as "suffering," "dissatisfaction," etc.—

---

69. And "grace," as we have seen, is not God but is a partaking in God's life.

the negative states associated with the incessant arising and passing away of all phenomena). The teaching of non-ego or non-soul affirms that the conventional self has no inherent existence but is, instead, an aggregate of five components or *skandha/khandha*: form (materiality), feelings, perceptions, volitions, and consciousness. Thus there is no substantive "person" as such: that which holds the conventional self together for the span of one life is karmic affinity, and this affinity is caused by attachments (the three basic attachments are greed, hatred, and delusion). That which is reborn is the karmic cluster, and this karmic cluster is "neither the same nor different" from that which preceded. That which is reborn is not a newly embodied "soul."

Most Buddhist schools affirm that samsaric rebirth can be in any of six destinies (*gati*, P. and Skt., "course," "destination"), depending on what karma is involved. Early Buddhist sources speak of five destinies, two of them relatively "good" and three of them "woeful." The two good destinies are to be reborn as a god (*deva*) or a human. The three woeful destinies are to be born as an animal, hungry ghost (Skt. *preta*; P. *peta*), or hell-being. Theravada Buddhism retains this enumeration. Big Vehicle schools include a sixth destiny, to be reborn as a "demigod" (*asura*). Demigods are extremely long-lived but bellicose and envious.

Liberation from the samsaric cycle of repeated birth-death-rebirth occurs when there is no more attachment. The various Buddhist traditions, as we have already seen, understand the precise state of non-attachment or liberation differently—depending on how the given tradition, in the particular, understands beatitude and the means to attain it. Theravada speaks of four stages of the Noble Path, namely "stream-winner," "once-returner" (only one more rebirth), "non-returner" (birth, instead, in the Pure Abodes, whence one can progress to *nibbāna*), and "arahant" (state of beatitude, i.e., perfect liberation). In Big Vehicle schools, the "Bodhisattva-way" progressively transcends the lower realms, usually in an enumerated series of stages (*bhūmi*, "level" or "stage"), until Buddhahood is achieved.

Regarding the Buddhist doctrine of *anātman/anattā* and its relation to "ordinary language," perhaps the following clarification is in order. Buddhists know, of course, that human language arises in and from the samsaric, that is, *conventional*, world, so the word "person," especially when it is used in relation to what passes over from one life to another, is understood to necessarily function according to mere *convention*. (Needless to say, this concession does not mean that conventional language cannot be deployed in order to "point toward" what Buddhism calls "ultimate truth": Buddhist scriptures and all words used to truthfully teach Buddhism are normally understood to abet liberation in this "skillful" way.) Given that most of my readers in this section are probably non-Buddhists, I recognize that to use the word "person" in connection with rebirth may encourage precisely the ongoing substantialization that Buddhism rejects. Ideally, I should follow the lead of R.W. Perrett and some others,[70] who use the word "agent" in lieu of "person" (because the karmic cluster is the agent of rebirth but is not a soul). Nonetheless, having deliberated over the matter for quite some time, I have decided—in this monograph's explanations of Buddhism—to retain conventional usage since that is what Buddhist masters routinely do in their public preaching.

Below are descriptions of rebirth from authoritative Buddhist sources representing major traditions. My explanatory glosses are within square brackets.

Several classic sources, on rebirth:

Beings are the owners of their *kamma*, heir to their *kamma*, born of their *kamma*, related through their *kamma*, and have their *kamma* as their refuge. . . .

There is a case where a certain woman or man is one who takes life—brutal, bloody-handed, violent, cruel, merciless to living beings. From performing and undertaking such *kamma*, then on the break-up of the body, after death, this person re-appears in the plane of deprivation, the bad destination, the lower realms . . . in hell. Or, if he/she does not reappear in the plane of deprivation . . . in hell, but instead returns to the human state, then wherever he/

---

70. See R.W. Perrett, in his treatment of Buddhism, *Death and Immortality* (Springer, 1986), p. 167.

she is reborn, he/she is short-lived. This is the way leading to short life, namely being one who takes life.
—Pali Canon, *Majjhima Nikāya*, 135[71]

By not seeing the four Noble Truths as they really are, long is the path that is traversed through many a birth; when these [Noble Truths] are grasped, the cause of birth is then removed, the root of sorrow rooted out, and there is no more birth.
—Pali Canon, *Mahā-Parinibbāna Sutta* 2, 2–3[72]

"Reverend Nagasena," said the King, "is it true that nothing transmigrates, and yet there is rebirth?" "Yes, Your Majesty." "How can this be? ... Give me an illustration." "Suppose, your Majesty, a man lights one lamp from another—does that one lamp transmigrate to the other?" "No, your Reverence." "So there is rebirth without anything transmigrating!"
—*Milinda-pañha*, Bk. III[73]

Expositions from contemporary teachers and masters, on rebirth:

Buddhism does not believe that anything comes out of one body and enters another. But we believe that everything arises from something before it and again gives rise to something after it. Now desire, the wanting of things, gives rise to clinging, gives rise to birth. So the last moment of the dying man gives rise to the life of the new-born child who inherits his *kamma*.

Change in the body cannot stop the flow of consciousness. After death, the body is burnt, but not the desire, so dependent upon conditions, a new being will arise, be it egg-born, born in a womb, moisture-born or of spontaneous birth according to its *kamma*.
—Ven. Dr. H. Saddhatissa (Theravada Buddhism)[74]

The relationship between birth and becoming can be compared to the process of falling asleep and dreaming. As drowsiness makes the mind lose contact with waking reality, a dream image of

71. *The Wings to Awakening: An Anthology of the Pali Canon*, trans. and explanation, Thanissaro Bhikkhu (Barre, MA: Dhamma Dana P., 1996), p. 49.

72. *Readings from World Religions*, eds. S.G. Champion and D. Short (New York: Fawcett World Library; orig. edition, Beacon P., 1959), p. 181.

73. See *The Buddhist Tradition in India, China, and Japan*, ed. W.T. de Bary (New York: Random House, Vintage Books, 1972), p. 25.

74. *An Introduction to Buddhism* (London: London Buddhist Vihara, 1976), p. 20.

another place and time will appear in it. The appearance of this image is called becoming. The act of entering into this image and taking on a role or identity within it—and thus entering the world of the dream and falling asleep—is birth. The commentaries maintain that precisely the same process is what enables rebirth to follow the death of the body.
—Thanissaro Bhikkhu (Theravada Buddhism)[75]

Some people do a lot of good in this life, but suffer a great deal. That may be the result of misdeeds in previous lives. Good deeds done in this life ripen by the next life, and harvest may be reaped when causal relations coincide.
—Dharma Master Hsin Tao (Chan, Chinese)[76]

There are three levels of meaningful or authentic motivation for the practice of *samatha* ("meditative quiescence"):—To attain rebirth in the form or formless realms;—To attain liberation or nirvana;—To attain full awakening.

Rebirth in the Form or Formless Realms: Such a rebirth can result in a life that lasts billions of earthly years and is filled with tremendous bliss. . . .

Some non-Buddhist contemplatives confuse rebirth in either of these two realms with the attainment of nirvana. With that in mind, they make its attainment the motivation for their practice of *samatha.* . . . However, if you follow this route and obtain such an exalted rebirth, after so many billions of years when the power of the *samatha* that got you there is exhausted, you fall from that blissful state and quite possibly could be born in hell realms.
—Gen Lamrimpa [Ven. Jampal Tenzin] (Vajrayana Buddhism, Tibetan)[77]

There is a path to the end of suffering—a gradual path of self-improvement, which is described more detailed in the Eightfold Path. It is the middle way between the two extremes of excessive self-indulgence (hedonism) and excessive self-mortification (asceticism); and it leads to the end of the cycle of rebirth. The lat-

---

75. *The Wings to Awakening*, p. 303.
76. *The Quality of Mercy*, trans. G. B. Talovich (Kungliao, Taiwan: Ling Jiou Shan Prajna Cultural and Educational Foundation, 1992), p. 27.
77. *Śamatha Meditation*, trans. B. Alan Wallace, ed. Hart Sprager (Ithaca, NY: Snow Lion, 1992), pp. 22–23.

ter quality discerns it from other paths which are merely "wandering on the wheel of becoming," because these do not have a final object. The path to the end of suffering can extend over many lifetimes, throughout which every individual rebirth is subject to karmic conditioning. Craving, ignorance, delusions, and its effects will disappear gradually, as progress is made on the path.
—Ven. Thich Nhat Hanh (Mahayana, Vietnamese)[78]

Catholicism and One Life-Span Only

Catholic doctrine posits only one life and definitively rejects both the teaching of rebirth[79] identified with Buddhism and the teaching of reincarnation identified in one form or another with Brahmanism and some other religions. Herewith some authoritative Catholic sources:

And just as it is appointed for men to die once, and after that comes judgment, so Christ, having been offered once to bear the sins of many, will appear a second time [the Second Coming of Christ[80]], not to deal with sin but to save those who are eagerly waiting for him.
—New Testament, Heb 9:27

The souls of these who, after having received baptism, have incurred no stain of sin whatever, and those souls who, after hav-

---

78. From online document devoted to the teaching of Ven. Thich Nhat Hanh: appendix to "Further Information about Buddhism," from http://www.peace.ca/beingpeace.htm (accessed June 11, 2006).

79. The term "rebirth" appears in the New Testament and Catholic teaching, but with an entirely different meaning: a human being in his one and only lifespan can be spiritually "reborn" in the sense that s/he can become, through Baptism, an adopted child of God partaking of God's life ("grace").

80. The New Testament in several passages describes the Second Coming of the triumphant Christ at the end of the world, at which time the "General Judgment" takes place. At the General Judgment, the body of each and every person who has already passed away will arise as an incorruptible or "spiritual" body (1 Cor 15:42–44) and, rejoining that person's soul, will participate in that person's eternal beatitude or deprivation. The term "Individual Judgment" is reserved for the judgment as it applies to a person's soul immediately upon death. (Those who are still alive at the time of the Second Coming will undergo immediate judgment and incur—in body and soul—the pertaining consequences.)

ing contracted the stain of sin, have been cleansed, either while in their bodies or after having been divested of them [i.e., cleansed in purgatory], as stated above, are received immediately (*mox*) into heaven, and see clearly [and continuously, for eternity] God himself, one and three, as he is, though some more perfectly than others, according to the diversity of merits.
—General Council of Florence (1439) [CF #2309, DS 1305]

Death is the end of man's earthly pilgrimage, of the time of grace and mercy which God offers him so as to work out his earthly life in keeping with the divine plan, and to decide his ultimate destiny. When "the single course of our earthly life" is completed, we shall not return to other earthly lives: "It is appointed for men to die once" [Heb 9:27]. There is no "reincarnation" after death.
—*Catechism of the Catholic Church*, #1013

In Buddhism, for those who are not yet liberated from the six *gati* ("realms," literally "destinations") of rebirth, these very realms enable purification from *kilesa/kleśa* (defilements, vices, and negative psychological tendencies), either passively, by retribution, so that bad *karma* runs its course until exhausted, or actively (normally limited to rebirth as a human being), through meritorious acts, meditation and its fruits, etc. While Catholic Christianity definitively posits only one life (as shown above) and thus definitively rejects rebirth, it is worth noting here, for the sake of its interest, that in the structural economy[81] of Catholicism the state or condition of "Purgatory" plays a somewhat analogous role. The following scriptural passages are taken by the Church to bespeak its teaching on Purgatory:

This was why he had this atonement sacrifice offered for the dead, so that they might be released from their sin.
—Old Testament (JB), 2 Mc 12:46[82] [taken to indicate that already

81. From the Greek, "rule of the house": the term takes on financial meaning only later.

82. 1st and 2nd Maccabees are books belonging to the official collection of biblical books called the Alexandrian Canon, a translation from Hebrew to Greek made by Jewish scholars in the third and second centuries BC. While Catholicism accepts, for its official list of Old Testament books, the Alexandrian Canon, Jews and Protestant Christians accept what is called the Palestinian Canon or Hebrew

in Old Testament times there was a belief among some Jews that souls could be purified after death.]

Now if any one builds on the foundation with gold, silver, precious stones, wood, hay, stubble—each man's work will become manifest; for the Day will disclose it, because it will be revealed with fire, and the fire will test what sort of work each one has done. If the work which any man has built on the foundation survives, he will receive a reward. If any man's work is burned up, he will suffer loss, though he himself will be saved, but only as through fire.
—New Testament, 1 Cor 3:11–15

Catholicism teaches that those who die in mortal (grievous) sin are condemned to an eternal hell. (Nowadays Catholic theology emphasizes more and more that in point of fact "damned" persons, by a freely willed choice, have opted for absolute selfishness and thus have actually condemned themselves to the hell-state.) Catholicism teaches that forgiven mortal sins and venial (smaller, i.e., non-mortal) sins still owe a debt to justice even when their guilt has been removed. This "penance," required by the equitable demands of justice, is traditionally called "temporal [non-eternal] punishment." Penance can be accomplished in this life or after death in a state of soul called Purgatory. Purgatory purifies the soul and brings it to perfection (whatever the perfection proper to it) so that it can participate fully in beatitude, the Beatific Vision. Nowadays, many Catholic theologians emphasize more and more the "perfecting" aspect of Purgatory—that we should not regard it so much as a punishment but rather as a positive "preparing" of the soul for beatitude. Herewith some authoritative Church statements:

... [I]f, being truly repentant, they [those who] die in charity [i.e., in the "state of grace"] before having satisfied by worthy fruits of penance for their sins of commission and omission, their souls are cleansed after death by purgatorial and purifying penalties, ...
—Second General Council of Lyons (1274) [CF 26, DS #856]

text. There is little historical doubt that St. Paul in the New Testament and the Church in its earliest or "Apostolic" era used the Alexandrian Canon, probably because Greek was the common language of the Mediterranean lands.

All who die in God's grace and friendship, but still imperfectly purified, are indeed assured of their eternal salvation; but after death they undergo purification so as to achieve the holiness necessary to enter the joy of heaven.
—*Catechism of the Catholic Church*, #1030

An important feature of Catholic teaching—and one which, in my experience, Big Vehicle Buddhists in particular find fascinating when they learn of it[83]—is that Catholicism, much like the Mahayana and Vajrayana, emphasizes that a human's dedicated merit can "alleviate the earned debt-of-suffering" of others (or "can smooth the purification process," to invoke the more forward-looking contemporary slant on the doctrine). "In and through Christ," Catholics in the "state of grace" can freely offer the fruit of their personal suffering to God in order to lighten the suffering of souls in Purgatory or still alive on earth. "Be imitators of me, as I am of Christ" (1 Cor 11:1), says St. Paul in Sacred Scripture, and in his Letter to the Colossians he provides a foundational New Testament text for participation in Christ's redemptive mission: "Now I rejoice in my sufferings for your sake, and in my flesh I complete what is lacking in Christ's afflictions for the sake of his body, that is, the Church" (Col 1:24). That members of Christ's "mystical body" (the Church community in union with the resurrected Christ) can participate in Christ's redemptive mission has long been at the heart of Catholic spirituality.

This teaching in no way impugns the doctrine that Christ's redemptive death and resurrection was, once and for all time, *perfectly efficacious* and infinitely sufficient. John Paul II, in his Apostolic Letter *Salvifici doloris*,[84] incisively draws the necessary distinctions:

---

83. See my "Afterword" in Park, ed., *Buddhisms and Deconstructions* (see full reference in the notes to the Introduction of this monograph), where on p. 255 and its endnote 106, p. 269, I discuss "participatory redemptive suffering" in my response to a Buddhist critique of my Catholicism. Subsequently, I was given reason to believe that this Catholic teaching strikes a positive chord with Buddhists, who compare it (analogously, of course) with the Bodhisattvic vows taken by many Big Vehicle Buddhists.

The sufferings of Christ created the good of the world's redemption. This good in itself is inexhaustible and infinite. No man can add anything to it. But at the same time, in the mystery of the Church as his Body, Christ has in a sense opened his own redemptive suffering to all human suffering. In so far as man becomes a sharer in Christ's sufferings—in any part of the world and at any time in history—to that extent *he in his own way* completes the suffering through which Christ accomplished the Redemption of the world.

Does this mean that the Redemption achieved by Christ is not complete? No. *It only means* that the Redemption, accomplished through satisfactory [expiatory] love, *remains always open to all love* expressed in *human suffering.* . . . Christ achieved the Redemption completely and to the very limits but at the same time he did not bring it to a close. . . . Christ opened himself from the beginning to every human suffering and constantly does so. Yes, it seems to be part *of the very essence of Christ's redemptive suffering* that this suffering requires to be unceasingly completed. (#24, para. 2–3)

Buddhism and Catholicism Appraising Each Other

The Locus for Catholics in the Buddhist Paradigm(s)

There are now very good books and articles in English that treat authoritative Buddhist attitudes toward other religions. I am particularly grateful for an informative article by John Makransky—one he published more than a decade ago (2003)—entitled "Buddhist Perspectives on Truth in Other Religions: Past and Present."[85] He

84. John Paul II, "Apostolic Letter *Salvifici doloris* ["On Salvific Suffering"]: On the Christian Meaning of Human Suffering," 32 pp., February 11, 1984 (available online via www.vatican.va).

85. In *Theological Studies: A Jesuit-Sponsored Journal of Theology*, Vol. 64, No. 2 (2003), pp. 334–61. (Also available on the Internet at http://www2.bc.edu/%7-Emakransk/buddhisttruth.pdf.) This same volume and issue of *Theological Studies* has an informative article by Ruben J. Habito, "Japanese Buddhist Perspectives and Comparative Theology: Supreme Ways in Intersection," pp. 362–87.

begins with the Sutras and their account of Sakyamuni Buddha's two basic paradigms of response to non-Buddhists, and then analyzes developments through the Theravadic, Mahayanist, and Vajrayanist paths, up to the present day. He also supplies an extensive and helpful bibliography. Among contemporary secondary sources that he cites, the reader may find particularly useful David Chappell's "Buddhist Responses to Religious Pluralism," in *Buddhist Ethics and Modern Society*, ed. Charles Fu (New York: Greenwood, 1991); and the papers in the section "Buddhist Perceptions of Christianity in the Twentieth Century," in *Christianity through Non-Christian Eyes*, ed. Paul Griffiths (New York: Orbis, 1990). K.N. Jayatilleke's *The Buddhist Attitude to Other Religions* (Theravada), though written several decades ago, remains a classic and is freely available online via the Buddhist Publication Society's website— www.bps.lk/olib/wh/wh216.pdf. There are, of course, quite a few other books and articles featuring Buddhist views regarding the other religions, several of them very recent as this topic becomes increasingly relevant for Buddhists, but most of these choose very selectively from the corpus of Buddhist teachings and practices and represent personal solutions and proposals[86] rather than the established Buddhist traditions.

I cite below, most often in the form of long passages quoted *en bloc*, the explanations of present-day established Buddhist teachers and masters as to the loci—in their respective Buddhist paradigms—of monotheists and of Christians in particular (both Catholics and non-Catholics). That Buddhist representatives, in the public forum, often define Christian belief so generically remains a problem, even though at the more specialized or "expert" level the venues for Buddhist-Catholic dialogue continue to expand and indeed proliferate.[87]

---

86. See, for example, Kristin Kiblinger's *Buddhist Inclusivism: Attitudes Towards Religious Others* (Ashgate, 2005); J. Abraham Vélez de Cea's *The Buddha and Religious Diversity* (Routledge, 2012); and Rita M. Gross's *Religious Diversity—What's the Problem? Buddhist Advice for Flourishing with Religious Diversity* (Cascade, 2014).

87. Besides the work of the constituent commissions of DIM/MID cited in an earlier note, the activities, sometimes including publications, of the following organizations frequently involve Buddhist-Catholic dialogue: quartered at the Vatican

Theravada

Among Theravada Buddhists in particular, there are those, like Gunapala Dharmasiri,[88] who confine themselves to a scholastic critique of theism, which they reject as both illogical and nonscientific. (Even these Theravada scholars, however, are not necessarily arguing that those who are Christians in this life cannot attain the

itself,—the Pontifical Council for Interreligious Dialogue and its journal, *Pro dialogo*; in Japan,—the Nanzan Institute for Religion and Culture (affiliated with Nanzan University, Divine Word Fathers and Brothers), with which the famous scholar James W. Heisig, SVD, has been associated for decades, and which now houses the *Journal of the Japan Society for Buddhist-Christian Studies*; and Shinmeizan: House of Prayer and Center for Interreligious Dialogue, founder Fr. Franco Sottocornola, SX, in cooperation with Ven. Tairyu Furukawa; in Taiwan—the Taipei Ricci Institute; in Sri Lanka, Tulana Research Centre for Encounter and Dialogue, founder Fr. Aloysius Pieris, SJ; in Europe,—the European Network of Buddhist-Christian Studies; the journal *Studies in Interreligious Dialogue* (The Netherlands, and all Europe—associated now with the European Society for Intercultural Theology and Interreligious Studies); association Voies de l'Orient (Belgium; director Fr. Jacques Scheuer, SJ); Lassalle-Institute (Switzerland; cofounders Fr. Niklaus Brantschen, SJ, and Pia Gyger); the Benedictine archabbey of St. Ottilien (Germany); Italy—Istituto Vangelo e Zen (founder, Fr. Luciano Mazzocchi) and Centro dei Focolari per il Dialogo interreligioso (director, Roberto Catalano); and in the United States,—the interfaith apostolate of the Benedictine nuns of St. Mary's Monastery (IL), and the Catholic nuns from several traditions who have participated in the Nuns in the West Conferences I, II, and III (Buddhist and Catholic nuns); the Society for Buddhist-Christian Studies (John Borelli, Frs. Leo Lefebure and James Fredericks, and the many many others whose paths I have crossed there) and its journal *Buddhist-Christian Studies*; Focolare-USA, and its Christian-Buddhist Dialogue (Don Mitchell and others); interfaith meetings at the Trappist Abbeys of Gethsemane (KY) and St. Joseph (MA); the apostolates of the Franciscan Sisters and Friars of the Atonement at both the Graymoor Ecumenical and Interreligious Institute (Fr. James Loughran, dir.) and the Graymoor Spiritual Life Center (NY), and of the Paulist Fathers (Tom Ryan, CSP, etc.) with whom they collaborate on interfaith matters. And this is only a *very* partial list based not on preference but on what people, organizations, and events have intersected my personal life-world. Nonetheless, I think the list serves to give the reader a good sense of the breadth of the Buddhist-Catholic encounter.

88. See Dharmasiri, "Extracts from a Buddhist Critique of the Christian Concept of God," in Paul J. Griffiths, ed., *Christianity through Non-Christian Eyes*, pp. 153–61. Dharmasiri is a Sri Lankan Buddhist who studied at the University of Lancaster, England. See Makransky, "Buddhist Perspectives," for a summary of Dharmasiri's arguments.

nirvanic state eventually; what these scholars are implying is that theistic belief, as such, can only act as an impediment.)

Other Theravadins choose to emphasize the positive. The enormously influential Buddhadasa Bhikkhu[89] maintains that there have been great teachers of "truth" in the world's many diverse cultures and that Jesus Christ was one of these.[90] Indeed, Buddhadasa even affirms that the New Testament's Mt 6:33, "But seek first His kingdom and His righteousness," points to authentic enlightenment, which is Truth at the highest level.[91] Thus, Catholic Christians, while remaining within their Church, can attain (at least a degree of) liberation, of beatitude. Buddhadasa makes it clear, however, that the individual Catholic's degree of progress is determined by his/her intuitive understanding and practice of wisdom and benevolence. Insofar as religion and authenticity are concerned, the natures of wisdom and benevolence are represented in what Buddhadasa calls "*Dhamma* language," which is the higher meaning hidden in more literal or "ordinary language." As a case in point, one can apply this hermeneutic to Mt 6:33, which in *Dhamma* language can mean, "But seek first the kingdom of truth and of morality." Buddhadasa says that the word "God," for example, can be taken literally or can be taken in its higher or *Dhamma* meaning, which is

---

89. Buddhadasa Bhikkhu (1906–1993) was a Thai Buddhist monk who pioneered in Theravadic countries the comparative study of religion. At an early age he withdrew from what he considered the excessive ritualism and internal politics of urban clerical life and founded Suan Mokh ("Grove of Liberation"), a *wat* (Thai: temple/monastery with resident monks) that cultivated the Forest Tradition and drew retreatants from all over the world. He championed social reforms to help the poor and often met stiff opposition from the Buddhist establishment and from governmental figures. A disciplined practitioner of Buddhist meditation, he is famous for the proposition that religions as such belong to the merely mundane world and often subvert the real Truth that is embedded in them.

90. See the treatment of Buddhadasa in Makransky, "Buddhist Perspectives," and Kari Storstein Haug, "Christianity as a Religion of Wisdom and *Kamma*: A Thai Buddhist Interpretation of Selected Passages from the Gospels," *Bulletin of the Council of Societies for the Study of Religion*, Vol. 35, No. 2 (April 2006), p. 43.

91. See Haug, p. 43.

"Truth."[92] In *The A, B, C of Buddhism* (p.11), Buddhadasa declares,

> The natural Law is comprised of six qualifications which all people regard as the qualifications of God: The Creator, the Controller, the Destroyer, Omnipotent, Omni-present, and Omniscient. We Buddhists have this natural Law [*Dhamma*] as God. This is the only God accepted by modern science. It creates both the positive and the negative, because it is only the natural Law. If it were a personal God, it would choose to create only the positive.[93]

For Buddhadasa, the diverse forms or appearances of the world's religious traditions are not to be confounded with the higher truth they carry:

> [O]ne who has attained to the ultimate truth sees that there is no such thing as religion! There is only reality.... Call it what you like—dharma or truth—but you cannot particularize that dharma or truth as Buddhism, Christianity, or Islam.... The label "Buddhism" was attached only after the fact, as it was in Christianity, Islam, and every other religion. None of the great religious teachers ever gave a name to their teachings; they just went on teaching throughout their lives about how we should live.[94]

This affirmation does not make Buddhadasa any less of a Buddhist "inclusivist," however, for one must keep in mind that for him "reality" is the "unconditioned, empty nature of things," a historically Buddhist formulation. Indeed, the very reason Buddhadasa supplies for why "reality" transcends the forms of religion is precisely that these forms are, in the Buddhist sense, "empty." Makransky explains:

92. See Buddhadasa Bhikkhu, *Christianity and Buddhism*, trans. Sinclaire Thompson, Memorial Lecture, Fifth series (Bangkok, Thailand: Sublime Life Mission, 1967).

93. Cited in Veerachart Nimanmong, "The Renewing of Thai Buddhist Belief in *Kamma*," Conference on the Bases of Values in a Time of Change, Council for Research in Values and Philosophy (Bangkok, Thailand, January 14–16, 1997), p. 21.

94. Bhikkhu Buddhadasa, "No Religion," in Donald Swearer, ed., *Me and Mine: Selected Essays of Bhikkhu Buddhadasa* (Albany, NY: SUNY Press, 1989), pp. 146–47. See Makransky's discussion in "Buddhist Perspectives."

Buddhadasa applies three levels of meaning to religious discourse. On the outermost level of meaning, religious traditions appear dissimilar in their expressions. On an inner level, all the great religions are the same in their essential concern to eliminate selfishness and to foster the inner freedom of love and humility. On the inmost level of meaning, historical religions in themselves are empty of substantial, independent existence.[95]

Likewise, it is clear that Buddhadasa affirms Jesus Christ to be a great teacher of "truth" because he regards Jesus Christ as analogous to those many Teachers of the *Dhamma* (understood in Buddhist terms) who function and have functioned in the world.

Mahayana and Vajrayana

In mainstream Mahayana and Vajrayana, the teaching that *all* sentient beings[96] will sooner or later realize Buddhahood[97] does much to allocate to Catholicism a role, though it be necessarily only a temporary one, in this process. That is, within a sequence of one life, or several lives, or many, many lives, a person may be a practicing Catholic, and these "Catholic stages" in a person's evolution toward eventual Buddhist awareness may or may not be helpful in that evolution. Understanding that Mahayanist and Vajrayanist "inclusivism" means that the ultimate end of all sentient beings is to realize Buddhahood, but that other religions play a role in this process, we can say that each of the authorities cited below presents a version of this inclusivism. According to Ven. Yin-shun (as we shall see), theism can play a positive or negative role. According to the current Dalai Lama, the theisms, and apparently Christian monotheism in particular (though such a conclusion can be only inferred), usually

95. In "Buddhist Perspectives."

96. A minority of these traditions, however, do not affirm universal liberation. And in the past, in early Chinese Mahayana the Fa-hsiang School famously affirmed that a particular class of beings, the *icchantika* (Skt.), lack the Buddha-nature or the potential for *bodhi*.

97. It is interesting to point out, here, that in some traditions, even non-sentient phenomena have the Buddha-nature. This is the case in Chinese Mahayanist schools such as Tiantai, Huayan, and Chan.

play a positive role, if the believer truly practices her/his religion's teachings. The Ven. Thich Nhat Hanh seems to concur, though, as we shall see, his rationale is somewhat different.

From the teachings of Ven. Yin-shun[98]

Ven. Yin-shun explains that "in order to suit people's various capacities, the Buddha Dharma is skillfully differentiated into Five Vehicles—Human, Divine, Sravaka, Pratyekabuddha, and Bodhisattva."[99] These all belong to the One Vehicle, also called the Great Vehicle, in that they are all subsumed under the Great Vehicle, though those in the Human, Divine, Sravaka, or Pratyekabuddha vehicles may not know it. The One or Great Vehicle Doctrine— "resolving to attain bodhi mind, practicing the Bodhisattva deeds, and accomplishing Buddhahood—is the real [ultimate] meaning of the Buddha Dharma and the real purpose of the Tathagata's teaching."[100] Yin-shun emphasizes that the religions other than Buddhism can lead, at most, to rebirth in the human or divine realms:

> If one's goal is to be born in the human world or in heaven, one is participating in the Human Vehicle or the Divine Vehicle. These vehicles are aspects to the Buddha Dharma that are shared in common with the world's religions. Confucianism is similar to the Human Vehicle, while Taoism, Christianity, and Islam can lead to the Divine Vehicle. Since people can thus reach the goals of rebirth in the world or in heaven by following the other religions of the world, one might ask why they should take refuge in the Three Treasures and practice the Buddha Dharma common to the Five

98. Ven. Yin-shun (1906–2005) is considered the foremost Chinese monk-scholar of contemporary times, and his books constitute an important part of the curriculum in most Buddhist institutes in mainland China and in Taiwan. Born in Zhejiang Province, China, he became a monk at the age of twenty-five and soon became a brilliant scholar/teacher at Gushan Buddhist academy there, and later in Hong Kong and Taiwan. In intellectual circles, he revived the significance of the San Lun tradition (Chinese Madhyamaka), but structured it so as to accommodate the whole range of Buddhist philosophy.

99. Ven. Yin-shun, trans. Wing H. Yeung, *The Way to Buddhahood* (Boston: Wisdom Press, 1998), p. 44.

100. Ibid., p. 203.

Vehicles. In fact, the Buddha Dharma does not say that whoever want to be born as a human or divine being must take refuge in the Three Treasures and practice the Buddhist [Sravaka/Pratyekabuddha/Great], Human, and Divine Vehicles. Taking refuge in the Three Treasures and practicing the Dharma common to the Five Vehicles is more secure than following other religions, however. When a person takes refuge and practices the Dharma, that person thereby enters the great door of the Buddha Vehicle. One then only needs to move upwards diligently in order to enter the world-transcending Dharma.[101]

Thus throughout his work, Ven. Yin-shun supplies exhortations like the following:

> If one sincerely wants to take refuge [achieve the ultimate], then it must be in the Three Treasures of Buddhism! One should differentiate between good and bad and not think that taking refuge in just any religion is the same. The founders, doctrines, and disciples of other religions cannot ultimately detach one from defilements.[102]

In short, only as a Buddhist can one achieve full Buddhahood, the ultimate. Human beings who are monotheists, for example, and who are sufficiently good and do good in the world, can be reborn in the "heaven" of their God, but—as Ven. Yin-shun and the Buddhist tradition in general warns—this heaven can block further progress in that its bliss can render one self-absorbed and complacent. Since Buddhism argues that one's sojourn in heaven can last only as long as one's store of merit lasts, the stay inevitably comes to an end. Then one can be easily reborn in a lower realm again. Buddhism argues on a much grander scale that the same pattern applies to the Gods themselves: they live in bliss for aeons and thus forget that their merit will eventually exhaust itself. "Common religions do not go beyond the scope of ghosts and spirits and the gods of polytheism and monotheism. None of these beings can save themselves; all have afflictions and are not yet liberated from birth and death."[103]

101. Ibid., p. 49.
102. Ibid., p. 27.
103. Ibid., p. 10.

Chinese Mahayana ranks the Realms of the Gods[104] according to the following (ascending) order: Desirous Gods (six levels), Form Gods (four Dhyana Heavens), and Formless Gods (four levels). The Desirous Gods retain greed and sexual desire, though in manifestations more far-reaching than those of human beings. Among the Desirous Gods, the sovereign Sakra-devanam Indra has the closest relationship with humankind and "rules the world through ghosts and spirits."[105] The Form Gods no longer have desire, but they have minds, subtle bodies, and dwelling places to which they are still bound. The lowest of the four Dhyana Heavens is divided in turn into three, the highest of which is the Heaven of Great Brahma. Though Great Brahma "has a spirit of compassion and universal love," he is bound by arrogance: "Because Brahma's mind was filled with arrogance, he unavoidably formed the conceited and erroneous ideas that he had created the world and that the people had come from him. After he had lived a long time—one and a half kalpas[106]—he announced to his people that he was everlasting with no beginning and no end."[107]

Above the realm of the Form Gods is that of the Formless. The Formless Gods have Heavens "where bodies and their dwellings do not exist; only the mind does. The Divine Beings in these realms are bound to the mind and its attributes." Thus, the formless Divine Beings too, like all the Gods, sooner or later (after billions of aeons) must undergo death and rebirth. The realm of formlessness has four heavens characterized by the four formless states of concentration: infinite space, infinite consciousness, nothingness, and neither perception nor non-perception.

104. Ven. Dr. Dhammadipa informs me that the Realms of the Gods as described in Chinese Mahayana are basically the same as those "listed in Theravada Nikaya (and certainly extensively explained in some Abhidhamma and commentary canons)," and by schools such as "Sarvastivada [for example]," in "the *Abhidharma-kośa*, etc." [email dated May 20, 2014].

105. Ibid., p. 9.

106. An "uncountable" *kalpa* (Skt. meaning "aeon") is variously said to be 10^{51} or 10^{59} or 10^{63} years.

107. Ibid., this quote and the preceding one, p. 10.

It is worth pointing out, as Ven. Yin-shun says, that these four formless states of concentration can also be acquired by human beings in meditative concentration and in the proper context can contribute much to one's spiritual advancement. He grants, in fact, that "non-Buddhists also can successfully practice and attain these concentrations."[108] (Presumably, a Buddhist could say that an apophatic Catholic mystic such as St. John of the Cross achieved them.) And Ven. Yin-shun goes on to explain that besides the four formless states of concentration, there are what are called the four infinite states: kindness, compassion, joy, and equanimity. Insofar as Confucianist and Christian virtues are similar to these states, Confucianism and Christianity can help their disciples make spiritual progress:

> When the Buddha spoke of the fortunate *karma* of practicing meditation for lay people, the emphasis was mostly on practicing these four infinite states. The maintenance of these states of mind and the constant mindful recollection of them is similar to the benevolence of Confucianism and the universal love of Christianity.[109]

From the teachings of Tenzin Gyatso, H. H. the 14th Dalai Lama[110]

In general, the Dalai Lama permits for the monotheistic religions a more efficacious role than does Ven. Yin-shun in the progress of sentient beings—over several (or many more) lifetimes—toward Buddhahood. Ven. Yin-shun's schema allows that theists, Catholics in our case, can achieve a degree of beatitude, and of course as a mainstream Chinese Mahayanist he affirms universal salvation, so

---

108. Ibid., p. 98.

109. Ibid., p. 99.

110. Tenzin Gyatso (1935–), who as the 14th Dalai Lama is the most influential figure in the Gelukpa school, fled to India after 1959, not having realized his hopes of cooperating with the Chinese forces that had entered Tibet in 1950 (historically the Dalai Lamas have functioned as the titular heads of state since the mid-eighteenth century). The 14th Dalai Lama has made interfaith dialogue one of his most important priorities, and his Buddhist scholarship, reflected in his many published books and in teaching activities throughout the world, is well known.

he expects that eventually each Catholic will be reborn as a Buddhist and eventually work her/his way up to ultimate Liberation.[111] The present-day Dalai Lama is more accommodating in that he argues that theisms, Catholicism in our case, can and sometimes do, via their own unique doctrines and practices, lead individuals to a recognition of the "unconditioned," the "subtle clear light" (the Gelukpa version of the "Dharmakāya" [*dharmakāya*]).

Given that Vajrayana belongs to that kind of Buddhism which evokes the Absolute in more "positive" terms, it is perhaps no surprise that uninformed Westerners tend to confound Vajrayana's Adi-Buddha (the "Primordial Buddha" or Clear Light that is the *pure* and *unconditioned* state of what we otherwise distinguish as phenomena) with a Creator-God. The Dalai Lama explains that the true nature of sentient beings *is* the Clear Light (a Tantric version of what we are calling Same-power), so the Clear Light *does* "originate," but not in the manner of a Creator-God who is an "independent and autonomous existence." Note the Dalai Lama's helpful clarifications when asked the following question, put to him during his visit to New Zealand in 1996: "You have said that according to Buddhist philosophy there is no Creator, no God of creation, and this may initially put off many people who believe in a divine principle. Can you explain the difference between the Vajrayana Primordial Buddha and a Creator God?" The Dalai Lama replied in part:

> I understand the Primordial Buddha, also known as Buddha Samantabhadra, to be the ultimate reality, the realm of the "Dharmakāya"—the space of emptiness [the unconditioned]—where all phenomena, pure and impure, are dissolved. This is the explanation taught by the Sutras and Tantras. However, in the context of your question, the tantric tradition is the only one which explains the "Dharmakāya" in terms of Inherent clear light, the essential nature of mind; this would seem to imply that all phenomena,

---

111. For our purposes here, the intra-Buddhist doctrinal controversies involving how quickly or how slowly Buddhahood can be achieved, of "gradual path" versus subitism, etc., do not seem to directly pertain—it suffices to point out that a Catholic in this life would in a subsequent life or lives conform to a Buddhist path.

saṃsāra and *nirvāṇa*, arise from the clear and numinous source.... We can say, therefore, that this ultimate source, clear light, is close to the notion of a Creator, since all phenomena, whether they belong to *saṃsāra* or *nirvāṇa*, originate therein. But we must be careful in speaking of this source, we must not be led into error. I do not mean that there exists somewhere, there, a sort of collective light, analogous to the non-Buddhist concept of Brahma as a substratum. *We must not be inclined to deify this luminous space* [italicization mine].... All the stages which make up the life of each living being—death, the intermediate state, and rebirth—represent nothing more than the various manifestations of the potential of clear light. It is both the subtle consciousness and energy. The more clear light loses its subtlety, the more your experiences take shape.... The ability to recognize subtle light, also called the Primordial Buddha, is equivalent to realizing *nirvāṇa*, whereas ignorance of the nature of clear light leaves us to wander in the different realms of samsaric existence.... This is how I understand the concept of the Primordial Buddha. It would be a grave error to conceive of it as an independent and autonomous existence from beginningless time.[112]

To the further question, "Do you think it is possible to be both Christian and Buddhist at the same time?," the Dalai Lama answered:

I previously replied to this question indirectly when I said that belief in a Creator *could be associated with the understanding of emptiness.*[113] I believe it is possible to progress along a spiritual path and reconcile Christianity with Buddhism. But once a certain

112. Tenzin Gyatso, 14th Dalai Lama, from a website designed by Sönam Tenzin of Dharmakara.net, prepared from official brochures, newsletters, and press kit of the Trust for the Visit of H.H. the Dalai Lama to New Zealand, with additional material compiled by Ven. Sönam Chökyi, a Trust publicity officer, as well as other sources: http://hhdl.dharmakara.net/hhdlquotes.html (accessed June 19, 2006).

113. The prestigious French scholar Jean-Luc Marion, and quite a few other contemporary theologians identified with the Catholic tradition, speak in one way or another of "God-without-Being." Catholicism is not univocally and exclusively wedded to Greco-Roman substantialism in its descriptions of God. In this present work, the two Annexes delve at some length into the problematic of God-as-unconditioned.

degree of realization has been reached, a choice between the two paths will become necessary.[114] [italicization mine]

In short, the Dalai Lama posits that to the extent that a Catholic's "God" is accessed as the unconditioned, i.e., emptiness, the Catholic is making progress, within her/his own Catholic religion, toward enlightenment. But the implication, of course, is that when—perhaps in a subsequent rebirth—she or he realizes that her/his own true nature *is* the emptiness, *is* the "Dharmakāya" or Clear Light, said person will then be a Buddhist. And we should note that our ongoing thesis is again confirmed, viz., that a founding difference between Catholicism and Buddhism is that Catholics affirm an ineluctable distinction between God and other beings whereas Buddhism affirms self-power (which, in Mahayana and Vajrayana, is understood in terms that we are calling Same-power).[115]

That the Dalai Lama reserves a degree of beatitude for those who live and die as practicing and faithful Catholics can likewise be inferred from his often-repeated statements that all the large traditional religions teach peacefulness, loving-kindness, etc., virtues conducive to eventual liberation, and that an individual under normal circumstances should "remain true to his or her traditional religion."[116] As the pertaining press statement also asserts, "At the same time His Holiness the Dalai Lama said that anyone could study any facet of Buddhism to supplement his or her spiritual growth, if anyone wishes to do so. To do this it is not required to embrace Buddhism and give up one's own religion."[117] Indeed, when visiting France, he acknowledged very warmly the ongoing exchanges—

114. Again from http://hhdl.dharmakara.net/hhdlquotes.html (accessed June 19, 2006).

115. Same-power of course is not to be confused with an independent (of the rest of reality) Source. In Big Vehicle Buddhism, Same-power does not transcend the rest of reality but *is* reality. In the Dalai Lama's version, Same-power is the Clear Light that is the true nature of all reality.

116. See "Press Statement: His Holiness the Dalai Lama has no plans of conversion of Hindus to Buddhism" (October 4, 2001), from "Tibet.Net: The Official Website of the Central Tibetan Administration, Office of His Holiness the Dalai Lama": http://www.tibet.net/en/prelease/2001/051001.html (accessed June 19, 2006).

117. Ibid.

described earlier in this present work—between Buddhist and Catholic monastics: "We have actually set up a very constructive programme of exchanges between monks and nuns of our two traditions."[118] The Dalai Lama has elsewhere noted what he considers an exception to his general advice against conversion, viz., that individuals may be justified in converting to Buddhism if their "causes and conditions" (karma and cooperating conditions) have rendered their case special in this regard.

Thus, this problematic too, observed from the Buddhist end, demonstrates how the Dalai Lama's version of Buddhist inclusivism assigns to the Catholic Faith a beneficial (though temporary) role in the progress, over many lifetimes, of the human race toward Buddhahood.

From the teachings of Dhyana Master Thich[119] Nhat Hanh[120]

Regarding the status of Christians in relation to truth and beatitude, the influential Vietnamese monk-in-exile Master Thich Nhat Hanh reaches many of the same conclusions as the Dalai Lama, but by a somewhat different route. Like some Buddhist masters in the Chinese, Korean, and Japanese traditions, he sees an individual's *karma* very marked by genealogy, both familial and cultural ("spiritual ancestry"). Many Buddhologists argue that this genealogical emphasis reflects the influence of Confucianism and its analogues

118. Ibid.

119. *Thich* is a name taken by all Vietnamese Buddhist monks and nuns, and is meant to associate them with the Sakya clan of Sakyamuni Buddha. Though Thich Nhat Hanh does not identify himself with Japanese Buddhism, he is often called Zen Master in English because the Sanskrit word *dhyāna* ("meditative absorption," Viet. *Thien*; Ch. *Chan*; Jap. *Zen*) is less recognizable to English speakers.

120. Dhyana Master Thich Nhat Hanh (1926–) is a globally known Vietnamese monk who has lived in exile (much of the time at Plum Village, in the Dordogne, France) since the mid-1960s, when his political activism made him unwelcome at home. Founder of nuclear Buddhist communities throughout the world, he has retained traditional Buddhism while adapting it to global needs—in particular, he has deployed "mindfulness" (Skt. *smrti*, "alertness" as the foundation of insight) and compassion against oppressive social and political structures. He is a prolific author and, living in France as he does, has engaged much in interreligious dialogue.

elsewhere, which so prioritize the cult of "filial piety." In one of his best-known books, Master Thich Nhat Hanh explains,

> We have blood ancestors but we also have spiritual ancestors. If you were born in the West there is a big chance you are a child of Jesus and that you have Jesus as your ancestor. Jesus is one of the many spiritual ancestors of Europeans. You may not consider yourself a Christian, but that does not prevent Jesus from being one of your spiritual ancestors because your great-grandfather might have been a good Christian. He has transmitted to you the seed, the energy, the love, and the insight of Jesus. If you do well, you will be able to help this energy to manifest within yourself.
>
> There are those [descendants of Christians] who think that they don't have anything to do with Christianity. They want to leave Christianity behind, but in the body and spirit of these people Jesus may be very present and very real.[121]
>
> . . . .
>
> A Buddhist is someone who considers the Buddha as one of his spiritual ancestors. . . . If you are a Buddhist, you have the Buddha as an ancestor.[122]

Master Thich Nhat Hanh, much like the Dalai Lama, clearly maintains that Christians *as Christians* can achieve holiness, holiness understood as "the spirit of love, of understanding, of peace, of Jesus."[123]

Much like the Dalai Lama, the Vietnamese monk maintains that the important role of dialogue is mutual cooperation in order to "heal" the world:

> A Christian is a continuation of Jesus Christ: He *is* Jesus Christ, and she *is* Jesus Christ. . . . A Buddhist is a child of the Buddha, he is, and she is, a continuation of the Buddha. . . . So it is true to say that when the Buddhist meets the Christian, the Buddha is meeting Jesus. They do it every day. In Europe, in America, in Asia, Buddha and Christ are meeting each other every day.[124]

---

121. Thich Nhat Hanh, *Going Home: Jesus and Buddha as Brothers* (New York: Riverhead Books, 1999), pp. 189–90.
122. Ibid., pp. 190–91.
123. Ibid., p. 195.
124. Ibid., p. 196.

. . . .

Buddha and Jesus are two brothers who have to help each other [each helps the other carry out his spiritual program to bring liberation to people]. . . . So instead of discriminating against each other, the Buddha and Jesus have to come together every day, ... Their meeting is the hope for the world.[125]

Thich Nhat Hanh, much like the Dalai Lama, affirms that in the normal course of events Christians should remain Christians and Buddhists remain Buddhists. The Vietnamese monk says that this in his experience should be the case even when Christians have become disillusioned and abandoned Christianity. When they are ready, they should go back "home":

Because they [disillusioned Christians] have suffered so much they want to have nothing to do with their family, their church, their society, and their culture. . . . They want to become a Buddhist because they have hated everything related to their roots. Have they succeeded in leaving everything behind in order to become something completely new? The answer is no. . . . My tendency is to tell them that a person without roots cannot be a happy person. You have to go back to your roots. You have to go back to your family. You have to go back to your culture. You have to go back to your church.[126]

Master Thich Nhat Hanh believes that Christians should continue on as Christians in this their present life, but clearly, again much like the Dalai Lama, he reinterprets Christ and Christian doctrine in Buddhist terms. This "Buddhist inclusivism" is clear from statements such as, "There is no conflict at all between the Buddha and Christ in me. They are real brothers, they are real sisters within me"[127]; and "Buddha and Jesus are two brothers who have to help each other."[128] In short, the mission or role of Jesus is taken to be analogous to that of an Emanation-Body (*nirmāṇakāya*) of a

---

125. Ibid., p. 200.
126. Ibid., pp. 182–83.
127. Ibid., p. 196.
128. Ibid., p. 200.

Buddha, which forms in order to teach the way to healing, to compassion and wisdom, and eventually to full enlightenment.

The statement we quoted earlier, namely, "A Christian is a continuation of Jesus Christ: He is Jesus Christ, and she is Jesus Christ," sidesteps the mainstream Christian teaching that a baptized person, while identified in a special manner with Christ by virtue of baptism (rendered "Christ-like" and indeed, in traditional Catholic terms, an "other Christ" or *alter Christus* in this sense), is not identical with Jesus Christ. On the other hand, in Master Thich Nhat Hanh's Mahayana Buddhism, an enlightened Buddhist is one who realizes that s/he *is* indeed the Buddha: his/her "true self" is the Buddha-nature.[129]

The Locus for Buddhists in the Catholic Paradigm

Whether non-Christians can achieve heavenly beatitude is a question whose theological history well demonstrates how the Catholic Church's understanding of teachings that belong to the *depositum fidei* ("deposit of faith") can mature and develop. Catholicism understands the *depositum fidei* to be the body of teachings or "saving truths" entrusted by Christ to the Apostles. In the form of Apostolic Tradition and Sacred Scripture, the whole Church, in proper union with the Magisterium, is understood to preserve and proclaim these teachings. Catholicism, unlike most Evangelical denominations, subscribes to a theory of "developmental theology": the Holy Spirit, in and through the evolving and often confused circumstances of concrete history, is gradually bringing the Church to an ever more mature understanding of the *depositum fidei*. The teaching of a scriptural passage such as the following belongs to the "deposit of faith" *and is thus unchangeable*,[130] but *how* the Church

---

129. Or, in the usage of this paper, so as to better clarify for non-Buddhists, the "true Self" understood as the Same-power that is the Absolute Unconditioned, in Thich Nhat Hanh's parlance the "Buddha-nature."

130. The teachings of Christ are taken to be unchangeable because they are the fruit of his historical mission: thus, they came to a close at the end of the Apostolic Age, and the Church is charged with passing them on intact.

understands this passage and its teaching has undergone slow but profound change:

> When Gentiles who have not the law do by nature what the law requires, they are a law to themselves, even though they do not have the law. They show that what the law requires is written on their hearts, while their conscience also bears witness and their conflicting thoughts accuse or perhaps excuse them on that day when, according to my gospel [Gk. *euangelion*, "Good News"] God judges the secrets of men by [Gk. *dia*, "through"] Christ Jesus.
> —Rom 2:14–16

This teaching, that the "natural law" written into the hearts of "Gentiles" can be enough—if they obey that "natural law"—to save them through Christ Jesus on the Day of Judgment, seems to contradict the many scriptural passages that insist on Christian faith and, through Baptism, literal membership in the Church. Indeed, we have already reviewed some of the many passages that establish the authority and indispensability of the Church, "pillar and bulwark of the truth" (1 Tm 3:15). The axiom "Outside the Church, no salvation," formulated in the early Church, was first directed toward heretics and schismatics who had intentionally separated from the Church. Its application underwent gradual extension but was, from early on, accompanied in one way or another by provisions that allowed for exceptions. Over time, the notion of "baptism of desire" (when one wants to be baptized but insurmountable circumstances prevent it) is formulated and recognized, as is the notion of "invincible ignorance" (when one cannot be held liable for lack of knowledge that is beyond one's control). Various understandings of "implicit faith" develop, and likewise, greater respect for other peoples and their traditions. During the pontificate of Alexander VII (1655–1667), the Congregation for the Propagation of the Faith included the following in its instructions to missionaries departing for Southeast Asia and China:

> Do not in any way attempt, and do not on any pretext persuade these people to change their rites, habits and customs, unless they are openly opposed to religion and good morals. For what would

be more absurd than to bring France, Spain, Italy or any other European country over to China? It is not your country but the faith you must bring, that faith which does not reject or belittle the rites or customs of any nation as long as these rites are not evil, but rather desires that they be preserved in their integrity and fostered.... Never make comparisons between the customs of these peoples and those of Europe; on the contrary show your anxiety to become used to them [the customs]. Admire and praise whatever merits praise. As regards what is not praiseworthy, while it must not be extolled as is done by flatterers, you will be prudent enough not to pass judgment on it, or in any case, not to condemn it rashly or exaggeratedly.

—"Instruction to the Vicars Apostolic of Tonkin and Cochinchina" (1659)   (CF #1109)

In the mid-twentieth century, Pius XII in the encyclical *Mystici Corporis* (1943) officially reaffirmed that non-Catholics can access the saving merits of Jesus Christ out of an "unconscious desire and longing" to belong to His Church. From this point in time onward, the modern-day momentum toward a more developed theology of *Catholic inclusivism* builds speed quite dramatically.

The "Leonard Feeney case"[131] in the United States provided an occasion for the Vatican to clarify the meaning of *Mystici Corporis* in the matter of "baptism of desire," in an official letter sent to Archbishop Cushing of Boston. The letter reads in part:

As regards the helps to salvation which are ordered to the last end only by divine decree, not by intrinsic necessity, God, in his infinite mercy, willed that their effects which are necessary to salvation can, in certain circumstances, be obtained when the helps are used only in desire and longing. We see this clearly stated in the Council of Trent about the sacrament of regeneration and about the sacrament of penance.

131. Leonard Feeney was a Jesuit who understood "Baptism of desire" to mean that explicit desire to belong to the Catholic Church is required. He was dismissed from the Society of Jesus (the Jesuit order) in 1949 and excommunicated from the Church in 1953.

The same, in due proportion, should be said of the Church insofar as it is a general help to salvation. To gain eternal salvation it is not always required that a person be incorporated in reality as a member of the Church, but it is required that one belong to it at least in desire and longing (*voto et desiderio*). It is not always necessary that this desire be explicit as it is with catechumens. When one is invincibly [i.e., not due to one's own fault] ignorant, God also accepts an implicit desire, so called because it is contained in the good disposition of soul by which a person wants his or her will to be conformed to God's will.

—"Letter of the Holy Office to the Archbishop of Boston" (1949) (CF #855, DS 3869–70)

Less than twenty years later, Vatican Council II (1962–1965) convened and went on to take several momentous strides forward. In *Lumen Gentium*, the council develops the fuller implications of Rom 2:14–16 (the natural law is "written on their hearts"), of 1 Tm 2:4 (God "desires all men to be saved"), and other scriptural passages, in order to declare: "Nor shall divine providence deny the assistance necessary for salvation to those who, without any fault of theirs, have not yet arrived at an explicit knowledge of God, and who, not without grace, strive to lead a good life" (#16).

In *Nostra Aetate*, the council addresses the non-Christian religions with respect and appreciation, affirming the goodness found in them. In this monograph's Introduction, we quoted the council's specific appreciation of Buddhism, and in the present context it is fitting to quote it again:

> Buddhism in its various forms testifies to the essential inadequacy of this changing world. It proposes a way of life by which men can, with confidence and trust, attain a state of perfect liberation and reach supreme illumination, either through their own efforts or by the aid of divine [i.e., supra-mundane] help. So, too, other religions which are found throughout the world attempt in their own ways to calm the hearts of men by outlining a program of life covering doctrine, moral precepts and sacred rites.
>
> The Catholic Church rejects nothing of what is true and holy in these religions. She has a high regard for the manner of life and conduct, the precepts and doctrines which, although differing in

many ways from her own teaching, nevertheless often reflect a ray of that truth which enlightens all men.
—From *Nostra Aetate*, #2 (VAT2D)

Gaudium et Spes goes so far as to say that God's grace can act invisibly in "all men of good will" and that "in a way known to God" (whose Wisdom we cannot fathom) the Holy Spirit offers to all the possibility of partnership in the "paschal mystery" (Christ's passion, death, resurrection, and glorification):

> The Christian is certainly bound both by need and by duty to struggle with evil through many afflictions and to suffer death; but, as one who has been made a partner in the paschal mystery, and as one who has been configured to the death of Christ, he will go forward, strengthened by hope, to the resurrection.
> All this holds true not for Christians only but also for all men of good will in whose hearts grace is active invisibly. For since Christ died for all, and since all men are in fact called to one and the same destiny, which is divine, we must hold that the Holy Spirit offers to all the possibility of being made partners, *in a way known to God*,[132] in the paschal mystery.
> —From *Gaudium et Spes*, #22 (VAT2D)

The *Catechism of the Catholic Church*, in #1260, after citing the paragraph above from *Gaudium et Spes*, adds:

> Every man who is ignorant of the Gospel of Christ and of his Church, but seeks the truth and does the will of God in accordance with his understanding of it, can be saved. It may be supposed that such persons would have *desired Baptism explicitly* if they had known its necessity. [italics in text]
> —*Catechism of the Catholic Church*, #1260[133]

That members of all religions (and indeed of no religion, if one means formal religion) can still be saved is now a settled question in Catholicism. In its declaration *Dominus Iesus*, the Congregation for the Doctrine of the Faith goes on to actually invite theology to

---

132. Italicization mine.
133. In #846–48, the *Catechism* presents the foregoing teachings as the fuller meaning of the old dictum, "Outside the Church, there is no salvation."

explore how positive elements in other religions "may fall within the divine plan of salvation":

> ... [T]heology today in its reflection on the existence of other religious experiences and on their salvific meaning in God's salvific plan, is invited to explore if and in what way the historical figures and positive elements of these religions may fall within the divine plan of salvation. In this undertaking, theological research has a vast field of work under the guidance of the Magisterium. The Second Vatican Council, in fact, has stated that: "the unique mediation of the Redeemer does not exclude, but rather gives rise to a manifold cooperation which is but a participation in this one source."
>
> —"Declaration *Dominus Iesus* on the Unicity and Salvific Universality of Jesus Christ and the Church," Congregation for the Doctrine of the Faith, #14[134]

The Pontifical Council for Interreligious Dialogue and the Congregation for the Evangelization of Peoples have declared the following, and in the Church such statements often herald what may be presented in a still more official way later:

> From this *mystery of unity* [alluding here to a speech of John Paul II to the curia; italics are mine] it follows that all men and women who are saved, share, though differently, in the same mystery of salvation in Jesus Christ through his Spirit. Christians know this through their faith, while others remain unaware that Jesus Christ is the source of their salvation. The mystery of salvation reaches out to them, in a way known to God, through the invisible action of the Spirit of Christ. Concretely it will be in the sincere practice of what is good in their own religious tradition and by following the dictates of their conscience that the members of other religions respond positively to God's invitation and receive salvation in Jesus Christ, even while they do not recognize or acknowledge him as their Saviour.
>
> —Pontifical Council for Interreligious Dialogue, Congregation for the Evangelization of Peoples (1991)   (CF #1059)

---

134. See Vatican website: http://www.vatican.va/roman_curia/congregations/cf aith/documents/rc_con_cfaith_doc_20000806_dominus-jesus_en.html.

Also a herald of what is ahead can be found, in my opinion, as early as 1970 in the "Communication" of the Federation of Asian Bishops' Conferences (FABC) in preparation for the 1970 synod:

> We [Asian bishops] accept them [Asian religious traditions] as significant and positive elements in the economy of God's design of salvation. (#14)

The bishops went on to ask,

> How can we not give them reverence and honor? And how can we not acknowledge that God has drawn our peoples to himself through them? (#15)
> —Communication of the FABC in preparation for the synod (1974)[135]

The pontificate of Benedict XVI was marked by caution in relation to interreligious dialogue in general. Actually, the pope's warnings against syncretism and relativism[136] were well-received by informed Buddhists as well, who resent the obfuscation of Buddhist doctrines often undertaken in the name of either a foundational "common ground" or a spurious version of inclusivism. In various contexts, Benedict XVI also issued clarifications in relation to Catholic prayer and meditation, and in relation to the divine "Rationality" (a term that has a subtle technical meaning in Catholic theology, to be treated ahead, in the First Annex). The reader should note that this present work carefully references and adheres to these cautions and clarifications wherever they apply to the specific subject matter being addressed.

As Benedict XVI met more and more visiting Buddhist monastics and devout laypersons, there were signs that he was learning more

---

135. "Evangelization in Modern Day Asia" (1974), in G. Rosales and C.G. Arévalo, eds., *For All the Peoples of Asia: Federation of Asian Bishops' Conferences, Documents from 1970 to 1991* (Maryknoll, NY: Orbis, 1992), pp. 11–25.

136. Syncretism, broadly speaking, is the mixing together of the distinctive doctrines of differing religions in an attempt at synthesis; relativism, broadly speaking, assumes that the validity of a truth does not transcend those who affirm said truth (so that a truth's only validity is established by its empirical history). Because Catholicism claims its official teachings are received from God, it has always gone on record in opposition to syncretism and relativism.

about authentic Buddhist teaching and practice and was coming to an increased appreciation for the Buddhist tradition. As has been often noted, Catholicism develops slowly but surely.

The official acts of the Pontifical Council for Interreligious Dialogue constitute a good index of papal sentiment in relation to another religion, so it is meaningful that on the occasion of Vesak (the annual Buddhist commemoration of the birth, death, and enlightenment of the Buddha), the council, on April 3, 2009—in continuing a long Vatican tradition of extending "congratulations" to Buddhists in advance of this celebration—included the following in its lengthy message:

> . . . . This annual celebration offers Catholics an opportunity to exchange greetings with our Buddhist friends and neighbors, and in this way to strengthen the existing bonds of friendship and to create new ones. These ties of cordiality allow us to share with each other our joys, hopes and spiritual treasures.   [see para. 1]
>
> While renewing our sense of closeness to you, Buddhists, in this period, it becomes clearer and clearer that together we are able not only to contribute, in fidelity to our respective spiritual traditions, to the well-being of our own communities, but also to the human community of the world.   [see para. 2]

The message points out that there are two very different types of poverty—a poverty to be chosen and a poverty to be curtailed. Christians believe the "poverty to be chosen" allows one to tread in the footsteps of Christ, "who for our sake became poor" (see 2 Cor 8:9). Christians "understand this poverty to mean above all an emptying of self, . . ." There is also the poverty that should be opposed, that which "offends justice and equality. . . ." Furthermore, "in advanced wealthy societies, there is evidence of marginalization, as well as affective, moral, and spiritual poverty," seen in people whose interior lives are disoriented and who experience various forms of malaise despite their economic affluence. The message goes on to applaud the Buddhist witness of non-attachment and contentment and Buddhism's commitment to the promotion of global good will:

> Whereas we as Catholics reflect in this way on the meaning of poverty, we are also attentive to your spiritual experience, dear Bud-

dhist friends. We wish to thank you for your inspiring witness of non-attachment and contentment. Monks, nuns, and many lay devotees among you embrace a poverty "to be chosen" that spiritually nourishes the human heart, substantially enriching life with a deeper insight into the meaning of existence, and sustaining commitment to promoting the goodwill of the whole human community. [para. 5]
—Pontifical Council for Interreligious Dialogue, Vatican City, April 3, 2009[137]

---

137. Available on the Internet at permalink http://www.zenit.org/article-2556 2?|=English.

PART TWO

Buddhist and Catholic Practice:
Fruitful Interrelations and the Future

You are the heirs and guardians of a venerable wisdom. . . .
—John Paul II, Address to the Representatives of non-Christian
Religions, Tokyo, February 24, 1981[1]

The majority of your fellow citizens embrace Buddhism. . . . as
people of Thailand you are heirs of the ancient and venerable wisdom contained therein.
—John Paul II, homily, Thailand, May 10, 1984[2]

Christians should recognize the divine Spirit operating outside the
visible confines of the Mystical Body.
—John Paul II, *Red. Hom.* 6[3]

The Spirit *who blows where he wills* is the source of inspiration for
all that is true and beautiful, according to the magnificent phrase
of an unknown author from the time of Pope Damasus (366–384)
which states: "every truth, no matter who says it, comes from the
Holy Spirit."
—John Paul II, Rome, December 5, 1990[4]

I BEGIN WITH a concrete circumstance, a scene of Buddhist monks/
nuns and Catholic monks/nuns meditating in their own religion's
respective ways in the same room and sending loving-kindness, in
their own religion's respective ways, to the members of the other

---

1. Cited in William Skudlarek, OSB, "John Paul II on Interreligious Dialogue,"
Dilatato Corde, Vol. IV, No. 1 (January–June 2014), DIM/MID.
2. Ibid.
3. Cited in Sebastian Painadath, SJ, "In Search of Harmony: Journeying with
John Paul II," *Dilatato Corde*, Vol. IV, No. 1 (January–June 2014), DIM/MID.
4. Ibid.

religion present. Since Vatican Council II, this scene has actually repeated itself many times already, and it continues to repeat itself, the Catholics doing so with the full permission of the proper ecclesiastical authorities.[5] The Church clearly senses that salvation history has reached a time ripe for this kind of encounter between Buddhism and Catholicism. Let us undertake a brief phenomenological description, broadly defined,[6] of key features of the above scenario as they pertain to the encounter of religions. I say "phenomenological" description, because from the Catholic perspective, there is also the work of grace operative in this scenario, and for Catholics this work is necessarily *the* most important, indeed the *sine qua non* of fruitful encounter. Grace orchestrates, enables, "determines" (while leaving human wills free[7]) all truly fruitful encounter, but mysteriously and from "underneath." Grace belongs to the supernatural order.[8]

The work of grace, hidden and humanly imperceptible, is thus by definition outside the realm of phenomenology, though manifestations of it can appear sometimes in the phenomenological realm. In short, we cannot and dare not try to "describe" *how* God's *grace* is working out salvation history in Buddhist-Catholic encounter. As the Catholic Catechism says, "Since it belongs to the supernatural

5. Indeed, some of the sessions described above have been open to lay participants as well, and I have participated very intently in some such events, deriving enormous benefit from them. I have also read, intently and at length, what the participating Buddhists and Catholics have reported about their "frames of mind" in relation to these sessions, and during the sessions themselves.

6. A phenomenological description, broadly defined, is a careful description of what appears in experience.

7. That this can be the case is a *mysterium* in the technical Catholic sense. A *mysterium* is a truth that we know because God has revealed it: if a *mysterium* is confounding, it is understood to be so because divine Rationality is too subtle for merely human rationality. Indeed, it has often been pointed out that if divine truths were fully understandable to humanity, humanity would be itself divine.

8. The "supernatural" refers to that which is not native to the capacity of human nature but is known and accessed only through divine revelation and its effects. It is one of those many Catholic technical terms that literally translate the Latin but that in contemporary English have, among the wider public, a very different sense or at least connotation. Another example would be the term divine "Mystery," the usual English translation of *mysterium*.

order, grace *escapes our experience*[9] and cannot be known except by faith"[10] (that is, faith in the truths revealed to us, taught to us, by the Lord Jesus Christ and elaborated by His Spouse, the Church). What Catholics should do, always, and especially during the meditation (and prayer[11]) session, is open themselves up as much as possible to the hidden workings of grace. (Repentance, adoration, petition, etc., sometimes as internal acts but always as a deep mode of "being-toward-God," should mark the Catholic's "waiting on the Lord" during meditation.[12])

A phenomenology of the joint Buddhist-Catholic meditation session notes, no doubt, that the Buddhists and Catholics practice the kinds of meditation/prayer that are respectively customary to them in other formal settings. To these, they usually add (or increase) other considerations and practices that reach out in a special way to the members of the other religion present. These practices (e.g., prayer, sending of *metta*, and even—in the case of some Buddhists—the use of benevolent "parapsychological" means[13]) are intended to spiritually "share" with the members of the other reli-

9. Though of course it can work *in* experience.

10. CCC #2005.

11. Usually internal and silent prayer, in the case of a meditation session. Mahayana and Vajrayana Buddhists pray too, in that they often invoke Buddha and Bodhisattvas for assistance (as is taught in the Big Vehicle's sutras), and doctrinal Theravadins pray in the sense of invoking the good example set by the historical Buddha, *arahants*, etc. A common Buddhist practice, especially during meditation, is to send sentiments of *metta* (P.; Skt. *maitrī*), i.e., "good will," "benevolence," toward others.

12. Otherwise, the falsities of quietism can insinuate themselves. In Catholic history, "quietism" is the name for several movements (the most notable occurring in the seventeenth century) that, among other features, so emphasized passivity and an "inward way" that, to one extent or another, they claimed freedom from religious obligations, from the sacramental system, and, in some cases, even from active deeds of charity. In the past, Catholic polemicists, fairly or unfairly, frequently accused Buddhists of spreading "quietist" teachings, so dialogists should, I think, familiarize themselves with this polemic.

13. The "parapsychological" refers to phenomena that belong to natural human capacity but are extraordinary in that they exceed the powers of ordinary human consciousness. Some better-known examples are telepathy, clairvoyance, and psychokinesis. Catholics would distinguish the parapsychological, which is still natural, from the supernatural.

gion, for the benefit of the members of the other religion, and for themselves too. In most cases, the Buddhist and Catholic meditators are very well informed, that is, very aware that Buddhists and Catholics, each according to their own tradition, are hoping for salutary effects on themselves and those of the other religion.

Those Buddhists and Catholics who are sufficiently informed realize what we have demonstrated at length in the preceding parts of this monograph, namely, that there are foundational differences between the core teachings of Buddhism and those of Catholicism. These foundational differences are not only conceptual or ideological but *existential*, i.e., they permeate, consciously or at least unconsciously, the whole life-world of each committed Buddhist and Catholic. In fact, especially during meditation, particularly group meditation, advanced Buddhist practitioners (and maybe very gifted Catholic meditators too, though Catholics do not normally aim to develop such skills) are able to discern or directly intuit ("parapsychologically") these "at-bottom" differences.

At this point, let us describe some pertaining features of the "existential project" characterizing informed Catholic practitioners at this meditative session. At least at the horizon of their awareness, the Catholics realize that the Buddhist tradition, over the course of 2,500 years, has no doubt generated hundreds of thousands, indeed millions, of holy and self-sacrificial disciples who have done enormous good for the human race. Anyone familiar with the history of religions knows that this cannot be gainsaid. Most of the Catholics should also know that only for the last 200–300 years has there been, between Buddhism and Catholicism in Asia, anything resembling meaningful contact such that Catholic teaching could be adequately explained; and even when such contact materialized, it involved only miniscule proportions of the Buddhist population.[14]

---

14. There is growing evidence that Eastern Christians (from Persia and elsewhere in the Middle East) established communities in China by the third century CE; Eastern Christians were surely in Changan (modern Xi'an), China, and probably in Tibet, by the seventh century. These communities died away or were assimilated. The Franciscan friars who accompanied Marco Polo to China in the 1200s had little chance to gain traction during their visit. St. Francis Xavier first went to

Only in the nineteenth century did Catholicism really gain a large audience for its preaching, but its message was often clouded because of associations with Western colonialism. In the twentieth century, and even now, only a fraction of Buddhists have meaningful access to Christian teaching. The Catholics at the meditative session also know that the Church teaches, as we have duly demonstrated already, that Buddhists who are not sent the grace of conversion and Christian belief can be nonetheless saved through the unique mediation of Our Lord Jesus Christ as long as they observe the law "written on their hearts" (Rom 2:15), i.e., the "natural" or moral law that inheres in human nature (CCC #1954–60). Furthermore, as we have seen, the Church very much respects the teachings and practices of Buddhism (Vatican Council II, *Nostra Aetate*, #2).

In sum, the Catholic meditator knows (1) that Buddhism has a flourishing religious culture which on the phenomenological level (that of human "life-worlds") can be said to generate very good, oftentimes wonderfully good, and holy people; (2) that the overwhelming majority of Buddhists have never had and do not now have meaningful access to Christianity; and (3) that Buddhists who have had or have meaningful access to Christianity may not have been sent the grace of conversion: God wills all human beings to be saved, but the grace of conversion to Christianity is gratuitous. God sends it, according to His own mysterious design, to whom He

---

Japan in the 1500s, but by 1635 fierce imperial opposition had put an end to all missionary presence in Japan. Matteo Ricci established himself in China in the 1600s, but he and the Jesuits and others who followed him worked with Confucianists. (As for missionaries to Tibet, the notes to the two epigraphs introducing this very monograph tell their story, which—inspiring as it is—ends in tragedy.) Catholic missionaries came to Indochina as early as the 1500s, but they endured persecution and other political vicissitudes. One of the few success stories is Bishop Lambert de la Motte's founding, there, of a congregation of native Sisters, the Lovers of the Cross (*Amantes de la Croix*) in 1670. Despite over 340 years of persecutions, wars, and other ordeals, this congregation now numbers almost 5000 Sisters in 24 communities, 18 in Vietnam, 3 in Thailand, 2 in Laos, and 1 in the United States. In Thailand, two Sisters from this congregation were my graduate students, and one of my fondest memories is of them walking to the bus station after class, joking and laughing with the six or seven Buddhist monks who were also my students.

wills[15]; others—including Buddhists—are still saved through Jesus Christ's merits, but by observing the natural law as it is enshrined and cultivated in their own tradition (the declaration *Dominus Iesus* speaks of "participated forms of mediation of different kinds and degrees" found in other religions,[16] though of course these forms "must always remain consistent with the principle of Christ's unique mediation"). How can a Catholic do other than conclude, then (even allowing for the lingering consequences of the Fall), that God in His mysterious design has disposed—at least at this time in salvation history and heretofore, and at least for those Buddhists to whom the above conditions apply—*that the situation be this way*?

If God has willed that all persons be saved but has not sent the opportunity of Christian conversion to all, how can we not conclude that God wills those good Buddhists in this latter category to live, flourish, and die as good Buddhists? *That God in His providence—at least for now—wants the situation to be this way?* That God—at least for now—wants Buddhism to be the setting for millions of good and noble people in the world? (This does *not* mean that Catholics should not witness to the Catholic faith or even—on the proper occasions and in a courteous way—consider it their duty to preach Catholicism to Buddhists, and to teach it mightily. But it *does* mean that Catholics would do well to remember that God alone sends the grace of conversion when and to whom He wills; Catholics should not "play God" or so anthropomorphize God that a profound respect is lost for the divine Wisdom and *Mystery*. Catholics should do all that they—on their own part—can do to further Christ's Kingdom, but then they should have the *humility* to leave the rest to God's Providence.)

---

15. Catholicism also teaches, of course, that God may send the grace of conversion to an individual, and said individual may freely reject it (for which wrong choice s/he is liable before God). The *Catechism of the Catholic Church* teaches that a person actually chooses Hell for himself/herself: "This state of definitive self-exclusion from communion with God is called 'Hell'" (CCC #1033).

16. Declaration *Dominus Iesus*, from #14, Congregation for the Doctrine of the Faith, August 6, 2000.

From their own frame of reference, the Buddhists at the meditative session are witnesses too, and in other formats, dialogic formats, they express their own heartfelt religious experiences and explain their own religious teachings to Catholics. Almost always, the Buddhists testify that a vital and most meaningful element of their religious practice is an ongoing dissolution of the "fiction" that is an inherent self; and that the doctrine of rebirth is one of the pivots of their religious life-world.

The Catholics at the meditative session realize that respect for their Buddhist counterparts entails a respect for what the Buddhists testify about themselves. In general, one can say that the respect Catholics owe is to the "existential project" of these Buddhists. In the Catholics' eyes, the distinctly Buddhist modes of "being-in-the-world" normally function on the *phenomenological* level but not on the supernatural level. The wellspring of grace won by Jesus Christ drives whatever good is accomplished on the phenomenological level by the doctrines/practices in the Buddhist life-world.[17]

In terms of Catholic respect for the Buddhist's existential project, even what the Church declares to be objectively wrong Buddhist teachings (such as "rebirth" and "no self-identical soul") figure here, insofar as they involve experiences testified to as essential in a Buddhist's life-world; a Catholic withholding such respect would in effect be telling her/his Buddhist counterpart that Buddhists don't report honestly or even understand (existentially) their most intimate religious experiences! Such a Catholic would be gravely violating the human dignity of her/his Buddhist friends.

The above formulation on the Catholic's part is not "relativist"[18] because (1) nowhere is the claim made or implied that Christ is not

---

17. So in this special and unusual sense, one can say that because what is "good" in the Buddhist doctrines/practices is driven by Christ, they are to this extent driven supernaturally.

18. In short, the Catholic would not be affirming that Buddhist convictions, when contradicting Catholic doctrine, are "valid for Buddhists" just as Catholic convictions are "valid for Catholics." Catholic supernatural truths are understood to be divinely revealed and to transcend human phenomenology (though they can work through human phenomenology).

in His historical incarnation, death, and resurrection once and for all the unique source of whatever divine grace is at work; (2) nor is the claim being made or implied that Buddhist doctrines, when contradictory to Catholic ones, are objectively true; (3) nor is the claim being made or implied that Buddhist practices are sacramental or equivalent in kind or degree to the sacraments,[19] which are uniquely efficacious.

How the Figure of Chiasm Pertains

If we return to our phenomenology of the joint meditation session, an intriguing configuration reveals itself. A *chiasm* reveals itself. This chiasm is best described in terms of an adapted form of what can be called a Derridean chiasm, where each of two contradictory "texts" is reinscribed in modified form as the subtext of its respective contradictory, thus:

Text X	Text -X	
x	-x	Primary Level
-x	x	Subtextual Level

19. Catholicism understands a sacrament to confer the grace signified by its outward sign, and to have been instituted by Christ Himself. There are seven sacraments (enumerated earlier, at the end of the section on "Catholicism and the Creator/Created Distinction").

At the joint meditation session, at least in the intentionalities[20] operative before and after the meditation proper (Buddhist forms of meditation, in particular, often suspend active intentionality), the Catholics and Buddhists mutually recognize that in crucial ways their operative intentionalities are contradictory to each other. The intentional field of the Catholics includes loving prayer for the Buddhists, who, if they are sincere and questing the good, ultimately are being saved by Christ's grace. The intentional field of the Buddhists includes the sending of loving benevolence (*metta/maitrī*) to the Catholics. This *metta* is accompanied in the case of Theravadins by the hope that the Catholics will ultimately find the meaning of impermanence, no-soul, and the root of suffering, and throwing off the fetters of attachment (to the self, to the "God-fabrication," etc.), will become liberated; in the case of Mahayanists, *maitrī* is accompanied by good wishes[21] that the Catholics' cycles of rebirths become quickly productive, leading to full realization of the Buddhist truths, so that they become fully enlightened (as already noted, most Mahayanists believe that all sentient beings will be ultimately liberated and in beatitude).

Thus, the intentionalities of the Catholics and the Buddhists, in terms of fundamental path and beatitude and the nature of beatitude itself, are ultimately contradictory—an irreducible difference (phenomenologically speaking) yawns between them. Two

20. In existential phenomenology, "intentionality" is a technical term not to be confounded with the looser English-language vernacular meaning of "intention." Adapted in the modern era by Franz Brentano from medieval epistemology, and further developed by twentieth-century existential phenomenologists, "intentionality" means "consciousness-of" an "object" ("object" = any something, in the broadest sense). A mind "intends," that is, moves toward (Lat. "stretches toward") its object. There are many modes of this "movement toward": intentionalities include "conceiving," "perceiving," "remembering," etc. An object can have many "horizons" toward which one's consciousness moves, though they are not one's purposeful or logical focus. Heidegger in particular emphasizes the subliminal and the affective modes of intentionality. The "objects" toward which "intention" moves can also be of various modes—"real," imaginative, ideal, etc.

21. And sometimes prayers to Buddhas and Bodhisattvas, that they may help; and sometimes by transfer of personal merit on the part of the Buddhist meditator.

contradicting "texts," X and -X, say. But how does the chiasm per se arise? The chiasm appears because the astute Catholics and Buddhists *mutually realize* that they in their good will are "intending" (in the technical sense) opposite paths/beatitudes for each other. In short, the Buddhists are internalizing, deep in their experiential fields, the image of the Catholics praying for them in Catholic terms, and the Catholics are internalizing, deep in their experiential fields, the image of the Buddhists intending, at least in the long term, a contradicting path/beatitude for them, the Catholics. In Derridean terms, each Buddhist and each Catholic has "inscribed" under her/his "text" (or lodged within her/his "text," if you will) a "subtext" which is the contradicting image of the other religion's good-willed intentions for her/him.[22] Thus the chiasm becomes:

Catholic	Buddhist	
Intends Beatific Vision of God for the Buddhist	Intends ultimate Buddhist beatitude for the Catholic	Primary Level
Image of Buddhist intending ultimate Buddhist beatitude for the Catholic	Image of Catholic intending Beatific Vision of God for the Buddhist	Subtextual Level

Perhaps for some readers the question has already intervened, and if not, it surely will intervene when we turn, in the forthcoming pages, to "double-bind," "obverse overlap," etc.: Why bother with all this? Why resort, here, to such "pretentious" thought-formations as

22. Here the subtexts are, in the language of existential phenomenology, "horizons" of the meditative intentionalities of the practitioners; sometimes, especially before or after formal meditation, these subtexts may become surface-texts, that is, they may become the phenomenological "objects" of conceptual attention (or "attending").

"Derridean" chiasm and the like?[23] The reasons are several, and in my firm opinion, almost incontestable on their face. The reason easiest to demonstrate, though perhaps in the ultimate sense the least significant, derives from religious studies, cultural studies, and similar disciplines. The phenomenology of religions, properly speaking, describes phenomenological fields, and the intentionalities of Buddhist-Catholic dialogue directly pertain to this study. Catholics need not be reminded that—*mutatis mutandis*—for the Christian *en pleine vie* "it is better for a human to know than not to know" all that is knowable about the teeming, awe-inspiring, subtle play of creation. The Church has long endorsed, even celebrated, the "humanistic" enterprise. The many descriptions of Buddhist-Catholic encounter with which I am familiar, while admirable in so many respects, for the most part ignore the complexity of its phenomenology, and especially they shortchange the crucial role of difference. I hope I am showing that very serviceable in this regard, most "accurate" and "discriminating" if you will, are the differential permutations that can be derived (and adapted) from Derridean thought in particular.

The second reason justifying the treatment of chiasm, above and thus far, is that it better enables Catholics and Buddhists to be more *discerning* of what is really going on, and thus to be more *sensitive* and more *charitable* toward each other.

The third reason is that a more subtle discernment of what is going on at the phenomenological level may enable Catholic theologians to better open themselves up to God's inspiration. Under the Magisterium's guidance, deeper insight may be had—God willing—into the roles (in the words of *Dominus Iesus*) "of other religious experiences and their meaning in God's salvific plan."

The fourth reason is that the chiasm supplies the Catholic theo-

---

23. Another variant of this complaint is that the Derridean thought-formations generate diagrams and obfuscating terminology for what is very obvious, namely, that Buddhists and Catholics disagree and know it and wish each other well and mutually know that too. In other words, I am making much fuss over the obvious. Actually, I think the attentive reader shall find the opposite to be the case. The diagrams clarify what would otherwise be less clear, and the terms pinpoint crucial distinctions not previously made, or at least not previously made in such a context.

logian a good way of thinking about how empathy with the intentionality of her/his Buddhist counterpart (cross-inscribed into the subtext of her/his own Catholic consciousness) can be vital and sincere while *not* reducing to common ground. Nor, let me add parenthetically, is "empathy" itself the common ground, since empathy is the vicarious experience of the "other." Empathy is necessarily an "infinite retreat" of chiasms, since the empathic act is always "split" (or "doubled," if you will): the empathic act requires that one simultaneously be and not-be the "other" intentionality. As for a non-Christic and generalized "essence-of-love," another common ground that can be advanced by a theology of "pluralism," Derridean difference—as we shall shortly see in more detail—better accounts for the phenomenological correspondences between Buddhist love and Catholic love as a "superjacent likeness" (not an "identity") raised up (or "constituted" in this sense) by a founding difference. (This is not at all to deny that a Buddhist can be saved through her/his loving acts if these acts are driven in the order of grace by Christ's redemptive love—but Christ's redemptive love belongs to the supernatural order, not the phenomenological order.)

How the Figure of Double-Bind Pertains

It should be clear from the situation as demonstrated thus far that Buddhist and Catholic dialogists who adhere to the authoritative traditions of their respective religions are at an impasse. We Catholics must acknowledge that Buddhists and Catholics respectively think that the most foundational teachings of the others' religion are wrong. God disposes, in the case of good Buddhists not sent the grace of Christian faith, that they normally live and die Buddhists (though what happens to them, in this regard, at the definitive moment of "crossing over" to Judgment we cannot know, as such is already beyond the phenomenological field).[24]

24. As for reports supplied by those who have had "near-death experiences," Catholicism can argue that these accounts, purportedly describing events after bodily death, cannot—even if some of them are true—be "final" in any sense. Any

Let us at this point recall the treatment of double-bind at the very beginning of this monograph, condensing it down to what is most serviceable here. Simply put, a double-bind is a bind, and a doubled bind. A bind is a situation of dilemma, that is, either option is conclusive against the agent. Derrida proposes and demonstrates, through his long career, several versions of double-bind. In his late phase,[25] he interprets the "doubling" of the bind to mean that, despite the dilemma that is the "bind," the agent cannot *not*-act. The agent cannot not-act because (1) to not-act is also conclusive against the agent *and* because (2) there is an irrefragable moral imperative (the "call of responsibility" at a given time and place) to act.[26]

In my ad hoc adaptation of this figure of double-bind, the application of "bind" is not in direct reference to Buddhist and Catholic dialogists (the situation of neither partner in the dialogue suits the definition of "bind"[27]), but rather to how the respective doctrines of the two religions contradict each other. That is, though each "side" in the dialogue considers the other's doctrines false, the fact remains that the two sets of doctrines on their face contradict each

person who has medically revived (from cessation of measurable heart and even brain function) obviously has not irrevocably "crossed over," has not yet come, finally, to the absolute moment of judgment.

25. Whereas the version of "double-bind" explained in this work's Foreword is drawn from Derrida's early phase.

26. A prominent example of Derrida's late-phase version of double-bind can be found in J. Derrida, "Force of law: The mystical foundation of authority," trans. accompanied by original French text, M. Quintance, *Cardozo Law Review*, Vol. 11, No. 5–6, p. 947 and passim; see also my analysis of this version of his double-bind on pp. 175–82 in R. Magliola, "Hongzhou Chan Buddhism and Derrida Late and Early," pp. 175–91, in Youru Wang, ed., *Deconstruction and the Ethical in Asian Thought* (London and New York: Routledge, 2007).

27. Buddhism and Catholicism are both "inclusivist" religions (in the technical sense), so each can accommodate, within its own doctrinal paradigm, the religion of the "other," that is, of the dialogue partner. This being the case, the situation of double-bind should not arise for either partner in the Buddhist-Catholic dialogue. Neither partner need encounter a set of options within herself/himself that negatively "bind" each other, that is, block or thwart each other. (Binds would arise for an individual only if her/his doctrinal belief system were partly Buddhist and partly Catholic: "cognitive dissonance" is the term frequently heard nowadays for an "internal split" of this kind.)

other (regardless of which set is ultimately true and which is ultimately false). For example, an imaginary agent seeking to affirm both Catholic "one mortal birth" and Buddhist "many mortal births" ("rebirth") finds that these opposing doctrines block each other—constituting, in this sense, a case of *aporia* ("no passage" through the horns of the agent's dilemma).

And how can the notion of a "doubled" bind apply, then? On the Catholic side, I propose that it applies very much to our present moment in dialogic history, when so many Catholic scholars in prestigious theological circles, and in the broader but related fields of religious studies and cultural studies, are revising—with the best of intentions—the Church's authoritative doctrinal formulations in the interests of "pluralism," "unity," "equality," and so on.[28] I propose[29] that for the Catholic dialogist, to "settle-for" such revisionism and to merge with it, is ironically *not*-to-act. This refusal to act is "conclusive against the agent" in its own right, because—legitimate development of Catholic doctrine aside—it would require violations of divinely revealed truths as the Church understands them. For the Catholic dialogist, this refusal to act is a refusal to acknowledge, to *face*, the reality of the bind, the reality of Buddhist/Catholic doctrinal contradiction. I argue that the very earnestness and mutual love and respect demanded, and indeed to an extent generated, by Buddhist-Christian dialogue lead the Catholic nowadays to an irrefragable moral imperative—the imperative to acknowledge irreducible difference.

In today's "pluralistic" climate most of all, the Catholic dialogist cannot *not*-act, and here "to act" means "to bravely take up one's responsibility." "Responsibility" implies a faithful development, ongoing through history, of the divinely revealed truths (the *deposi-*

---

28. Curiously, or maybe not at all so curiously, a book aimed at a "popular" readership bucks this elitist trend, what Pope Francis would call this "gnostic" (in the sense of pretense to a higher, secret knowledge) trend. Stephen Prothero outlines—though admittedly with strokes that are not careful enough sometimes—the radical differences between religions in his *God Is Not One: The Eight Rival Religions That Run the World—and Why Their Differences Matter* (HarperCollins, 2010).

29. Knowing all the while that thereby I shall be shunned in some quarters and vilified in others.

tum fidei) entrusted by Christ to the Apostles and by the Apostles to their successors and the whole of the Church. To back off from difference, to circumvent, is to retreat from this very responsibility.

How the Figure of Overlap-in-the-Obverse (or "Obverse Overlap") Pertains

"Overlap-in-the-obverse" is a metaphor representing in spatial terms a kind of relationship, in our case, a kind of relationship belonging to Buddhist-Christian dialogue.[30] The metaphor operates within the context of four notions: "field-in-common," "positive overlap," "negative overlap," and "overlap-in-the-obverse." "Field-in-common" represents the common territory of two parties[31] (but see the important observation at the end of this paragraph). "Positive overlap" represents, on this field-in-common, those areas where the two parties overlay or extend on top of each other (thus "positively coinciding" in this sense). "Negative overlap" represents, on this field-in-common, those areas where the parties fall short, that is, do not occupy the field-in-common. The deficits or defaults of the parties overlay each other. That is, they "negatively coincide" in this sense. "Overlap-in-the-obverse" represents, on this field-in-common, those areas where one party is in occupation and the other party is not (or is less so). They "obvertly coincide"[32] in this sense (one side is in occupation and the other side is in total or partial default). (It is *very* important to note too, given our commitment to samenesses erected by pure difference, that even in the case of positive overlap [the "samenesses" here], the two parties remain absolutely different: they do not synthesize, merge, or "unify" into

30. Please understand that I use so cumbersome a metaphor because experience has taught me that a succinct mathematical or other more abstract representation would seem too "unnatural" to many of my readers.

31. Or more than two, but we are dealing in this paper with two parties, Buddhism and Catholicism.

32. The Latin *obvertere*, "to turn toward" or "face," generated, in the English etymological history, the sense "to make the more conspicuous of two sides," so an "obverse relationship" is one in which one side predominates over the other side (see *Webster's Third New International Dictionary*).

"one." Indeed, the positive overlap is erected by the pure difference between the two parties. As for "field-in-common" itself, it too is erected by pure differences [pure differences necessarily "off the page" of our ad hoc discussion, but correlating to our earlier deconstruction of so-called "common ground"].)

Overlap-in-the-obverse pertains here to that relation between Buddhist and Catholic dialogue partners where exposure to (and even familiarity with) the teachings/practices of one's counterpart in the other religion can stimulate the revival of dormant but important analogous teachings/practices in one's own religion.[33] In Buddhist-Catholic dialogue, the mutual benefits of overlap-in-the-obverse have already proven themselves very tangible, and they hold even greater promise for the future. An extraordinarily interesting example of this mutuality is reported by the well-known Buddhologist and theologian Fr. Aloysius Pieris, SJ, whose Tulana Research Centre for Encounter and Dialogue in Sri Lanka features statues and bas-reliefs created by Buddhist artists and depicting Jesus and Mary.[34] Fr. Pieris tells us, "In the traditional missiology, the Church tells the Buddhist who Christ is. We do the opposite; we ask the Buddhists who Christ is." He goes on to explain that after the Buddhists have read and pondered on the Christian Scriptures, "They tell us who Christ is, and in that dialogue they tell us not only who Christ is for them, but also who Christ is for us in Asia." In the light of Christ's teachings, the Buddhists *both* revisit the counterpart but dormant features of their own Buddhist tradition *and* show the Catholics what they have neglected or refused to see in their own Catholic tradition.

It is my place here to propose some salient cases in which the doctrines and practices of Buddhism can stimulate the Church, prompting it toward a more fruitful harvesting of its own counter-

33. An immensely helpful example of precisely this kind of interaction with Buddhists, in relation to celibacy, is Fr. William Skudlarek's *Demythologizing Celibacy: Practical Wisdom from Christian and Buddhist Monasticism* (Liturgical Press, 2008). This book should be a "must read" for all Catholics, celibate or married.

34. See Aloysius Pieris, SJ, "Jesus and Mary as Portrayed by Buddhist Artists," in *Dilatato Corde*, Vol. II, No. 1 (January–June 2012) at the DIM/MID website (five YouTube videos accompany the printed text).

poised reserves (in the *depositum fidei* and the flowering thereof through history). The edification (in the aforementioned sense) which Buddhism can afford the Church ranges in a continuum from the most practical to the most theoretical and refined. It is, for example, a longstanding practice in Chinese Buddhism[35] to identify oneself with the Buddha, one's "true nature." There are in fact intriguing statuettes of monks with an open flap at their abdomen, showing the embryonic Buddha within: the monks are "pregnant" with the Buddha in the sense that, proportionately to their spiritual progress, their "realization" of their true nature will develop until they realize they are and have been the Buddha all along. In order to develop this awareness, and simultaneously behave like the Buddha in relation to others, thus spreading kindness, wisdom, and practical help in whatever form required, practitioners remind themselves throughout the day—no matter where they are or what they are doing—that they are in fact the Buddha. According to Catholic teaching, Christ—while not being identical to us—is present in us through the Holy Spirit (Rom 8:9–10; 1 Cor 3:16; etc.); we are to have the "mind of Christ" (1 Cor 2:16). "You are not your own," says St. Paul, so "glorify God in your body" (1 Cor 6:19, 20). The "justified," i.e., "graced persons" or "persons-in-grace," must realize that "it is no longer I who live, but Christ who lives in me" (Gal 2:20).[36] Those Chinese Buddhists who, having recognized their "true self," realize that it is the Buddha who is "looking out through their eyes" and thus behave accordingly, are analogous to[37] Catholic Christians who, recognizing that they have put on the "new nature" (Gk. literally *ton kainon anthrōpon*, "the new man," Eph 4:24), realize that Christ is looking out through their eyes and behave accordingly. But how many Catholic priests in their sermons urge Catholics to treasure their role as *alteri Christi*, "other Christs" who, consciously, kindly, prudently, allow Christ to act through them in every encounter (*every* encounter) throughout the day?

35. With correlates in Tibetan Buddhism, Korean Buddhism, and so on.
36. The New Testament is replete with such passages. See, for example, Jn 14:17; Rom 8:15, 26; 2 Pt 1:4; 2 Cor 6:16; Phil 2:13.
37. With the determinate differences already discussed.

If for Chinese Buddhists, the Buddha is looking out through their eyes, it is also the case that the Buddha is looking back at them through the eyes of all others, and thus must be treated accordingly (though relative to concrete situations, of course). Among many Mahayanists and Vajrayanists, besides the general awareness that all sentient beings[38] have the Buddha-nature, there are specific daily practices by which one enacts this conviction. Buddhists who uphold the Lotus Sutra, for example, try to follow in the path of the monk "Never Disparage," who greeted everyone he met, even those who most reviled him, as an incipient Buddha (who would attain full Buddhahood someday).

In Catholic teaching, there are several degrees of God's presence in creation. Broadly speaking,[39] one can say that according to Catholic teaching, (1) God is present in all people and things (Acts 17:28; Rom 11:36; Col 1:17; etc.) by way of the divine "essence, presence, and power"; (2) God is in a fuller way present in all human beings, since they are made in the "image and likeness" of God, i.e., they have intellect and free will (thus, all people are neighbors, Lk 10:29–37, etc.); and (3) God is most fully and intimately present in those who are united in the communion of grace, the "Mystical Body of Christ" (Rom 12:5; 1 Cor 6:15, 12:27; Eph 4:4–6, 15, 16, 5:30; Col 1:18, 2:19; etc.). God looks at the believer through the eyes of others and even from out of all inanimate things. Throughout history Catholic saints have put this teaching into practice, even heroically, and insisted on it (think of St. Patrick's Breastplate Prayer, for example, or St. Ignatius of Loyola's "finding God in all things"). The problem, rather, is that nowadays most of all, the daily moment-by-moment *practice* of this noble teaching is so widely ignored. Catholics can be enormously edified by the counterpoised Buddhist moment-by-moment practice (and to this edification I can give personal witness).

Freedom from dependence on sensory gratification, as well as from palpable "religious experience," is important in Buddhism, and especially in the modern world the many Buddhist techniques

38. As already pointed out in an earlier footnote, in some very sizable traditions it is the case that not only sentient beings but all things have the Buddha-nature.

39. There are further nuances, but they are not necessary for our purposes here.

for cultivating such a freedom can be adopted/adapted by Catholics with great effect for the (differing) purposes of their own Catholic spirituality. Breathing, prostrations, fasting, ritualized gestures, and other deployments of the body have great value in Buddhism, and can summon Catholics, especially Western Catholics, to a rediscovery and enhancement of the vital role the body has traditionally played in Catholic religious life. Likewise, Buddhist emphasis on the *impermanence* of worldly power and pleasure, and on the importance of silence, repentance, and purity of intention; and the importance of proper preparation for the moment of death, and the offering of suffrages for the dead—all these can summon contemporary Catholics to a renewed observance of their own counterpoised teachings.

The daunting resolution of a committed Buddhist to make spiritual gains, no matter how overwhelming the obstacles, may be driven by Buddhist "self-reliance,"[40] but contemporary Catholics, tempted by self-indulgence on the one hand and—especially in the United States of America—by Protestant Fundamentalist "fideism" on the other, would do well to be more resolute in their own discipline, penitential practices, and "good works." The maxim attributed to St. Ignatius of Loyola holds true today more than ever: "Pray as if everything depended on God *and work as if everything depended on you.*"[41]

In the matter of doctrine per se, Catholicism of course cannot and should not and shall not deviate from the truths that Jesus Christ revealed during His public ministry on earth. But as we have already emphasized, Catholicism is very committed to a "developmental theology" in the sense that the seeds of His public Revelation shall flower through history. The time may now be upon us to develop an Oriental flowering of this same public Revelation. Just as Greek logic abetted Catholic theology in its early movement into Hellenistic culture, the Indian tetralemma may abet Catholic theol-

---

40. This is not to deny that Buddhist "self-reliance" can be inspired by the teaching and example of Buddha, of course.

41. Cited in CCC #2834, with a reference to Joseph de Guibert, SJ, *The Jesuits: Their Spiritual Doctrine and Practice* (Chicago: Loyola UP, 1964), p. 148, n. 55.

ogy in a Catholic movement eastward. Buddhist thought often enacts various versions of the tetralemmic sequence: "x is, x is-not, x both is and is-not, x neither is nor is-not." Buddhist teaching often emphasizes what would be conventionally called the "impersonal" in the West, but in fact Buddhists often take this "impersonality" to be an application of the fourth lemma, "x neither is nor is-not." The *dharmakāya*, for example, is "unconditioned" and is variously spoken of in terms of the fourth lemma and even in terms of that which is ineffably beyond the fourth lemma. It can be argued (see ahead in this monograph) that the God of Catholic Tradition and Scripture, while of course "personal,"[42] and astonishingly and dazzlingly so, can be expressed *in addition* by the "impersonal" (God as *both* personal and impersonal), especially since all concepts and words, even the most appropriate ones, fail to adequately represent the divine mystery.

On "Waiting":
A Proposed Mental Site for Dialogic Meditation

We described, earlier, how the intentionalities of experienced Buddhist and Catholic meditators, in the context of a joint meditation session, can exhibit an intriguing chiasmic formation. The Buddhist and Catholic meditators mutually realize that they in their good will are "intending" eventual beatitude for their counterparts in the other religion, but they also realize that Buddhist and Catholic understandings of beatitude contradict each other (as do also their understandings of the path to beatitude). One can say, mindful of our recent discussion of "overlap," that the mutual wishes for the beatitude of the dialogic "other" *positively overlap*, i.e., positively coincide insofar as they wish the good of the other. This "sameness"

---

42. Here I do not indicate divine "Person" precisely in its technical theological sense, but rather the word "personal" in its more conventional sense, as in the expression "a personal God," where the word "personal" usually signifies that God is One and is a "living" God of wisdom and love (thus human persons are made "in the image and likeness of God" because human persons have intellect and free will: see CCC #356–57).

means "co-extension" and not merger or unity or identity, since pure differences between Buddhist beatitude and Catholic beatitude are what appoint whatever sameness there is.

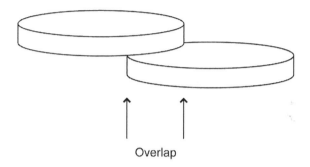

Overlap

So plastic a model[43] (and so prolix a description as was just given) may seem needless to the reader, but again I think there is a reason for such elaboration. At the beginning of a meditation, meditators in each of these two religious traditions often mentally *"place"* themselves."[44] At some level of consciousness, this locus often continues throughout the meditation itself, so that the meditator "inhabits" it. Our plastic model of the positive overlap becomes important because—sometimes at least—it can provide the mutual locus for sessions of the Buddhist-Catholic joint meditation. (In this sense, the locus is somewhat analogous to what is called *nimitta*, or "form for apprehension," in Buddhist meditation.[45]) The Buddhists can imaginatively place themselves there and send benevolent energies

43. Again, I remind the reader that we are adapting, not adopting, some thought-*practices* of Derrida. And when I resort to words like "model" and "diagram," and associate them with Derrida, I *only* mean that he uses the pertaining formations again and again and again in his thought: they constitute leitmotifs of his *thinking* style.

44. Catholic mystics are known to have imaginatively placed themselves in the "enclosed garden" (a site evoked by the Bible's *Song of Songs*), and many Catholic meditators follow in this tradition; Vajrayana Buddhists use visualizations in order to relate to their *yi-dam*, etc.

45. In another stage of their practice, the Buddhists may go on to "empty" (in the sense of dissolve) the *nimitta*, for which an analogous but orthodox Catholic practice could be to dissolve the positive overlap, or locus here, in the *mysterium* of

toward the Catholics, all the while realizing that the Catholics occupying the same "place" are "intending" within a frame of reference ultimately very different from theirs. Alternatively, the Buddhists may choose to rest in the locus without any purpose, idea, or focus whatsoever while meditating (compare Korean Zen Master Seung Sahn's "don't-know mind," i.e., the mind of "I don't know"). It suffices, for the kind of meditation I am describing here, to simply rest one's mind in the "place" of positive overlap.

During the joint session, the Catholics, for their part, also meditatively place themselves in this same locus of positive overlap, recognizing that their Buddhist counterparts may not have been sent the gift of Christian faith, and that God is thus working out the divine will for them in and through what is good/true in their Buddhist lifeworld. Earlier, we reviewed the provisions and rationale justifying for Catholics this respect for and openness to Buddhists. Here I move on to further considerations that should become very involved as the Catholics meditatively enter the *locus*. If they adhere to the following sequence, I think they will find their entry smooth and fruitful.

(1) Silently and devoutly, send love and good will, in the Name of the Lord, to the Buddhist counterparts. (2) Open mentally, heartfully, to the Buddhists: receive their loving-kindness and learn from their virtuous example. (3) Direct your attention to what we have called the "chiasm"—that the Church in this age is encouraging Buddhist-Catholic dialogue, including joint meditation, but that your Buddhist counterparts have existential projects that at this very moment run radically contrariwise to yours. Pray: "What do *You* want, Lord? Let me know *if* You want me to know, and give me the grace to learn. *If* You want me to wait, and to rest in the waiting,

---

God, who is distinct from the positive overlap or locus but creates it and all other things and is present in them by divine "essence, presence, and power." In this "moment" of meditation, by dissolving the locus the Catholic would be recalling the truth that all things are from God, and God alone knows and disposes the full reach (the "depths") of the divine design. Given that at this point in the text I am addressing the concrete relationship of the dialogue-partners to each other, I do not develop the notion of "abrogation of locus" here. Ahead, however, toward the end of the Second Annex, in the treatment of Catholic meditation, I present a Catholic version of "emptiness" that may interest the reader.

please give me the grace to wait and to rest in the waiting." In simple yet deep *humility* and *serenity*, mentally prostrate yourself to the divine Wisdom, to the divine Mystery. With the "certain hope" that is so precious, be open to the future, to the Oncoming, knowing that the Parousia is oncoming . . . the Parousia when we shall better understand how beautifully, how subtly, God worked in history, and works.[46] (4) Here, the figure of positive overlap is serviceable, too, in that visually the adjacent inner sides of the mutual overlap— where indeed the two religions actually "touch"—are *hidden* from view. . . . Hidden from both parties to the overlap. Michael Barnes, SJ, alludes to an unknowing that is applicable to the Catholics here, an unknowing that discomfits at the beginning but can be deeply salutary:

> [E]xperiences of passivity, dislocation, and vulnerability in the face of the other are to be understood . . . as "something to do with God."
> —Michael Barnes, SJ, *Theology and the Dialogue of Religions*[47]

For the Catholics, this hiddenness—precisely because of the per-plexity it can induce and the "release" that can follow—mutely points to the *mysterium* of God's design. Catholics at this point can stop images and concepts and simply "rest" in the *locus*. Advert to your breath, slow inhalation-exhalation, breathing in, breathing out, breathing in, breathing out. . . . Rest in the Holy Spirit, who is called in the New Testament's Greek *hagion pneuma* (the root meaning of *pneuma* is "breath" or "wind"). Wait without "demand-ing a sign," that is, without greed for an immediate "answer" or "solution." Wait in simple trust, as Mother Teresa of Calcutta (like so many other saints down through the ages) always taught us to wait. This is Christian "waiting on the Lord," which in English turns out to be an apposite pun, since "to wait on" can also mean to be the "handmaid" and "to serve at table." It is quite remarkable how transformative such "resting in the waiting" can be, once one calmly and simply maintains it for one or two or three hours or much

46. Even in the darkest and most terrifying history.
47. Cambridge: Cambridge UP, 2002, p. 183.

more. With Buddhist monks arrayed in meditation in front and to the sides of me, I have meditated this way for long periods of time, and can testify to this practice's fruitfulness.

Some Buddhist readers, especially those who identify with Subitist teachings, may at this point be eager to remonstrate, "You Catholics 'wait' because you believe in a linear theory of history and the Second Coming of Christ, and because, on the personal level, you're awaiting Heaven, but we Buddhists affirm that the Buddha-nature is already our true nature *now*, and even though most Buddhists may not yet be enlightened enough to experience this 'original nature', the practice of 'waiting' is surely *not* going to help!" My reply would be to grant indeed that Catholic waiting differs from Buddhist waiting (a conclusion consonant with a major thesis of this monograph, in fact); but I would go on to point out that in the kind of Catholic meditation I am describing here, Catholic waiting, like Buddhist waiting, eschews "instrumentalism"—that is, a "method," or even the mental placement of a concept or image, would do no more than thwart the meditation. And Catholicism affirms that God's *presence* abides *now* in a special way in what we have been calling in this monograph the "graced soul." Fr. Yves Raguin, SJ, a great Jesuit dialogist who worked so many years in Asia, and whom I had the good fortune to interview in 1983 at the Ricci Institute, Taipei, Taiwan, puts this teaching well in his letter to a Catholic nun: ". . . [T]he last step of the Gospel is taken when Christ says: 'It is good for you that I go' [Jn 16:7]. We would comment,—'You will not see me any more before you; you will not be able to rely on my external presence, but I will be in you.'" And Fr. Raguin explains elsewhere, "We no longer see Him before us as an object of thought. Henceforth it is He Himself who through His Holy Spirit turns our regard toward the Father and makes us cry, 'Abba, Father.'"[48]

Because waiting without a "waited-for" can only happen if one

48. Both quotations from Fr. Raguin can be found in Michael Sasso, "'In the Footsteps of Matteo Ricci': The Legacy of Fr. Yves Raguin, SJ," pp. 2, 3 (at http://www.michaelsaso.org/?p-972 [accessed April 14, 2010]). On "waiting," see also Francis X. Clooney, SJ, "A Final Word on the Wisdom of Watching and Waiting," in his *Hindu Wisdom for All God's Children* (Wipf & Stock Pub., 2005), pp. 134–138.

"lets go," many Buddhist masters point out that waiting has an extraordinary ability to open up to the "openness," the *dharmakāya*. Buddhist waiting of this kind is described well by Stephen Batchelor:

> A meditative attitude is eternally prepared to *wait*. Freed from any pretensions of knowing, nothing in particular is expected to happen. Such waiting is content to let things be while at the same time acknowledging that, concealed within the mystery, there is an unknown. That which lies hidden cannot be coaxed forth. It has its own time beyond the time of what can be recollected and anticipated. Waiting waits; it is alert to every moment but has no expectations.[49]

In one of the quotations at the very end of this monograph, a Buddhist motif of waiting appears again. The Buddhist masters would tell you to let go of that quotation too.

---

49. Stephen Batchelor, *The Faith to Doubt: Glimpses of Buddhist Uncertainty* (Berkeley, CA: Parallax, 1990), p. 46. On the topic of Buddhist waiting, I recommend his sub-section, "Unknowing, Waiting, and Listening," pp. 43–49, and then all that follows through at least p. 87. Batchelor quotes many authoritative Buddhist sources, and on "letting-go," even several Catholic ones.

FIRST ANNEX
On God and Dissymmetry

Through the opening of the fourth surface or through the empty
box in the center of the four squares, you shall have been swept off
[*entrainés*], overcast [*surjetés*] in a still unended, unending labor
[*travail*]. The square or, as you wish, the cube, will not close itself
up.
—Jacques Derrida, *La Dissémination*,[1] p. 398 (my translation)

THE ABOVE EPIGRAPH is cited from one of Derrida's early deconstructions of the square/cube.[2] He often takes "squareness" (be it
the flat square of a plane surface or the six squares of a cube's sides)
as an emblem of what he considers holistic structure,[3] be that structure Hellenic rationality (syllogism, symmetry, centering, framing,
etc.), a Hebraic holism (the "four-squaredness" of the Tetragram-
maton,[4] etc.), a modernist organicism (so even Sigmund Freud's
mechanicism and Lévi-Strauss's Structuralism are "holistic" in this

1. *La dissémination* (Paris: Éditions du Seuil, 1972).
2. Derrida is commenting on a work by Philippe Sollers.
3. "Holism" is taken here in a broad sense, as synonymous with the tacit or
overt assumption of a "wholeness" of any kind. "Whole" means "free of defect,"
"lacking nothing belonging to it." A "whole" is "complete" ("filled up," "not lacking
anything necessary to it") and "comprehensive" ("grasped [totally] around"). Its
formulation or process or methodology stays "within its frame" ("is framed") in
this sense and thus is "*consistent*" ("standing fixed in unity"). "Consistency" is
marked by "harmony, regularity, and steady continuity throughout." Ideals of
holistic systems are often "equilibrium" and at least an underlying "self-identity"
(see *Webster's Third New International Dictionary* for the preceding definitions).
4. For a Christian believer, the epigraph can mean that the divine Tetragram-
maton is self-deconstructive in the orthodox sense that God reveals through the
divine Name but breaks out of and transcends the divine Name (or—to phrase this
problematic better—breaks out of and transcends the literality of the Name *as
humanly perceived*).

sense), or any other transformation of "wholeness" whatsoever.[5] What is often egregiously misunderstood is that Derridean decon- struction does *not* negate or deny that which is deconstructed. That the square/cube is not closed up presumes that there must always be this configuration in the first place, and that this configuration is ongoing. Indeed, the deconstruction depends on the square/cube because deconstruction is a "nothing" of itself.[6]

That deconstruction is "nothing of itself" becomes clear when one considers that *all* thought and *all* communication presume a "consistency" of some kind (so it goes without saying that decon- structive discourse, too, cannot function without some "holism"). The early-phase Derrida devotes much time precisely to the decon- struction of *logos* (Gk. "Reason," "rationality"), the "foundation" of "coherent" thought; the ongoing result of deconstruction is that Reason continues on and does so *without becoming something other than reason*, but Reason continues on with *fissures* showing its own structural imperfection or inadequacy. In short, rationality persis- tently "puts in question" its own foundations (though, says Derrida, most minds, compulsively chasing after security at all costs, uncon- sciously mask the "fissures"). Next, Derrida proceeds to examina- tions of more elaborate "coherences" ranging along the micro- scopic-macroscopic scale, with deconstructions of formal logic and the "principle of non-contradiction" ("whatever is, is"), of mathe- matics ("study of quantitative operations") and enumeration ("counting"), and of macroscopic representations of many kinds (philosophical, socio-political, etc.). A macroscopic formulation is a

---

5. It is interesting to note that the square that "will not close itself up" applies to the Buddhist *catuṣkoṭikā* ("four-cornered logic") as well. In Chinese Buddhism, Jizang (Chi-tsang) is perhaps most famous for his deconstruction of what had become quite static renderings of the *catuṣkoṭikā* (the "four-cornered logic" associ- ated with Madhyamikan and various other Buddhist schools of thought). See R. Magliola, "Nagarjuna and Chi-tsang on the Value of 'This World': A Reply to Kuang-ming Wu's Critique of Indian and Chinese Madhyamika Buddhism," in *Journal of Chinese Philosophy*, Vol. 31, No. 4 (December 2004), pp. 505–16.

6. For a discussion of Derridean deconstruction as a "nothing" in itself, see R. Magliola, "Hongzhou Chan Buddhism, and Derrida Late and Early" (as in earlier note), pp. 179–81.

logos (here, Gk. "rationale") in the grander sense—a theory or other "comprehensive" formation. The more "centered" the theory is (in terms of "equilibrium," as one "centers" or "balances" content within a frame), the more "logocentric" it is said to be.[7] The deconstructive aim, throughout, is to do no more than turn the pertaining holism against itself (the holism's presumptions against themselves, etc.), thus generating a better ad hoc "clue" as to how life-worlds go on.

For our purposes here, the above epigraph from Derrida is intended to signal the dissymmetrical effect and power of Divine Providence, which can open up and de-center all representations, but can simultaneously *reveal* through them and through this very process. Ironically and providentially, this "postmodern" epigraph—in its Catholic adaptation—points to a dissymmetry deriving *not* from Catholic heterodoxy but from Catholic orthodoxy. Indeed, those recent formulations of interreligious dialogue that are conventionally labeled "avant-garde" or even "postmodern" turn out in a Derridean context to be the more "modernist."

"Modernism" in the nomenclature of Continental philosophy (and here I do *not* mean to single out the in-house nineteenth- and early-twentieth-century ecclesial term "Modernism" as such), and more specifically, "Modernism" as Derrida understands it, refers to post-Romantic displacements and recuperations of holism (up until the present day). These recuperations, like all structures-of-the-whole, overtly or covertly assume and project a unified formation of some kind. In the very broadest sense, the ad hoc subject-matter of any modernist formulation can be emblematically repre-

---

7. Though Derrida "lived and moved in a life-world at a very distant remove from that of Pope Francis," as I say in this book's Preface, it astounds me sometimes how "deconstructive" Pope Francis's words and behavior are. He is particularly adept at the technique of "reversal," the crucial first step in "classic" Derridean deconstruction. In his address to the Pontifical Gregorian University in Rome (referenced earlier), he "deconstructs" that institution's "centrism" by insisting that according to the "logic" of God, "evangelical form ... reaches the center *from* the periphery and *returns* to the periphery" (rather than vice versa). Likewise, he not infrequently stops his Catholic visitors short, before they can kiss his papal ring: instead, he kisses *their* hands, thus acting out his role as "Servant of the Servants of God."

sented as *enclosed*[8]: a closed square or cube marks off its inside content or "space." Holistic structures can have many permutations—positive/negative, polar, symmetrical, dialectical, and many other forms of latent *equivalency* (thus "relativism," for example, is *modernist* because it presumes a latent equivalency of values). Even "infinity" can be such a formulation, when it is understood to mean the absolute negation of "finitude" (or vice versa).

Holistic thought, including Modernism, claims that its undertakings are somewhat commensurate with their subject-matter and that subject-matter's "truth" (even if the "truth" be that there is no truth). "Modern" structure characterizes many disciplines: "modern art," for example, may claim to be equivalent to the artist's subjectivity, or to the "laws of chance," or to the "texture" of its own medium (and so on); "modern" architecture, whether it belonged to the school of "simple functionality" or to the school of organic "playfulness," or to any of a number of others, presumed the value of *unity* (or any transformation thereof).

In the epigraph above, Derrida describes square-as-deconstructed (or cube-as-deconstructed). The square or cube remains, but as-deconstructed (or, better put, as-deconstructing, since the process is ongoing). Square or cube remains because deconstruction is a "nothing"—it just enables the emblem to be a more fruitful trace[9] of the way matters go on. One's undertaking "within" the "whole" is continually swept off and overcast—one is inside and outside the quadriform box that will not "close itself up." And the quadriform here as always is—to use one of Derrida's *jeux de*

---

8. Catholic mysticism's "enclosed garden," referenced elsewhere in this book, is—in Catholic terms—a "box . . . swept off" that will "not close itself up"!

9. In the 1970s and 1980s, avant-garde literary critics associated with the English-language tradition made Derridean deconstruction out to mean that texts yield no "clue" or "trace" but are the "mere free play" of language. Derrida often made clear that these avant-gardists did violence to his project, which was both to engage and deploy a "rigorous logic" and to rigorously use logic against itself. See Christopher Norris's discussion in Norris's *Derrida* (London: Fontana, 1987), pp. 43–44. The term "clue" and more particularly the term "trace" almost always indicate for Derrida that which is "there" but "*not* there": "not there" in terms of self-centered content but there as a "directional" (compare/confer, in Appendix Two of this book, the second note to the English translation of Derrida's letter to me [1997]).

mots—a *quadrature*, referring in French to the problem of "squaring the circle," colloquially meaning in turn an "insoluble problem."[10] *Quadrature* also has the noun *rature* embedded within it, the verb *raturer* meaning "to cross out something." Not only will the box not close up, but this very figure of a deconstructing box is under ongoing erasure too, in an "unended, unending labor." (Favorite Derridean maneuvers such as either "going over into extra" or, conversely, "falling short," play a role similar to the figure of box-as-deconstructed/ing: they deconstruct the perfect delineation of content by boundary.)

It should be clear by this point that from a deconstructionist's point of view, any formulation of interreligious dialogue that posits an "ultimate reality" reflected by diverse but equal paths is simply too "framed" and equilibrated to be—on the face of it—"true" as it stands (though, to phrase the matter in a distinctively Derridean way, possibly the formulation can display "the true with cracks in it"). A fortiori, any "Catholic" formulation of Buddhist-Catholic dialogue that presumes that God is equally accessed by Buddhism and Catholicism would be—if taken at face value—too centered/symmetrical to be "true" as it stands, especially if the argument of this monograph is affirmed, viz., that the two religions are at bottom contradictory (for then God would necessarily be a mystical unity who/that equally originates the two contradictories,[11] a most "balanced" and holistic notion).

In terms of this monograph, perhaps the "centrist" temptation can come from our earlier discussion of "pure difference" and the analogy drawn from Bateson's work on perception. With some crucial changes in our interpretation, God would be analogous to a Pure Difference, and a divine "event of switching" would be effectuating Buddhism in time and space and Catholicism in time and space. Two contradictory but equal "paths" would be arising in the world (that such a model can have "multiple switches" accommodating many more than two paths could "work" in terms of a

---

10. *Quadrature* has other meanings too in French. See a French dictionary.
11. Indeed, for its part, Catholicism has declared irrational or non-rational mysticism such as this to be heretical.

finessed Batesonian model, but it is a topic not within the purview of this monograph). Wonder of wonders, though, that authentic Catholic teaching, as presented at length above, sets forth a model that is much more *askew* and *lopsided*, and thus postmodern in the Derridean sense: God sends one Savior into the world, saves only through Him, and yet enables the disciples of other religions to follow their own religions and still be saved! Indeed, God does not even send Christian belief to all, yet He allows for all to be saved. Christ's Life-Blood vitalizes not only His own Rose, but the Buddhist water-lily too, beautiful in its own color and configuration. And wonder of wonders, sometimes that water-lily can strengthen ("edify," from Lat. *aedificare*, "to build up") the Savior's own Rose. (There are other vitalized and edifying flowers too, as Vatican Council II points out.)[12]

From a strict deconstructionist's point of view, the issue here is *not* that the unbalanced, the dissymmetrical, is intrinsically better than the holistic. Rather, the dissymmetrical is more serviceable as an emblem primarily because it signals the inadequacy of "human-

12. The accusation that such Catholic inclusivism is unfair and fundamentally unworthy of God disregards what shall have to be the case: that there is no mundane "comparison" in the heavenly state and persons shall shine to the extent that they fulfilled the celestial proddings sent uniquely to them. The Jew will celebrate what was her/his unique Jewish role in life, the Muslim will celebrate what was her/his unique Muslim role, the Buddhist her/his unique Buddhist role, the Hindu her/his, the "secularist" her/his unique role in life, and so on. Nor should vain comparison taint how a Catholic should approach other religionists or non-religionists in this *present* world. The Jews or Muslims or Buddhists or Hindus or secularists, and so on, may be holier than the unloving Catholic if they are doing what the celestial design is beckoning them to do. In this scenario, the non-Catholics are the faithful servants, and the condescending Catholics are the runaway sons. Sometimes the policies of the institutional Church itself have been wrongful, grossly wrongful: John Paul II in particular, in his many public acts of heartfelt repentance in the name of the whole Church, has acknowledged these ecclesial sins. For a very informative book collection of many of John Paul II's official acts of repentance, see Luigi Accattoli, *Quando il Papa chiede perdono* [When the Pope Asks Forgiveness] (Milan: Arnaldo Mondadori, 1997); the subsequent English translation bears a title which—perhaps intentionally or perhaps unintentionally—seems to downgrade the repentance to a personal one: *When a Pope Asks Forgiveness: The Mea Culpa's of John Paul II*, Luigi Accattoli, trans. Jordan Aumann, OP (Boston: Pauline Books and Media, 1998).

ist" harmony, balance, and other holistic ideals if they are left to stand purely and simply as such. Dissymmetry in this context unsettles by virtue of its *is-not*-ness. Any formulation that is so constructed that it can claim to enclose *all* of its subject-matter tends to be too glib to be true, indeed, too merely "human" and prideful to be true. (Such is exponentially the case, a Catholic would say, when dealing from the human side with subjects such as God, ultimate reality, and the like.) What is crucial to understand is *not* that we should on this account jettison holism. Rather, what we are to learn is that an intact holism is not *enough*. In many deconstructive scenarios, this often plays out to mean that we are (1) to keep the holism and (2) to keep the holism-as-deconstructed, i.e., the holism with a crack or fissure in it.

Clearly, there are many features of Derrida's deconstructive project that are more radical and extreme than anything Catholicism can incorporate. A Catholic adaptation and application of deconstructive insights is a delicate task, but one, I claim, that is nonetheless worthwhile and more than worthwhile. At the outset, one must cautiously distinguish between (1) conventional "talk" about God, (2) more developed theological discourse, and (3) God's Revelation and its representation in official Church teaching. A demonstration of how deconstructive insights can serve conventional religious talk and theological discourse, while difficult to make, is easier—needless to say—than to show how deconstructive insights serve Sacred Scripture and official Church teaching. Nonetheless, I think it is still worth our while to make some initial efforts at the latter. God may have sent us divinely inspired Representations with fissures in them, fissures providentially designed so as to better *instruct* us.

Divine Revelation as represented in Sacred Scripture is divinely inspired and inerrant,[13] so how—for a faithful and orthodox Catholic—can deconstruction be of help? How can deconstructive insights edify her/his faith? The matter can be broached from the side of human frailty, I think. Divine revelation is gloriously true, and we embrace it with humility and gratitude, but we must also

---

13. See CT #95, 99, etc. (DZ 783, 787, etc.).

remind ourselves that divine Revelation is necessarily directed toward us as *finite* beings: grace and faith indeed open us up to truths that we cannot know on purely human grounds, *but we remain nonetheless only finite beings* and not God. Revelation and its propagation in Church teaching are gloriously true, but they necessarily remain *clues*, supereminently privileged traces of that which is infinitely "*more*." They are supereminently precious clues to the absolutely ineffable truths they represent: they necessarily cannot be the "full" reality.

Needless to say, though Our Lord declares "I and the Father are one" (Jn 10:30), we cannot plumb the depths of this most profound *mysterium*. And even so straightforward a teaching as "God is Love" cannot ever plumb the plenitude of God's love. And so on and on and on. The often-cited incident of St. Thomas Aquinas and his ecstasy of December 6, 1273, is much to the point and bears repeating in this context. He had quoted and meditated on Sacred Scripture all his life, and discoursed magnificently on Church teaching throughout his career, but he stopped writing the *Summa* after his ecstasy, declaring: "All I have written seems to me like so much straw compared to what I have seen . . . ." And even what he had seen in ecstasy was not the "fullness +," since he remained and would forever remain finite, after all. "O the depth of the riches and wisdom and knowledge of God! How unsearchable are his judgments and how inscrutable his ways! 'For who has known the mind of the Lord, or who has been his counselor?'" (Rom 11:34).

Down through the centuries, the Church has in various contexts authoritatively declared that reason and revealed truths are compatible.[14] God is Truth, and divine Truth is "true" to itself, i.e., is "rational." Revealed truths open the door to matters we cannot know otherwise, but these truths are rational. We cannot know them of ourselves because our human wisdom is inferior to God's wisdom. In short, the issue is competence rather than rationality: the more transcendent and refined the divine truths involved, the less we can understand them, though they are true in themselves. God's

14. See Vatican Council I's summary of authoritative teaching on this matter, and its added clarifications: CF #133–36 (DS 3017–20), or CT #77–80 (DZ 1797–800).

"incomprehensibility" (God is "incomprehensible," says Vatican Council I [CT #355, DZ 1782], as do many earlier authoritative sources) is in exponential relation to God's transcendence. Writing as a theologian before his elevation to the papacy, Joseph Ratzinger (Pope Benedict XVI) described this teaching succinctly: ". . . how little we are capable of defining God, much less fathoming him. After all, God's answer to Job explains nothing, but rather sets boundaries to our mania for judging everything and being able to say the final word on a subject, and reminds us of our limitations. It admonishes us to trust the mystery of God in its incomprehensibility."[15]

In this regard, too, it is crucial to recall that it is ultimately the theological virtue of *love* ("charity"), namely, the movement of the will toward God the perfect Good, that empowers the human being to grow more and more in both the love and the *knowledge* of God, until finally the graced soul is swept up into heaven, where the graced soul can experience (in proportion to its individual capacity) God the perfect Good and Truth. Indeed, St. Paul tells us:

> Love never ends; as for prophecies, they will pass away; as for tongues, they will cease; as for knowledge [merely human or "mediated" knowledge], it will pass away. For our knowledge is imperfect and our prophecy is imperfect; but when the perfect comes, the imperfect will pass away. . . . For now we see in a mirror dimly [Gk. "through a mirror in a riddle (*ainigmati*)"], but then face to face. Now I know in part; then I shall understand fully [i.e., full to one's individual capacity], even as I have been fully understood. So faith, hope, love abide, these three; but the greatest of these is love. (1 Cor 13:8–13)[16]

In this sense, the theological virtue of love, *deconstructing* merely human knowledge, enables the beatific experience of God as Goodness and *Truth*. Benedict XVI takes great care to affirm that graced

---

15. Joseph Ratzinger, "Introduction to Christianity: Yesterday, Today, and Tomorrow," *Communio*, Vol. 31 (fall 2004), p. 492. I am indebted to Gerhold Becker, who alerted me to this quotation from Ratzinger, cited in Becker, "Reason, Faith, and Secularization: Jurgen Habermas meets Joseph Cardinal Ratzinger," *Prajñā Vihāra*, Vol. 7, No. 1, p. 41.

16. See also Col 2:2, 3; Eph 3:19.

souls are led by love to a contact with God's higher Rationality: "Certainly love, as St. Paul says, 'transcends' knowledge and is thereby capable of perceiving more than thought alone (see Eph 3:19); nonetheless it continues to be love of the God who is Logos."[17]

In an adapted form, deconstruction can play a useful heuristic role in the above-described Catholic theology, which poses both (1) the divine provenance of reason, and (2) the incomprehensibility of God. Deconstruction, as already explained, does not negate holistic structure but rather, depends on it: deconstruction exposes the shortcomings of a formulation but refuses to supply a substantive formulation in its place. When Derrida deconstructs *logos*—regardless of whether the logocentrism is in microscopic or macroscopic form—he very strictly limits himself to *logos* in order to do so. That is to say, he affirms the enduring uniqueness and necessity of reason, so much so, in fact, that he seems to eschew other forms of knowing. For Derrida, reason-as-deconstructed/ing is a process that opens up the inexorable defects of reason but, significantly, does not on this account betake itself either to irrationality or to a non-rationality.[18] Rather, reason-as-deconstructed/ing is *reason at its most refined*, i.e., reason as *most sensitive to itself*. Catholicism and Derridean deconstruction both prioritize "rationality" in relation to truth (though the Church affirms in God a higher-order rationality, a divine Rationality, and Derrida does not).

Because Derrida turns a logical structure against itself, two constituents make up the narrative of his ad hoc deconstructions, namely, the formation and the formation-as-deconstructed. (It is crucial to remember too that for Derrida there are no definitive and final deconstructions: any formation can be deconstructed in many ways, and any one formation-as-deconstructed can in turn be posed

---

17. Benedict XVI, address at the U. of Regensburg, September 12, 2006, para. 6. (Available online via the Vatican website, http://www.vatican.va.)

18. For its part, it is interesting to note that the Catholic Church does likewise, rejecting both irrationality and non-rationality, and this is especially the case in approaching the Divine. (Of course, unlike Derridean thought, Catholicism affirms a supernatural order that, while neither irrational nor non-rational, is "above" the human being's natural rationality, and can be known and accessed only through God's gratuitous gift.)

as a formation and deconstructed, so the process is unending.) The (1) positioning of the formation and (2) ensuing deconstruction of said formation is graphically/emblematically represented in some Derridean texts by the sign of the X, since calligraphically one composes an X by a stroke and then a counter-stroke. The X's configuration is understood to act-out the positioning and then the deconstruction—a stroke and a counter-stroke.

If we apply the X[19] to the *relationships* between humanity and the (divinely revealed) Johannine *Logos* (Jn 1:1–18), i.e., if we attempt to service these relationships in a Derridean way, the surprising heuristic relevance of (an adapted) deconstruction to an orthodox Catholic theology[20] may become apparent. Of course, the meanings of John's *Logos* in the Gospel's prologue and in Church teaching are much more specialized than the Greek philosophical term *logos*; nonetheless, when the inspired Johannine writer came to represent the culmination of the Hebrew tradition in the Word of his prologue, he was writing in Greek and he chose the precise term he did because its Greek meaning cross-pollinates with the Hebraic sense so as to generate the meaning he intended.[21]

My suggestion is that as a heuristic tool, the X of "formation/formation-as-deconstructed(ing)" can be fruitfully applied to the *encounter* between humanity and the Johannine *Logos*, and especially so as an ongoing re-summoning of Catholic and all Christian believers to *humility* and *awe* in the face of the Divine. Perhaps unexpectedly, our Catholic deployment of the X can claim to go forward under the flying colors of Benedict XVI himself, at least inasmuch as one of his essays provides us a fine demonstration of it:

19. It is an interesting serendipity that Derrida's X, which is the Roman alphabet's X, approximates the configuration of the Greek *chi*, whose configuration was the first letter of early Christianity's XP (*Chi-Rho*), a cryptic emblem for the Christ.

20. Of course we are *choosing* to adapt Derridean deconstruction this way. Derridean deconstruction can just as well be deployed in contrary ways, since, as already explained, deconstruction involves a complex of strategies whereby any holism can be disassembled and its less apparent or hidden "subtext" made more apparent.

21. See Benedict XVI, address at the University of Regensburg, para. 5, where he argues for the far-reaching significance of this cross-pollination.

"God has become quite concrete in Christ, but in this way his mystery has also become still greater. God is always infinitely greater than all our concepts and all our images and names."[22]

"Concepts" ("senses" or "signifieds," in linguistic terms[23]) and "names" (the "signifiers," i.e., unique phonic/graphic patterns) and sometimes "images" (mental representations of sensory data associated with concepts) are constitutive of "verbal signs." A "verbal sign" is thus a link of a unique concept and its coordinated phonic/graphic pattern. "Referents" are ordinarily nonlinguistic and exist in the actual world (though there are many *modes* of actuality—the empirical, the imaginary, the mathematical, etc., and for most religious believers, a supernatural[24] mode as well). A "verbal sign" relates to a "referent." The above quotation from Benedict XVI posits as the first stroke of its X, "God has become quite concrete in Christ," and as its second or counter-stroke, "God is always infinitely greater than all our concepts and all our images and names." Let us probe a bit into how linguistics can help us here.

In authoritative Catholic teaching,[25] the Johannine "Logos," the divine "Word,"—*when taken as a verbal sign*—is constituted of a primary concept and several correlated concepts (as its "signified") and of the Greek phonic/graphic pattern λόγος [*logos* in its Latin transliteration, *verbum* in its Latin translation, *word* in English, and so on] (as its "signifier"). The concepts constituting the "signified" of the verbal sign "Logos" are, in more detail, the following: the primary concept is "divine Word" or the Second Person of the Most

22. Ratzinger, "Introduction to Christianity: Yesterday, Today, and Tomorrow," p. 492.

23. I am, in the main, invoking "Continental" Saussurean linguistics here, though in modified form in that my understanding of reference invokes a more conventional realism, whereas Saussure aims to be strictly structuralist (in the "Continental" sense).

24. The "supernatural," as we have already indicated, refers to that which is not natural to human capacity, but is known and accessed only through divine Revelation and its effects.

25. As is well known, there are some contemporary Catholic theologians and Catholic biblicists who do not read St. John's prologue according to the definitions of the pertaining Church councils, but my intention, for reasons explained earlier, is to reflect Magisterial teaching.

Holy Trinity; the concepts correlated to the primary concept are the union of the Son with the Father, and the union of Christ's divine and human nature (or "hypostatic union"). There are other correlated truths too, pertaining to the Logos as such, and officially defined, but these two are ordinarily taken to be the most significant, given the theological history of the early Church.

The verbal sign "Logos" properly bespeaks these truths. That is, the Church assures us that the two aforementioned scriptural/theological concepts (signifieds) are properly and truthfully linked to the phonic/graphic pattern, the signifier or name, "Logos." But here is where the problematic *becomes* infinitely complicated,[26] because the *referent* for the verbal sign "Logos" is the actual divine Word. The "signified" (the concepts) of the verbal sign "Logos" accurately mirror the reality of the divine Word (otherwise the verbal sign would not be referentially true), but necessarily the reality of the divine Word, the *referent*, also infinitely transcends this signified. For example, the reality of the union of the divine Father and the divine Son, and the reality of the union of the divine and human in the Christ, are mirrored in the verbal sign's concepts signifying these realities, but are also infinitely *more* than these concepts can possibly mirror. "God is always infinitely greater than all our concepts and images and names" (and this is so even when they belong to revealed truth, because—no matter how accurate—they are still not God *in Se* and thus are *limited*).

Let us now examine in more detail how an (adapted) Derridean X, stroke and counter-stroke, may contribute some helpful insights regarding the above template, the theology of which of course has been known for a long time. Inasmuch as the verbal sign "Logos" expresses or mirrors the reality of the actual Incarnate Word for human beings, it functions as the "formation." But inasmuch as the verbal sign "Logos" falls short of the divine reality, the verbal sign is "marked" or *fissured*, and stands as "formation deconstructed" (deconstructed by the divine Infinity that "always already" transcends it). The formational "box" or "cube" that is the verbal sign

---

26. Or ultimately complicated because so "simple," in Thomistic terms.

continues to stand but is "swept off . . . in a still unended, unending labor": it "will not close itself up."

In more general terms, we can say that God has represented the divine reality through scriptural words that are precisely designed to instruct us *progressively*. That the divine artistry has designed the words to be a progressive heuristic is a point well-made by the Church Fathers, following, for example, from St. Gregory of Nyssa's principle that "the language of God's revelation is accommodated to our capacity to understand."[27] God has providentially designed these inspired and inerrant signs to both stand firm and be split open: thereby, God intends to lead us, as the epistle to the Hebrews says of scriptural signs, to ever greater "maturity" (Heb 6:1) in interpreting that which it calls the *logia* (literally "oracles," Heb 5:12) of God.

Besides its application—as above—to the relation between sacred verbal signs and their referents, the (adapted) Derridean X can also be applied, I think, to our encounters, both devotional and theological, with the Incarnate Word Himself and the Most Holy Trinity Itself. Let us turn to the Incarnate Word first, returning in this new context to the passage quoted earlier from Benedict XVI, which bears repeating here: "God has become quite concrete in Christ, but in this way his mystery has become still greater. God is always infinitely greater than all our concepts and all our images and names." The second clause of its first sentence does not pertain to verbal signs, but to the actual Incarnate Word.

Christ the Incarnate Word, both at the time He walked the earth and afterward, in His Glorified Body, is the "*kharaktēr tēs hypostaseōs autou*" (Heb 1:3), the perfect "representation of the reality [of God]," and the "*eikōn tou theou tou aoratou*," the perfect "image of the invisible God" (Col 1:15). He thus "concretizes" God, but paradoxically *this very concreteness* (the "in this [concrete] way" in Benedict XVI's passage) renders "His mystery . . . still greater." The "concrete" is that which can be phenomenologically experi-

27. See endnote 163 in *Gregory of Nyssa: The Life of Moses*, trans., intro., and notes by A. J. Malherbe and E. Ferguson, with preface by J. Meyendorff (New York: Paulist Press, 1978), p. 174.

enced, so the reference here is to the human nature of the Incarnate Word. How can it be that via the Sacred Humanity (hypostatically united with His Divinity, of course), the "mystery" of God has become "still greater"? Or—in terms of the Derridean X—how can the very "concreteness" of the Sacred Humanity be both a stroke and counter-stroke? If we keep in mind that it is precisely the Derridean counter-stroke that enables X-as-clue, the following scenario can take shape: the humanity of Christ is absolutely God-as-present (the stroke), but the humanity of Christ is paradoxically a *clue* to God's "more," the infinite reaches (of the infinite God) that are, at some point (even in the Beatific Vision), necessarily "absent-to-us," "beyond" us (thus, the counter-stroke), or otherwise—as theology reminds us—we would become God ourselves.

In relation to the Sacred Humanity of Christ, another scenario for the Derridean X regards in particular the vulnerability to which His human corporality subjects Him, for—during His passion and death—the embodied Christ becomes, in the prophetic words of Isaiah, "marred, beyond human semblance" (Is 52:14), and in the Psalms, "a worm, and no man" (Ps 22:6, IB). The Sacred Humanity is absolutely God-as-present (the stroke, the "formation"), but the Sacred Humanity is disfigured (the counter-stroke, the "mark of the fissure," the deconstruction). In this scenario, the divine clue comes by way of the disfigurement, the "mark of the fissure": Christ is beckoning us to pure sacrificial love, and He is calling us to service of the poor, the suffering, the deprived—they are His most treasured and precious ones.[28]

At the resurrection, the glorious Christ rises up as Victor, His body the tangible sign of the divine X—"intact" but "split open" on the right side (whence the sacred blood and water flow). That the body is "intact" emblematizes the *plenum*, the saving "fullness" that is always "enough and more-than-enough." That the body is punctured and slashed inscribes the "clue." "Whoever wishes to come after me must deny himself, take up his *cross*, and follow me" (Mk 8:34, S/A). That Christ's body inscribes this Way is made painfully, gloriously clear in the epistle to the Hebrews:

28. And other lessons too, I am sure.

151

Therefore, brethren, since we have confidence to enter the sanctuary by the blood of Jesus, by the new and living way which he opened for us through the curtain [Gk. *katapetasmatos*, "veil," alluding to the veil of the Temple], that is, through his flesh. (Heb 10:19–20)

Through the slashes in Christ's body, in Christ's side, we enter the heavenly sanctuary where the Tri-une God is the living temple (see Rv 21:22).

Having surveyed some possible services that an adapted Derridean mode of thinking can offer Catholic teaching on the Incarnate Word, we can now broach some ways in which such an approach may serve Catholic teaching on the Most Holy Trinity. This task we can begin here and then extend further in portions of the Second Annex that follows. What is clear, of course, and indeed became clear already during the heated Trinitarian controversies of the Patristic Age, is that the divine Trinity confounds human rationality. The many scriptural passages bespeaking the Most Holy Trinity send us privileged clues, divinely inspired and inerrant clues that steadfastly refuse recuperation into a holistic formation, even a complex dialectical formation. For God's "higher Rationality"—insofar as it can be accessed by humanity at all—*chooses to show itself* as a "rationality-deconstructed/ing." (*Not* that God's "higher Rationality" *is* itself "rationality-deconstructed/ing," but rather that God sends us "traces" of the divine nature that deconstruct merely *human* rationality.) The Church has faithfully correlated and studied the many scriptural clues to the "nature of God" and assembled them into its authoritative teachings on the Most Holy Trinity. For example, the doctrines of the co-equality and consubstantiality of the three Persons deconstruct a model of the Trinity based on causality, be it ontological or temporal. The doctrine of the co-eternality deconstructs temporal causality. That the three Persons are consubstantial yet *really* (not "virtually") distinct deconstructs a spatial or numerical model, as does the *circumincessio* (the Persons, though really distinct, are absolutely "in each other"). And so on.

As has just been remarked, that these truths bewilder and confound human *ratio*, human logic (from Gk. *logikē*, from *logikos*, from *logos*, "reason") has been known and philosophized and theologized for many centuries already. In an earlier work,[29] I have tried to format—in Derridean terms—several configurations of this necessary "bewilderment." Indeed, there are cases when a set of God's revealed truths, and the Church's teachings that manifest them, seem to generate in a particularly glaring way their own special impasse (in Derridean terms, *aporia*).

The Derridean thought-motif I bring into play here, and reserve for such cases of *aporia*, is the notion of "glitch": Derridean "glitches" are not just exposures of a "not-knowing," but in their specific engineering accomplish ad hoc their own veiled emission of truth. In short, in these cases, "glitches" arise as a concrete impasse *generated* in at once a spectacular/blinding fashion *by what is already defined and we know to be true*. My argument in these special cases is that these snags are themselves dim clues from God, dim clues precisely about the theological subject-matter in situ (whatever it may be), but seen "through a mirror in a riddle." The glitches are not in God per Se, but are in each case a slender passageway to a higher understanding of God (and God's higher or divine Rationality) in relation to the particular issue at hand. The reader can find a demonstration in my treatments, elsewhere, of the "virtual" status of the "active spiration" of the Holy Spirit.[30] Precisely because the Trinitarian *hypostases* (Persons) by definition must be defined oppositionally, the "one principle" (Father *and* Son) that spirates the Holy Spirit can *neither* be real (or it would be a Fourth Person) *nor* be the divine Unity (that by definition does not have distinction or relativity). Thus this Magisterial bind, this glitch, generates the theological notion of the *virtual* status of the active spiration. While

29. See my *Derrida on the Mend*, pp. 133–49.

30. "Two Models of Trinity,—French Post-Structuralist versus the Historical-Critical: Argued in the Form of a Dialogue," in O. Blanchette, T. Imamich, and G. McLean, eds., *Philosophical Challenges and Opportunities of Globalization* (Washington, DC: Council for Research in Values and Philosophy [RVP], Catholic U. of America, 2001), pp. 407–8, 413–20. (Also online at the CRVP website, http://www.crvp.org > publications > Series 1, Culture and Values > #1.19: *Philosophical Challenges and Opportunities of Globalization*, Vol. 2, ch. 22.) See also my *On Deconstructing Life-Worlds: Buddhism, Christianity, Culture* (Scholars P. of American Academy of Religion, 1997; Oxford UP, 2000-), pp. 187–90.

the Church has not officially defined this virtuality, it has defined the procession of the Holy Spirit from the Father and the Son as "from one principle," and its other official definitions pertaining to the Trinity and the Unity necessarily generate the neither-nor status of the "one principle" as described above. My "Derridean" suggestion is that on this count the active spiration, as neither divine Personhood nor divine Unity, somehow emits a veiled clue to some special *difference* between Personhood and Unity (of course all the while still remaining absolutely *one-and-the-same* divine nature, again by definition). I am not suggesting that veiled clues point to matter requiring doctrinal development or further Church definition: the clues may be divinely meant for private religious experience (in which case they should be discussed with a qualified spiritual director, of course).

For the divine crosshatches and binds and glitches, the emblems can be, again, the wounds that slash open Christ Our Lord's body— the punctures of the nails and the rips in the flesh are "glitches" in the somatic "wholeness" of His body, after all. Scripture tells us that these wounds, significantly, accompany Christ's glorified body after the resurrection, and in the Celestial City itself. The punctures and slashes are not His body, but they are marks that can open up His body. In regard to these emblems, it is worth recalling what the great thirteenth-century Franciscan mystic, Blessed Angela of Foligno (who has been dubbed the "master-teacher of theologians"), reports to us about the puncture and gash in Christ's right side: "At times it seems to my soul that it enters into Christ's side, and this is a source of great joy and delight; it is indeed such a joyful experience to move into Christ's side that in no way can I express it or put words to it."[31] And the thirteenth-century Franciscan James of Milan (Giacomo da Milano) tells us, "His wounds are always open, and through them I will once again enter his womb."[32]

---

31. Blessed Angela of Foligno, from ch. VI of *Memorial*, quoted in William J. Short, *Poverty and Joy* (New York: Orbis, 1999), p. 106, citing Paul Lachance, trans. and ed., *Angela of Foligno* (New York: Paulist Press, 1993), pp. 175–76.

32. James of Milan, from ch. XIV of *Stimulus amoris*, trans. William J. Short, OFM, in Short, *Poverty and Joy*, p. 108. Short informs us that *Stimulus amoris* was

The final point in this First Annex pertains to a kind of idolatry that can tempt the Christian, and in our context specifically the Catholic believer. For Jean-Luc Marion, in relation to God, the prioritizing of God's "being" rather than His love produces idolatry, since God's first and primary self-revelation is His love, and it is love's deeds in this world that reveal His being to be in fact love. A theologian adapting from the early-phase Derrida, as this work does, would take another tack, namely: in relation to God, undeconstructed formulations, whether their pertaining intentionalities involve conceptualization or sensing/imagining or affectivity, tend—insofar as they are human—to exalt holism beyond its adequacy, i.e., tend to idolize holism and its objects. What secular deconstructionists, among others, have shown is that the many kinds of "oneness" (so we should speak of "onenesses") functioning within the human purview are all—directly or indirectly—conditioned by time and space, and given our understandings of time and space (a fortiori nowadays with the discoveries of the "new physics," and so on), even in the finite world there is no "oneness" that ever properly holds itself together as a "oneness" pure and simple. This applies a fortiori to more complex unities—dialectical or whatever. (See, for example, the Derridean treatment of time/space in this monograph's Foreword.)

The great temptation for devoted Catholics is to extrapolate *from* an undeconstructed perception of human time and space *to* a "symmetrical" Tri-une God, for then God becomes a perfect "synthesis" for the theologian and an imagined and felt object for theologians and laypersons both (Christ in His human nature is another question, though surely the resurrected-Christ-in-His-human-nature transcends the capacity of the earth-bound human imagination). God's "nature" insofar as it has been revealed to us seems in many ways to be gloriously *asymmetrical* (though again, we must remind ourselves that asymmetry too is only a divine trace that has been sent

first translated into English, with commentary, by an English Augustinian friar, the English mystic Walter Hilton (d. 1396), as *The Goad of Love*; and that a modern English version can be found in C. Kirchberger, *The Goad of Love* (London: Faber and Faber, 1952).

to us; indeed, if our limited and fallen human nature had been such as to privilege asymmetry instead, God would have sent many *symmetrical* clues precisely to destabilize our bias toward asymmetry).

The Church's teaching that God is reflected in all creation means that a "'universe' (Lat. translation of Gk. *to holon*, from *uni*, "one," and *versus*, p.p. of *vertere*, "to turn")-as-deconstructed/ing" points to the "Tri-une God-as-deconstructed/ing." (Again, we must continue to remind ourselves that the latter, too, is only a trace.) The *mysterium* of God's "unchangeability"[33] is not to be framed by or confounded with stasis, the static, the humanly predictable. There is a regrettable tendency among believers and nonbelievers alike to take the Beatific Vision to mean a stationary encounter with a stationary God. St. Catherine of Genoa, who experienced many an ecstatic foretaste of heaven, takes care to disabuse us of this naive analogy to human seeing:

> ... [W]hen the creature is purged, purified, and transformed in God, then is seen that which is pure and true; and this vision which strictly speaking is not seen, can neither be thought nor spoke of.[34]

And St. Gregory of Nyssa tells us:

> This truly is the vision of God: never to be satisfied in the desire to see him. But one must always, by looking at what he can see, rekindle his desire to see more. Thus no limit would interrupt growth in the ascent to God, since no limit to the Good can be found nor is the increasing of desire for the Good brought to an end because it is satisfied.[35]

---

33. The New Testament, in line with the Old Testament, tells us: "Every good endowment and every perfect gift is from above, coming down from the Father of lights with whom there is no variation or shadow due to change" (Jas 1:17). In Scholastic terms, theologians point out that "change" would imply a "composite" and thus finite God. Also, a mutable God would imply that God is not true to His own Rationality (the theological error of Voluntarism). My point here is completely different: namely, that God's immutability is too often confused with the human experience of the static or stationary.

34. St. Catherine of Genoa, as quoted in H. A. Reinhold, ed., *The Soul Afire: Revelations of the Mystics* (Garden City, NY: Image Books, 1973), p. 362.

35. *Gregory of Nyssa: The Life of Moses*, trans., intro., and notes by A. J. Malherbe and E. Ferguson, with preface by J. Meyendorff (New York: Paulist Press, 1978), p. 116.

SECOND ANNEX
"Hellenized" Catholic Theology and Its Encounter with Buddhism—Some Future Possibilities

No one can reasonably deny that the philosophical framework in and through which authoritative Catholic teaching, that of popes and councils, expresses itself is a synthesis of Judeo-Christian faith and Greek rationality. Catholicism subscribes to a developmental theology: the Holy Spirit, in and through the evolving and often confused circumstances of concrete history, is bringing the Church to an ever more mature understanding of the "deposit of faith." In this sense, there is no "going back," and the efforts of some "liberal" theologians to de-Hellenize Catholic doctrine fly in the face not only of orthodoxy but also of the sedimented nature of history (Derrida in his own way argues to the same point: [1] he "stays with the body," as we have seen, and [2] in his "oto-autobiographical" *Jacques Derrida*[1] and elsewhere, he acts out how—though we are not trapped in our past—we are necessarily entangled in it).

1. Geoffrey Bennington and J. Derrida, *Jacques Derrida*, trans. G. Bennington (Chicago and London: U. of Chicago Press, 1993). In this fascinating book, Bennington streams, in a continuous band along the top two-thirds of each page, his exposition of Derrida's philosophical thought; and Derrida streams, in a continuous band along the bottom one-third of each page, a narrative that "plays off," tangles up, and escapes from Bennington's exposition above it. Derrida's narrative is simultaneously an oto-autobiographical "Circumfession" exhibiting how Derrida's life and work are entangled in his past and in *the* past. For readers developing an interest in Derridean thought, I add Geoffrey Bennington's books on Derrida to those I have recommended already. Bennington is a most unreligious person and scholar, but his familiarity with the world of Derrida's thought is quite unmatched.

In comparison with the work of proper theologians (and many of them brilliant besides), my own minimal efforts are inconsequential indeed, but nonetheless, I can say that I have tried, at least in my own small way, to go forth to meet Buddhism while carrying, in my hands, the Catholic tradition as it *now* stands. (Please note also, dear reader, that after further consultation I am even revisiting what I have published thus far in this regard: apropos, see ahead several paragraphs.)

In treating the Tri-une nature of God, my effort has been to draw out, precisely from the Magisterial declarations on this question, those aspects that would be most congenial to South- and Far-Eastern (and specifically Buddhist) philosophical sensibilities, aspects such as (1) impersonality and what can be loosely called (2) "positive emptiness" (non-entitativeness). For example, as is readily seen from the following passage (which summarizes a rather long argument on the workings of the Most Holy Trinity[2]), I depend directly on the conciliar[3] definitions of Nicaea I, Ephesus, Chalcedon, Constantinople II, and Florence, the theology of which is of course "Hellenic" in form and expression:

> Keeping in mind that Conciliar *hypostasis* as a term is meant to avoid identification with either the Unity (which would be "modalism") or human personhood (which would be anthropomorphism), we can go on to propose—according to the postmodern but orthodox protocols limned above—the following scenario (and here I distinguish between "Person," as in the Trinitarian Persons, and "person," as in human personhood):—(1) the Divine Unity is devoid[4] and impersonal, (2) the Trinity—because of its internal voiding oppositions—is Personal, and (3) the Triune God

2. Developed later in the same paper via Thomistic philosophy.

3. "Conciliar" is meant here in the sense of the normative first dictionary sense, viz., belonging to the councils of the Church, and *not* in reference to the heresy of "Conciliarism."

4. In French, Derrida sometimes plays off the meaning of the prefix *dé-* (English *de-*) in its meaning "to be apart from," "to reverse" (these senses derive from its Latin etymon). In my own analogous usage, adopted for a long time already in my work, "devoid" signifies "away from voidness," a voidness complected or spotted with lack-of-voidness (so it is a "mixed voidness," if you will). The adjective "void" I reserve for any state of pure emptiness.

is "impersonal" (except for the Son, insofar as the Son is incarnate in Jesus Christ, who in His human nature has "human consciousness").[5]

It is because of the "internal voiding oppositions" between the Persons that each of them is a Person (*hypostasis*). So declares the Council of Florence, which defines that "everything is one" in God "except where an opposition of relationship [*relationis oppositio*] occurs." Each of the Persons *as* a Person is constituted *only* by oppositional relation between the Persons. Whatever would be common to the Persons belongs to the Unity *instead*. The oppositional relations between the Persons are "voiding" in two senses—(1) the Persons *quā* Persons are, strictly speaking, void (empty) of whatever is ascribed by Scripture to more than one Person (these ascriptions belong to the Unity *instead*); and (2) the Persons are defined exclusively by *purely negative reference* (so the Father is *only* Paternity, the Son is *only* Filiation, and the Holy Spirit is *only* Passive Spiration: that is, the Father is constituted as Father because and only because He purely *is-not* the Son, and *mutatis mutandis*, the Son and Holy Spirit likewise are defined by what they purely *are-not*).

My access to the "immanent Trinity," where there is room for dispute (despite their precision, the councils have left much room), is in most cases Rahnerian, as the theologians among my readers have already detected. I conclude that the divine Unity is "devoid" (a mixed or impure voidness) because the Unity holds all the definitions of God except what is unique to each *hypostasis*. The divine Unity is "impersonal" in that the anthropomorphic is strictly excluded (nor is God gendered, as the *Catechism* reminds us[6]). For the same reason, it must be said that the Tri-une God (the divine Unity and the Trinitarian Persons *consubstantially* united) is "impersonal," excepting of course the human nature of Jesus Christ that is hypostatically united with His divine nature.

Having heeded the objections of some eminently qualified colleagues, I have of late revisited my fumbling efforts to apply—in a

---

5. Magliola, "Two Models of Trinity-," p. 408.
6. CCC #370.

postmodern[7] but orthodox manner—several (adapted) Derridean protocols to our Catholic understanding of the Most Holy Trinity (as indicated in the above brief summary, for example). My intention has always been to humbly suggest some proposals that can further abet a Catholic opening to Oriental thought, especially insofar as non-entitativeness can be brought into play. But I realize now that a due respect for the mystery of the divine consubstantiality requires that I factor in, more than I do, the consubstantiality of the Trinity and the Unity. For example, when I say the Unity is "devoid" because the Unity omits what is strictly unique to each Person, I seem to offend against the Unity and its *simplicity*. And when, in my books and—in more developed fashion—the pertaining published paper,[8] I argue that the pure differences among the Persons are constitutive (in the Derridean sense) of the Unity, I seem to offend against the consubstantiality of the Unity and the Persons.

Perhaps it would be more helpful to restructure my presentation, so that it proposes just that an Augustinian emphasis can bring with it the risk of an exaggeration, namely, the heresy of modalism: but that notwithstanding, to come at God from the side of the divine Unity may, quite possibly, still work—for our feeble human minds—as some kind of tenuous clue to God's incomprehensible *mysterium*. And on the other hand, perhaps we should grant that a more "postmodern" emphasis, such as I have suggested, can surely bring with it—if taken univocally, unilaterally—the risk of a heresy, a tritheism favoring the Persons over the Unity: but that notwithstanding, to come at God from the side of the Trinity may, quite possibly, still work—for our feeble minds—as some kind of temporary clue to God's incomprehensible *mysterium*. What rescues us from these dire straits is, of course, the faith-filled recognition that the so-called two sides are in fact one-and-the-same, and infinitely

---

7. As pointed out already, Derrida took care to distance himself from "postmodernism": when I invoke the term here, I mean it only in a broad sense that can accommodate Derridean thought as well, that is, as an umbrella term for intentional programs of operation that disrupt holisms.

8. "Two Models of Trinity-," pp. 404–5, 408–21.

more, because God is perfectly Tri-une, a *mysterium* indeed. In the final analysis, ours is simply to adore, to simply and humbly adore.

If we are attentive to the diversity around us, near us, we must deny ourselves the easy confidences that keep the other at a distance. But as believers, we must also be able to defend the relevance of the faith of our community, deepening our commitments even alongside other faiths that are flourishing nearby. We need to learn from other religious possibilities, without slipping into relativist generalizations.

—Francis X. Clooney, SJ, *Comparative Theology: Deep Learning Across Religious Borders*[9]

History has shown that the Church's progress toward the Parousia is often not smooth: the Church's growth often comes in fits and starts, but the point to keep in mind here is that the growth *does* continue. Along with many others, I think we are entering a time when a South- and Far-East Asian Catholicism can flourish like never before. Asian churches—through their glorious histories of martyrdom, through their steadfastness in the face of persecution and many other obstacles,[10] and more recently through their missionary outreach to the whole world—have been a heroic and luminous inspiration to the global Church. It is also well-known that outstanding South- and Far-East Asian theologians have been at work in Catholic theology for quite some time already. My point, rather, is that perhaps we are entering a time when Asian modes of thinking can initiate a quantum leap in the Church's theology at large, and that such a development would do much to leaven the Asian Church while simultaneously abetting the Church everywhere.

My own work has been as a Catholic among Asian Buddhists, and the most I intend to do here is humbly offer some suggestions

9. Malden, MA, and Oxford: Wiley-Blackwell, 2010, p. 7.

10. In the case of the Philippines, for example, the Church was of course powerful from the very arrival of the Spanish onward, but for centuries there were limitations on the clerical roles permitted the indigenous population. The Church today, under Filipino auspices, is a glorious beacon of the Faith in Asia and sends missionaries all over the world.

based on my experience in Chinese and Thai academic circles. It seems to me that to achieve a more significant growth in Asia, the Church must absorb, in an orthodox way, what are uniquely Oriental emphases. "Impersonality," as I have pointed out, is an important thought-motif for Buddhists in particular, and the function of "impersonality" in the problematic of the Tri-une God can bring this motif to the forefront. Likewise, the motif of non-entitativeness is crucial for Buddhists, and the Church, in my opinion, must address, absorb, and transform this notion. Associated with non-entitativeness is the *salubrity of fracture*. Occidental thought has been more than once seduced by a facile and complacent holism.

In general, European theology has identified lack-of-wholeness exclusively with the consequences of Original Sin, and healing has been taken to mean, almost always, the restoration of wholeness. But cannot fracture-in-wholeness also be a clue to God, a "trace" of God in this sense? (Though a clue, of course, that is necessarily "under erasure," i.e., under the sign of the X, in that it is no more than a trace that will someday cede for us before the divine reality.) In fact, it seems to me that these two understandings, brokenness as flaw and brokenness as divine trace, can in many ways be one-and-the-same. Let us remember the theology of the *felix culpa* (the "happy fault"). "From all eternity" the God of Mystery willed a scenario whereby God the Son would be broken and rise gloriously broken, and thus save creation from Original Sin. Somehow, beyond our ken, this scenario is a sign of God.

Other lines of thought that, in my opinion, "go out to meet" the Buddhist mind-set include (1) the Thomistic God-without-attribute (see ahead, the treatment of Thomism and meditation) and even, if given a unique turn, (2) the theology of *analogia entis* ("analogy of being") so prominent these days in ecumenical circles.[11] The Schoolmen deployed "analogy of being" so that one

---

11. An important symposium on the legitimacy of the *analogia entis* as a way of coming to knowledge of God took place at the John Paul II Cultural Center, Washington, DC, April 4–6, 2008, on the eve of Benedict XVI's papal visit to Washington. Sponsored by the Pontifical Faculty of the Immaculate Conception (at the local Dominican House of Studies), and Eerdmans Press, it drew together theologians from the Catholic, Orthodox, and Protestant traditions.

could reason from effects (creation) to the Cause, the Ultimate (God). Though the Scholastics and their predecessors attributed lack-of-wholeness to the limitations of creaturehood (the world of "effect") and wholeness to God (the Whole, or Perfect), can it not be, sometimes, that lack-of-wholeness in the effect *reflects* lack-of-wholeness in God? (Though again, we are talking here only of the human concept of "wholeness" and its adequacy; in short, sometimes lack-of-wholeness as a human concept may be a better *clue* to God's nature than what human beings understand by "wholeness.")

In the main, Catholic theology adopted/adapted structures of conceptual thought from the Hellenistic tradition. Catholic theology can go on now to learn from, adopt/adapt, structures of South- and Far-Eastern thought. For example, Indian and Chinese thought emphasizes the value of what can be called "both-and" thinking, and in my experience Westerners who are sensitized to/by Oriental culture over a long period of time almost inevitably come—at least selectively—to think this way. Oriental "both-and" thinking tests whether the conventionally taken "incompatibility" of a given two elements is real or *merely* conventional. If the two elements are in fact compatible, and it is better (in terms of the value-system involved) that they both be affirmed, then the "both-and" mode is brought into play. It is quite remarkable how an *unreal* "incompatibility" can become entrenched sometimes and stubbornly taken for real, though the solution, the affirmation of *both* elements, is right there in front of us. (Of course, *discernment* is crucial here: in the contexts we are discussing, one must test whether morality is served and—in theology—whether truth is served.) The point I am making is that "both-and" thinking should become encoded into our experience as an active *possibility*. In my view, the "both-and" should become a structural "reserve" in our overall mind-set,[12] the possible application of which is spontaneously at hand.

By way of example, we can appeal to a very concrete case deriving from the busy world of scriptural redaction and exegesis. There has been much controversy in some circles over the redactions of the "messianic Psalms" and the critical search for their *Ur*-texts. This is

---

12. That is, in our *Vor-Struktur*, as a Heideggerian would say.

especially the case with Psalm 110 (Vulgate, Psalm 109),[13] which has been traditionally taken by the Church as prophetic of the Incarnation (this use can be liturgical and edifying, of course—the text is in no way necessary as proof of the doctrine). The traditional reading is more difficult to support in terms of the Masoretic redaction, but may depend on earlier versions of this same Psalm. There are lacunae in the Hebrew texts, and the meanings of some of the Hebrew words are "philologically unavailable." There are at least three versions that are critically justifiable in one way or another—the "reconstructed" Hebrew text (reconstructed from alternative ancient Hebrew manuscripts), the Septuagint Greek text, and the currently "accepted" Hebrew text. The Greek text aligns itself most often with the reconstructed Hebrew. Given that intensive and sustained research seems to have met an impasse, the relevance of "both-and" thinking can present itself.

A Catholic can, of course, simply accept that God has allowed this impasse, these uncertainties—indeed, in some textual instances, these literal contradictions—to stand. But I would strongly suggest that if God has allowed, for us, these intransigently heterogeneous scriptural texts to arise, this condition is meant not just to be accepted but to be heuristically cultivated and, indeed, *celebrated*. If, for example, the currently "accepted" Hebrew puts Yahweh, in verse 5, at the right hand of the Messiah-figure, and the reconstructed Hebrew, instead, puts the Messiah-figure at the right hand of Yahweh, why cannot this be a case of "both-and," that is, a case in which each of these two formulations communicates a special divine truth? In short, each can be true in its own way. In my view, it is not at all "begging the question" (*petitio principii*) to apply to this site of unsolved heterogeneity the assurance that "every scripture is God-breathed and profitable for teaching. . . ." (2 Tm 3:16).

For a second demonstration, broadly speaking, of "both-and"

---

13. In Taiwan, I became so intrigued by the "both-and" structure and its relevance to the critical problematic of Psalm 110 that I devoted a study to it, entitled "Postmodern Literariness and the Bible: On Psalm 110, Piquant Piqué," *Studies in Language and Literature* (National Taiwan University, Vol. 4 (October 1990), pp. 31–41.

thinking and its pertinence, we can draw from the Catholic social world at large. A merit of the "both-and" in these cases is that it often violates the proprieties of the typical Western "First World" life-styles. A case in point is the United States of America, where— driven by the Holy Spirit—the Church, in particular through Vatican Council II, teaches configurations of truths that turn out in an American social setting to be *chiasmic,* and chiasm, no matter what its elucidation,[14] tends to violate proprieties. The chiasm's "both-and" shows, sometimes with great rigor, that elements deemed to be incompatible are really compatible (and, in the case of Church teachings, often in fact *obligatory*). What can be loosely called the "conservative" or "right-wing" American Catholic readily affirms the grave sinfulness of abortion, but backs off from the Church's vigorous denunciations of hegemonic First World politics/economics. The "liberal" American Catholic takes to heart the Church's "option for the poor," but tends to be lax in terms of Church teachings on marriage and sexuality.

"I came to cast fire upon the earth" (Lk 12:49), roars the Lion of Judah who is also the Sun of Justice. In short, the Church's configuration of truths demands of/for many Catholics a painful *reconfiguration.* This reconfiguration according to the Holy Spirit *dislocates* lifestyles (thrusting them into "chiasm," if you will, crucifying their proprieties), so that the conservative Catholic comes to oppose, for example, *both* abortion *and* American (global) political-economic triumphalism, and the liberal Catholic comes to support, for example, *both* the anti-superpower politics of the Third World *and* campaigns against "easy divorce" and "gay marriage." Such redistributions of "natural" preference crucify egoism and remake us into conformity with Christ. (Can it even be the case, in the West, that the "natural" gravitations of "conservative" congregations of Catho-

14. The history of philosophy has given us several elucidations of chiasm. Maurice Merleau-Ponty's chiasm, for example, differs somewhat from the "Derridean chiasm" that we adopted/adapted earlier in this monograph. In its elucidation as "both-and" thinking, the Orient's deployment of chiasm has been much more pervasive than chiasm has been in the West, in large part because "both-and" thinking is not restricted to academic discourse in the Orient. In Taiwan, I found that it actively pervades the life-world of almost every Chinese person.

lic religious Sisters and "liberal" congregations of Catholic religious Sisters toward what have become their respectively stereotyped agendas may need some readjustment, a remaking in terms of the chiasmic "both-and"? Do we need more Sisters, perhaps, who *both* actively motivate the laity to oppose torture and unjust war and wealthy lifestyles *and* also wear religious habits, teach grade school, and organize forty-hour Eucharistic vigils? I do not mean to suggest, of course, that these various apostolates *necessarily* belong together. These questions pertain to a congregation's charism, so surely we should affirm that the Sisters must work out these answers for themselves.)

Another conceptual mode much emphasized in Indian and Chinese thought is the "neither-nor," and like the "both-and," it too pervades the individual and social life-worlds in much of Asia. Classical Indian logic is tetralemmic: x is y, x is not y, x both is and is not y, x neither is nor is not y. Parallels to these four lemmas pervade the Far East too, and date from a time long before Buddhism brought their more Indian formulation to China, Vietnam, Korea, and Japan. The "neither-nor," or fourth lemma, can be understood according to either of two contrary senses, depending on whether the "positive" or "negative" tetralemma is being invoked.[15] In the negative fourth lemma, "x neither is nor is not y" means x is *not at all* either y or non-y, so x totally escapes or transcends y and non-y: $x = -(y$ and $-y)$. In the positive fourth lemma, "x neither is nor is not y" means x is not y but x is also *not* non-y, so x is somehow entrammeled in y: $x = -y$ and $-(-y)$. The Buddhist website "Twelve Links: Notes from Samsara" gives the following example of positive tetralemma: "The self is neither real nor not real (neither ultimately real nor completely nonexistent)."[16] Especially as Orientals deploy it, this open-ended but fragile entanglement of x in y can be very subtle. (For example, to say

15. See "Notes on the Tetralemma" (January 26, 2006) on the website "Twelve Links: Notes from Samsara": http://twelvelinks.blogspot.com/2006/01/notes-on-tetralemma.html. Another helpful source is "LNC and the Buddhist Tetralemma" on the web page on "Contradiction" in the online open-access *Stanford Encyclopedia of Philosophy*: http://plato.stanford.edu/entries/contradiction/#LNCBudTet, pp. 12–15.

16. "Twelve Links," p. 2.

"x is not not-correct" sends a differing and more subtle message than to say "x is correct" or even "x is not wrong.")

In my opinion, the ongoing inculturation of Catholic theology into South- and Far-East Asian thought can adopt/adapt the Oriental mode of "neither-nor" for/to the problematic of grace and free will, for example. And I intentionally choose *this specific example* because—while the neither-nor correctly applied does not at all jeopardize the teaching that God saves us and we do not save ourselves (indeed, this teaching, as my whole preceding monograph argues, is the *pivot* on which the pure difference between Buddhism and Catholicism *turns*)—the neither-nor can perhaps better display for Orientals the full subtlety and sophistication of Church teaching on grace and free will.

The *Catechism of the Catholic Church*, despite some adjustments in frame of reference, declares of course the traditional teaching that "the grace of Christ is not in the slightest way a rival of our freedom when this freedom accords with the sense of the true and the good that God has put in the human heart" (#1742). As the compilers/editors of *The Christian Faith* put it, the Magisterium has "refrained from systematically developing a treatise on the life of grace," however, because theology "can never exhaust the treasure contained in revelation and tradition." Rather, the Magisterium "tries to address issues that, from time to time, promote a partial, limited understanding of the life of grace, one that falls short of the gift God made to humankind."[17]

At the Council of Trent, the Church, when speaking of "prevenient grace," sought to express the delicate balance between God's role and ours by juxtaposing two beautiful scriptural passages: "Hence, when it is said in Sacred Scripture, 'Turn ye to me, and I will turn to you' (Zec 1:3), we are reminded of our freedom; when we answer, 'Convert us, O Lord, to thee, and we shall be converted' (Lam 5:21), we acknowledge that God's grace prepares us."[18] Not that the "balance" is an equilibrium as such, of course. The paradox is that God "does it all" but still the free human being freely "does it."

17. *The Christian Faith* (CF), p. 791.
18. CT #561 (DZ 797).

I would suggest that—whether dealing with "prevenient," "concomitant," or "subsequent" grace[19]—the "positive" version of the neither-nor speaks well to the Oriental mind-set. That is, "a human being neither determines nor does-not-determine" her/his salvation, in the sense that a human being certainly does *not* determine her/his own salvation but on the other hand does *not not* determine her/his own salvation (somehow her/his free choice is present and necessary in the process). The human being, as the recent *Catechism of the Catholic Church* puts it, is justified by the "grace of God," and "Grace is favor, the free and undeserved help that God gives us . . ." (#1996), but on the other hand, the human being does not *not* determine her/his salvation, because "The soul only enters *freely*[20] into the communion of love" (#2002).

The paradox aforementioned, viz., "God does it all but still the human being freely does it," baffles the human mind and is a *mysterium*. But if the positive fourth lemma can apply here, the negative fourth lemma can also apply in its own way. The *mysterium* to which the paradox points, without of course in any way solving it, is expressible as the negative version of the neither-nor: "a human being neither determines nor does-not-determine her/his salvation" means, in this version, that the *mysterium* of *how* the paradox happens *transcends* the framework of the question posed, that is, the framework of the human definition(s) of "determining/not-determining."

It would be typical of Oriental thinking that *both* the positive *and* the negative versions of the above be used together, so as to express *both* the theology of grace insofar as the Church has tried to explain this *mysterium* and the theology of grace insofar as the Church has silently, humbly prostrated itself before the necessary inexplicability. I would ask Western theologians to entertain the notion that this Oriental way of proceeding not only can "speak well to the Oriental mind-set," but also can contribute to the ever-maturing theology of the universal Church.

The Church's teaching on the nature of the Beatific Vision is

19. CT #573 (DZ 809).
20. Italicization mine.

another example where perhaps the fruitfulness of the neither-nor can be demonstrated. I choose *this specific example* because—while the neither-nor correctly applied does *not at all* jeopardize the teaching that God remains forever distinct from us (indeed, this teaching is another *pivot* on which the pure difference between Buddhism and Catholicism *turns*)—the neither-nor can perhaps display for Orientals the full subtlety and sophistication of Church teaching on the Beatific Vision.

Scripture reveals that God, the Creator, forever transcends the created: God "transcends creation and is present to it," as the *Catechism* summarizes the matter (#300), and it goes on to gloss the nature of this transcendence with the words of St. Augustine, "God is 'higher than my highest and more inward than my innermost self.'"

Nonetheless, Scripture reveals that grace makes us "partakers [Gk. *koinōnoi*, "sharers"] of divine nature" (2 Pt 1:4), so that "we shall be like" God for "we shall see him as he is" (1 Jn 3:2). "Grace is a participation in the life of God" (CCC #1997), and celestial beatitude brings grace to full flower so that there is "perfect communion with God" (#2550). In short, the paradox is that we are forever distinct from God but still somehow like God through "sanctifying grace," what the *Catechism* also calls "deifying grace" (#1999).

My suggestion here is that, while the negative version of the neither-nor does not seem well-suited to express this paradox, the positive version suits it very well indeed: to wit, the "graced" person is definitely *not* God but somehow is *not not-God* either. Perhaps in the future this formulation, maybe even in a much more developed form, can fruitfully serve the Church in the Orient and the Church universal.

The process of adapting to and learning from South and Southeast Asia, and the Far East, necessarily entails the development of new but orthodox Catholic meditative forms. These forms—besides other differences—must be much more somatically disciplined than the meditation modes of contemporary movements such as

"Centering Prayer"[21] or the "World Community for Christian Meditation,"[22] both of which—though somewhat influenced by Yogic and Buddhist practice—are basically Occidental in provenance (Eastern and Western Church). The development of truly Asian meditative forms has been going on for several decades, in relation to both Hindu and Buddhist cultures, and the Congregation for the Doctrine of the Faith has already published official documents on it.[23] Inculturations of Catholic meditation into Zen modes, and to a lesser extent into various Theravadic forms, are already well-known in the Western Church, at least among many of those Catholics who research and/or practice meditation. In particular, religious orders and congregations—the Benedictines, Trappists, and Jesuits, among others—have taken the lead worldwide in these developments.[24]

Here I take the opportunity to recommend more work in the use of Vajrayana Buddhist form. Visualizations associated with chakrasites and accompanied by mantra-recitation, characterize much Vajrayana practice. In my experience, few Catholics are temperamentally disposed toward Zennist "no-thinking," but many Catholics take readily to visualizations (e.g., Ignatian "mental image of place" and "seeing the personages" in the *Spiritual Exercises*) accompanied by prayerful recitation (the Jesus Prayer, devout "aspirations," etc.). In 1999, my presentation of Vajrayana form, set in

21. Centering Prayer, founded by three Trappists associated with St. Joseph's Abbey, Spencer, Massachusetts—William Meninger, M. Basil Pennington, and Thomas Keating—grows largely out of the Church's ancient format of *lectio divina*. Fr. Thomas Keating has gone on to found "Contemplative Outreach," which promotes Centering Prayer and is expanding to many dioceses. Sr. Catherine Cleary, OSB, also associated with Buddhist-Catholic dialogue, does much teaching for Contemplative Outreach.

22. The World Community for Christian Meditation (WCCM) was founded by an English Benedictine, Fr. John Main (1926–1982). Fr. Laurence Freedman, OSB, assumed leadership after the founder's passing. Influenced by both the Church's Hesychastic tradition and Yogic chanting of mantras, the meditative format of the WCCM involves the chanting of Christian mantras, such as the ancient Jesus Prayer. The WCCM, like Centering Prayer, is undergoing steady growth.

23. For example, the "Letter to the Bishops of the Catholic Church on Some Aspects of Christian Meditation," October 15, 1989 (see the official doctrinal documents of the Congregation for the Doctrine of the Faith online at http://www.vatican.va/roman_curia/congregations/faith/doc_doc_index.htm).

accordance with Buddhist breathing mode and meditative posture, but using a chakra-method thematized in an utterly orthodox Catholic way, was very well received by the Pontifical Council of Culture and the Federation of Asian Bishops' Conferences.[25]

Here in this monograph, a work more concerned with doctrinal issues, I would like to point out that there is even a specifically *Thomistic* counterpoint available to Catholic meditation in relation to that moment in Vajrayanist tantric meditation when both "visualization of the deity" and "identification with the deity" are "dissolved" into "emptiness." That is, in a typical tantric *sādhana*, the meditator at the moment of dissolution aims to *become* the unconditioned state that is "emptiness" or "Buddhahood."[26] More specifically put, in a tantric *sādhana* the meditator follows the following sequence: first, s/he visualizes and venerates a tutelary deity, a symbolic figure representing wisdom or compassion or some other aspect of enlightenment; then s/he identifies with the tutelary deity so as to transform into the aspect of enlightenment the deity represents; and finally, s/he dissolves all objectivity and subjectivity, and

---

24. Quite a few priests and nuns/sisters/brothers of religious orders and congregations, as well as some diocesan ("secular") priests, have undergone intensive training from Buddhist teachers who are recognized masters of their respective Buddhist traditions or lineages (terminology varies according to the provenance of the Buddhist teachers involved, as do the titles of the certifications they impart). Some of these Catholic clergy and Religious adhere quite carefully to the Church's official guidelines regarding meditation and interreligious relations, and some do not. Among the contemporary Catholic clergy and Religious who are trained by established Buddhist teachers and are certified by them to teach, in the United States alone one can already point out quite a few examples. Among the most well-known are the following: In Zen,—the Jesuit Robert E. Kennedy and three of his practice-heirs—Janet Richardson, CSJP; Kevin Hunt, OCSO; and Michael K. Holleran (diocesan, formerly Carthusian); and the Redemptorist Pat Hawk, CSsR (d. 2012); and, in Theravada practices,—Sr. Mary Jo Meadow, SFCC; and several Discalced Carmelite friars—Kevin Culligan, Daniel Chowning, Mark DeVelis, and Anthony Haglof. Again, this is only a *partial* list.

25. See R. Magliola, pp. 71–82, in *Proceedings: The Convention on "Christian Humanism: Illuminating with the Light of the Gospel the Mosaic of Asian Cultures"* (as in earlier note).

26. See Lama Anagarika Govinda, *Foundations of Tibetan Mysticism* (New Delhi: B.I. Pub., 1991; rpt. of the same from London: Rider and Co., 1960), pp. 206–9.

all phenomenal traces, in order to become the one unconditioned and pure emptiness (or Buddhahood). At the end of the meditation, the meditator returns to everyday life, while trying to live these three phases at the same time, namely, veneration, pure behavior (manifesting wisdom, compassion, etc.), and pure emptiness. On the other hand, in a Catholic meditation following a Thomistic model, "dissolution" would be a moment necessarily functioning for the *opposite* reason, namely, so that the meditator could freely "open up to" the grace of God, God who is "purely existent" and thus *in Se* beyond human knowing. (Nor, in a Catholic meditation, would a moment of dissolution preclude many other moments in a meditation when God's "attributes" [in the Thomistic sense] can be the meditative focus.)

How we can appropriate from St. Thomas in this regard requires some detailed treatment, here, of his theology of God and existence. In terms of Scholastic philosophy, which in turn derives from the Greek philosophical tradition that the Church has adopted and adapted in order to doctrinally express its (largely) Hebraic sources, God is "absolutely simple" because a "compound being" is necessarily contingent and finite. God purely *exists* because God's existence and essence are one-and-the-same (otherwise, God would be "compound" or "conditioned"). This does not mean that God *is* all existents (or individual beings), but rather that God causes all existents. Kevin Hart, in a *JAAR* review essay entitled "Of Love and How,"[27] gives us a concise description of the Scholastic formulation as Aquinas presents it: "God is his own act of being, not *ens commune*, and we can grasp God as wholly undetermined *ipsum esse subsistens* only by analogy."[28] (I might add here that, from the Catholic perspective, it is for this very reason that those pluralists who identify God as the *esse* or "being" common to all entities and then draw parallels to the Buddhist *dharmakāya* already miss the point on the Christian side, not even to mention their questionable understanding of *dharmakāya*.)

---

27. *Journal of the American Academy of Religion*, Vol. 77, No. 3 (September 2009), pp. 712–33.
28. Ibid., p. 717.

In the Middle Ages, intense disputes took place over how to understand God's pure existence. Robert C. Koons discusses this controversy with great clarity,[29] showing that Aquinas addressed two ways of taking "pure existence": one is to regard pure existence as that which remains when all qualifications are stripped away (implying that qualifications are "positives"), and another is to regard pure existence as "positively" excluding all qualifications because all qualifications would involve subtractions (implying that qualifications are "negatives"). Aquinas argues that only this second way applies to God's existence. Koons supplies a helpful analogy:

> Here's an analogy: we could think of "gold" in two ways. I could think of "gold" as an element that is present, to varying degrees, in such things as gold ore, 14- or 16-carat alloys, sea water. All these things are, to varying degrees, gold. Alternatively, I could think of "gold" as a name only for specimens of absolutely pure, 24-carat gold. In this sense, a 14-carat "gold" bracelet isn't gold at all. These correspond to the two ways of thinking of "pure existence": (1) as something shared, in varying degrees, by all existing things [so in the analogy, the sea water is gold plus other positive things[30]], and (2) as something that exists in a state of pure, unqualified existence [so the non-gold in the sea water blocks the sea water from status as "gold"[31]]. God is identical to existence only in the second sense.[32]

Koons further explains why Aquinas argues this way:

> Why does Aquinas think this is so? He argues that it is impossible to add anything to existence (*esse*). If you were to add something to an act of existence, you would be adding either (1) another, distinct act of existence, or (2) something non-existent. When you add two acts of existence together (alternative 1), you have two

---

29. Robert C. Koons, Phl 349, Lecture #15 (U. of Texas at Austin), "Aquinas's Proof of God's Existence: Part II": http://www.utexas.edu/cola/depts/philosophy/faculty/koons/phl349lec15.htm (accessed July 21, 2008). Much of my treatment of Thomism's "pure existence" is a paraphrase of Koons.

30. This parenthetical gloss is my notation.

31. Again, my notation.

32. Koons, p. 4.

beings, not one, so such a process cannot explain how one thing could be "more" than merely existent. If you add something non-existent to a being, you have added nothing to it, and so haven't modified it at all. . . . To explain how things [that is, creatures[33]] can have a variety of degrees of excellence (clods of dirt, worms, men, angels), we must instead suppose that in each case the act of existence has been "determined" or limited by a definite potentiality, a nature or essence. These definite, finite essences can have the effect of negating existence to varying degrees.[34]

What I am proposing is that in a Catholic meditation, a moment of "dissolution" (possibly at the "third eye" chakra of the head) can appropriate from Aquinas in the following way. Before the "dissolution" (or more accurately, the "bracketing-out"), the (new) meditator can recall that God *in Se* cannot be the "object" of human acts of the intellect or will. But what can we do, then, if—from this perspective—God strictly speaking cannot be our "object," an "object" of our intellect and will? We can either use words, concepts, images, feelings, etc., anyway, knowing all the time that they "fall short"; or we can, for a measured period of time, suspend words, concepts, images, feelings, and simply rest in awe and "waiting." In the moment of "dissolution" ("bracketing-out"), we are choosing, for a limited amount of time, the latter alternative. (In a way, we are choosing to "lose ourselves in God" while knowing that God is experientially unfathomable.[35] To invoke our earlier analogy, God is such inconceivable "gold" that all gold next to divinity is no gold at all: bracketing-out is one kind of temporary response to this "overwhelming" fact.) In short, awe and waiting can be, for a measured

---

33. This parenthetical gloss is my notation.

34. Koons, pp. 4, 5.

35. As the Church often warns us, we should not be so pretentious as to expect any kind of "mystical contemplation": such is given only to a very few human beings, and those who are so blessed affirm how humbled they are by what is so obviously, even for them, "pure gift." In this regard, the passage we quoted earlier from St. Catherine of Genoa in another context here bears repeating: ". . . [W]hen the creature is purged, purified, and transformed in God, then is seen that which is pure and true; and this vision which strictly speaking is not seen, can neither be thought nor spoken of" (see pertaining earlier note).

period of time, a silent kind of image-free, concept-free prayer.[36] The meditator should thus proceed into the "clearing" by gently clearing the mind of images and concepts and words and attention to sensations. When any of these arise (as they will, especially at the beginning and sometimes very insistently), allow them to pass and die without attending on them.

Of course, such a "moment" of meditation should be preceded and followed by traditional form, the use of words, concepts, ideas, etc.[37] Not only has the Church—in the face of Quietism and Semi-Quietism—insisted on these for many insuperable reasons (with the Incarnation, of course, as the most salient reason of all), but indeed the use of traditional form makes sense in terms of the very argument from Aquinas that we have been invoking. For Aquinas, what are conventionally called God's "attributes" are simply other names for God's pure existence. Again, Robert Koons's clarifications are very helpful:

> Absolute existence includes everything that could be included in any perfection, such as goodness, power, wisdom, joy. God is good, but God's goodness is not something distinct from God, nor something distinct from God's existence. Instead, "God's goodness" is simply another name for God Himself, and for His existence. In other words, the following series of equations are correct (where the final "P" stands for any perfection, any purely positive attribute): God = God's existence = God's essence = God's goodness = God's power = God's P. In this way, we can truthfully attribute any perfection to God without compromising God's absolute simplicity. Since existence is the most noble thing, absolute existence must contain every possible perfection of any possible creature.[38]

I conclude with a final suggestion bearing on adaptation from

---

36. Needless to say, even a limited form of image-and-concept-free mind is extremely difficult to achieve. There are various "steps" one can undertake toward such a state of mind, such as imagining that the mind is entering an endless cloud, or light, or sky-blue azure.

37. And indeed, in terms of Catholic chakra-meditation, words, concepts, and ideas can be used at several or all of the chakras.

38. Koons, pp. 5–6.

Buddhist meditative practice. As mentioned earlier, there has been already for quite some time a lively assimilation of Zen form into Catholic meditation.[39] Insofar as I know, such has not been the case, however, in the matter of a particular discipline associated most with Linji Chan (Lin-chi Ch'an) and its disseminations (e.g., Rinzai Zen in Japan), namely, the use of *gong'an* (literally "public case," but in Chinese Chan practice a brief phrase or story given by master to disciple in order to prompt the disciple's spiritual development). Many functions and kinds of *gong'an* (Japanese *kōan*) exist,[40] but I would recommend for Catholic adaptation the kind that presents a puzzle that—in order to "work"—must be *solved* at a deep personal psycho-spiritual level. This kind of *gong'an* is "telic" or purposeful in the sense that it is not a "mere" paradox the very insolubility of which is the occasion for a leap to a supra-rational state. Rather, the puzzle occasions a breakthrough to a specific psycho-spiritual solution or "answer" that, indeed, is rooted in the supra-rational but that is nonetheless pointed and maybe even expressible (though the expression is by no means *equivalent* to the solution: it is at most a sign of the solution).

Christian *gong'an* of a telic kind can—under the guidance of a competent spiritual director—open pathways so that the Holy Spirit, *Sua sponte*, can bring forth the fruits of (1) further and specific transformation in/into Christ (*metanoia*) and/or (2) an epiphanic "Christful" solution to a personal problem. Holy Scripture is by nature the most fruitful source of Christian "phrases" and "stories,"

39. Almost all of the Catholic assimilation from Zen has been transmitted to Westerners in the form of a "silent Zen," in which from very early on in the process one is trained to "let go" of all images, ideas, emotions, and, as soon as possible, all "thought" as such (whereas in Vajrayana Buddhist meditation, one follows a path through images, ideas, and emotions to the stage of "no thought"). Quite a few Catholic clergy and Religious have received Zen Dharma-transmission via the well-known Japanese Zen monk Yamada Koun Roshi and his Sanbo Kyodan lineage: for example, Fr. Niklaus Brantschen, SJ; Fr. Willigis Jäger, OSB; and Sr. Elaine MacInnes, OLM; or via the lineage of Shogaku Shunryu (Suzuki Roshi): for example, Fr. Patrick Hawk, CSsR; and—Suzuki Roshi > Bernard Glassman Roshi > Fr. Robert Kennedy, SJ.

40. See *The Koan: Texts and Contexts in Zen Buddhism*, eds. Steven Heine and Dale S. Wright (Oxford UP, 2000).

but to function as telic *gong'an* they must be not only *conductive* ("conductive" in a way analogous to the use of sacramentals) but also specifically *problematic*. (The personalized "solution" to the posed "puzzle" and its "question" should *directe aut indirecte* lead, of course, to the sacraments and the sacramental life.)

Listed below are some examples of possible *gong'an* drawn from Scripture. What is crucial to understand in this regard is that—if the phrases or stories are to function properly as *gong'an*—possible historico-critical resolutions to their posed "problems" are to be bracketed-out.[41] (However, the scriptural contexts of the given scriptural texts *can* be involved in the practitioner's meditation on her/his given *gong'an*, much as in the Chan collections such as the *Biyan Lu* and the *Wumenguan*, *gong'an* frequently allude to other pertaining *gong'an* or to commentaries surrounding them.)

(A) Inter-Gospel variants from the same narrative stock

For example: Lk 11:23 says, "He who is not with me is against me, and he who does not gather with me scatters," but Mk 9:40 has otherwise, saying, "For he that is not against us is for us." Question: Why—for you—this difference?

Another example: Lk 17:37 says, "Where the body [Gk. σωμα, *sōma*, "living body"] is, there also the eagles/vultures [Gk. αετοι,

---

41. In the Jewish tradition, rabbinical exegesis and debate feature a pious wrangling over meaning that sometimes much resembles the to-and-fro movement of meaning in *gong'an* texts. The fluid movement of meaning in Midrashic interpretation of course operates in a mode other than the historico-critical, as does also the allegorical mode of the Church Fathers. In an interview at the Gregorian University in Rome while serving as McCarthy lecturer there, Robert Louis Wilkin, author of *The Spirit of Early Christian Thought: Seeking the Face of God* (Yale UP, 2003), points out that at the same time (mid-twentieth century) one group of Catholic biblical scholars were receiving permission to develop and apply the historico-critical method, another Catholic group were reviving, with approbation, the classical Christian mode of reading the Bible, a mode dedicated (largely) to allegorical reading and operating outside of the "historico-critical." Indeed, the "imaginative world of the Bible, a world of images and metaphors, of story and history," should live perennially in our spirituality: Divine inspiration, properly discerned, can breathe through them as much now as ever. See "Reading the Bible with the Church Fathers: Interview with Historian Robert Louis Wilkin," ZENIT, June 19, 2003: http://www.zenit.org/english/visualizza.phtml?sid=37499 (accessed June 20, 2003).

aetoi, "birds of prey," can refer to eagles or vultures] will be gathered together"; but Mt 24:28 says, "Wherever may be the body [Gk. πτωμα, *ptōma*, "dead body"], there the eagles/vultures [Gk. αετοι, *aetoi*, "birds of prey") will be gathered together."[42] Question: Living body? Dead body?

(B) Problems of textual/redactional/recensional criticism

For example: Ps 110:5 in the current Hebrew text translates as "The Lord [Yahweh] at your [the Messiah's] right hand shatters kings in the day of his anger," but the "reconstructed" earlier Hebrew text reads, "At his [Yahweh's] right hand, the Lord [the Messiah] shatters kings in the day of his anger"—see unabridged *Jerusalem Bible* (1966), note f, p. 897. Question: The Father at Christ's right hand, Christ at the Father's right hand? What to do?

(C) Exegetical cruxes

For example: Heb 11:11, literally in Greek, "Σαρρα δύναμιν εις καταβολην σπέρματος έλαβεν," "Sarah received power to throw down [or 'forth'] seed"; see F. Gaebelein, gen. ed., *Expositor's Bible Commentary*, Vol. 12, Leon Morris, ed., *Hebrews*, p. 119—"The difficulty is that on the face of it the verse ascribes to Sarah an activity possible only to males." Question: Why so?

Though Sacred Scripture seems ideally suited as material for *gong'an*, other sites and sources may very well be appropriate depending on situation and need. In some situations, sacred Chris-

---

42. As already indicated, unless they can abet the *ad hoc* function of the *gong'an* in terms of the practitioner's spiritual growth, the historico-critical and even exegetical contexts of the scriptural passages can be bracketed-out for the time being, since *gong'an* deal with "private" truth rather than public truth. However, let me point out for the interested reader that the historico-critical and exegetical problematics of Lk 17:37 and Mt 24:28 are fascinating and much controverted, and well worth scholarly pursuit. The accreted secondary literatures involve reconstruction of Hebraic sources, examination of the pertaining older Jewish exegetical traditions, and research into what were the newer apocalyptic appropriations. Some scholars argue that the references to the "birds of prey" are Midrashic-style permutations of Gn 15:11. In general, Mt 24:28 is understood to be about the fall of Jerusalem to the Romans, and Lk 17:37 about the Second Coming.

tian art, because of its visibility and immediate concreteness, can function as very effective material. The following are some examples:

—The icon of the "Virgin with Three Hands," called in Greek the "Tricherousa" (see those many eighteenth- and nineteenth-century versions in which the third hand has been assimilated to the Virgin herself[43]). Question—Why does the Virgin have, here, three hands?

—A painting or statue of Our Lady of Mt. Carmel (choose one with the characteristic addressed in the following question[44]). Question—Of the twelve stars around Mary's head, why is one star[45] hidden so it cannot be seen?

When a competent spiritual director supplies a *gong'an* that s/he judges (situationally) suitable for the advisee, s/he imparts it, and the advisee prays, then (rationally) thinks about it, and then—during meditation—lets it rest in the *dantien* (*tan t'ien*), a locus about three finger widths below the navel and two finger widths inside from the skin surface. (Thus, this practice resembles traditional Catholic *lectio divina*, but with the specific differences that the *gong'an* is puzzle-like and is "somatically" placed in the Chan/Zen manner.) After the meditation, the advisee should confide the

---

43. As in the eighteenth-century northern Russian "Tricherousa" icon displayed at http://campus.belmont.edu/honors/Virgins/virgins.html (accessed February 1, 2010). In earlier forms of the "Tricherousa" (and in the original icon housed at Mt. Athos), the third hand represents the severed and then miraculously restored hand of St. John Damascene (eighth century), whose hand had been severed by order of the caliph through the machinations of the Byzantine Emperor, an iconoclast who fiercely opposed St. John's defense of the veneration of icons. The Virgin Mary having then gone on to heal St. John's hand, the saint attached a silver replica of his own hand onto Mary's icon in gratitude.

44. Many paintings and statues of Our Lady of Mt. Carmel conceal one or more of the twelve stars (Rv 12:1, "and on her head a crown of twelve stars"), in most cases by placing one or more stars either behind her head or somehow within her head covering. By reviewing any of the many online "galleries" of artwork featuring Our Lady of Mt. Carmel, one can readily find several examples. In this regard, I recommend http://carmelnet.org > galleries > Carmelite image galleries > OLMC main > set 5 (and set 6), accessed December 2, 2009.

45. Or more than one, depending on the example the director chooses. And in some works of art, it is even the case that half of a star is concealed.

gong'an to the Holy Spirit's care and treasure it within the body, subconsciously bearing it about while traversing the normal routine of the day. During the rounds of the day, it is often the case that the *gong'an* rises spontaneously, demands one's full attention, and then subsides again. The hope is that sooner or later its "personalized" solution will spontaneously crystallize, either while one is alone or during a to-and-fro exchange with the director (or, indeed, anytime, since such epiphanies are known to sometimes occur at the most unexpected moments).

Perhaps some hypothetical examples can better demonstrate this process. It may be the case, for example, that the director senses that the advisee's spirituality is too self-satisfied. Persistent admonition having failed, the director may choose to hand-pick for this situation the *gong'an* "living body, dead body" cited above, and when imparting it remind the advisee that vultures eat dead bodies and eagles typically prefer live prey. Sooner or later, under the influence of the Holy Spirit, the truth may suddenly dawn: If there are vultures (*aetoi*) gathering around me, I am dying or dead (*ptōma*); if there are eagles (*aetoi*) gathering around me, I am a living body (*sōma*). I should no longer trust my inner-directed "intuition" of whether I am making spiritual progress or not—whether I am "dead" to actual graces[46] or "alive" to them. Rather, I must look to my *effects* in/on the world *outside*, and try in a selfless way to serve other-than-myself. "You will know them by their fruits" (Mt 7:16).

Or it may be the case, for example, that an advisee is too taken up in the activities of the world and would benefit from some "prompt" whereby the Holy Spirit may deign, possibly, to impart a flashing insight—some "golden key" that can open up for the advisee the "secret" (subjectively speaking) of true recollection for the remainder of her/his days! The director may choose, for example, a suitable icon of the Virgin with Three Hands and instruct the advisee to take it as a *gong'an*. The icon depicts the upper right hand of Mary underneath and supporting the Christ Child, implying her role as Mother. The Holy Child's right hand is raised in benediction,

---

46. "Actual grace," that is, grace which is *ad actum* ("to or for a specific act") is God's special intervention to help us perform a salutary act.

and Mary's left hand is open to receive that blessing, implying her role as Daughter. Mary's mysterious third hand is placed palm-inward on her midriff.

Without researching the traditional readings of this icon, the advisee should confront its imagery in a kind of naked simplicity and go through the meditative process as described earlier. Sooner or later the Holy Spirit may deign to inspire the advisee, who may come (for example) to the following personalized realization: Mary's third hand is held to her midriff, where she once in time and space carried the precious Embryo who matured and was born and is now in her arms. But Mary's third hand still tenderly clasps the site where the Child had been *because the Holy Spirit still engenders the Christ there.* The Child in Mary's arms will develop into manhood, will undertake the public ministry, suffer, die, resurrect, and ascend. But like Mary, because I am in sanctifying grace I bear about in myself, all the time, *the Christ* (who is present there in the company of the other two divine Persons, an indwelling "which is attributed in a particular manner to the Holy Spirit"[47]). Knowing this, how can I do otherwise than be recollected, consciously or subconsciously, all the time!

Or it may be the case that a Religious feels unappreciated, over-looked, and alone in his or her religious community, and this feeling of non-existence may make the vows, and especially the vow of celibacy, seem a crushing burden. Having exhausted other means of providing inspiration and guidance, the spiritual counselor may, for example, offer to the Religious, as a *gong'an,* one of the paintings or statutes of Our Lady of Mt. Carmel described above. Perhaps sooner or later in the meditative process, with God's grace, a solution such as the following may suddenly crystallize, empowering the Religious with firm insight and an indomitable will. The twelve stars circling Mary's head represent the twelve Apostles, and the

---

47. "Now this wonderful union [of God and the graced soul], which is properly called indwelling and differs only by reason of our condition or state from that in which God embraces and beautifies the citizens of heaven, is most certainly produced by the divine presence of the whole Trinity: 'We will come to them and make our home with them' [Jn 14:23]; nevertheless it is attributed in a particular manner to the Holy Spirit" (Leo XIII, *Divinum illud* [1897], CF #1994, DZ 3331).

hidden star among the twelve represents the Apostle John. John's star is hidden behind Mary's head because he among the twelve is the only one known to be celibate—he is the Virgin Apostle who by the very fact of his consecrated virginity belongs to the Virgin Mary in a special way ("'Woman, behold, your son!' Then he said to the disciple, 'Behold, your mother!' And from that hour the disciple took her to his own home," Jn 19:26, 27). John's glory is precisely that he is effaced by Mary's face, so a viewer looking at the Carmelite painting sees Mary where otherwise the hidden star would appear. Because of his or her consecrated chastity, the Religious in a special way can exclaim John Paul II's Marian motto, "Totus Tuus," O Maria!—Oh Mary, "totally yours!" Mary occludes John precisely so her shadow can revalorize his darkness.

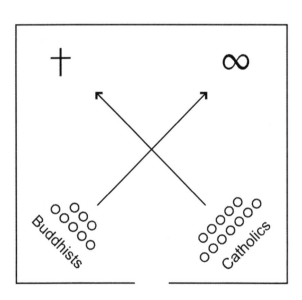

Regarding the above diagram, see footnote 4, p. 184.

A Conclusion:
Closing/Opening

THIS MONOGRAPH draws to its close by way of another quadrature,[1] for my proposal is that sometimes when Buddhists and Catholics meditate together, they arrange themselves (in "Zen-sitting" posture when possible; or alternatively the Catholics can kneel[2]) in the same room but in respective rows that are at right angles to each other. Indeed, the Buddhists can face toward a statue of Buddha (or another appropriate Buddhist symbol) and the Catholics toward a Crucifix (or another appropriate Catholic symbol). Thus the respective anterior foci or force-fields of the two rows intersect each other in a kind of X or chiasm, marking the difference between the two religions yet involving the two religions in each other. Such a configuration is in accordance, it seems to me, with Vatican stipulations that "prayer" *between* religions be arranged in "multi-religious" rather than "interreligious" formats because religions differ as to their spiritual objectives.[3] At the same time, the configuration models the several themes of this monograph in ways that the reader at this point can recognize. Finally,

1. See diagram on facing page.
2. Of course other postures should be accommodated too, depending on circumstances.
3. Benedict XVI already made this clear in his book *Fede, verità, tolleranza: Il cristianesimo e le religioni del mondo* (Siena, Italy: Cantagalli, 2003) when he was still prefect of the Congregation for the Doctrine of the Faith; the Italian book is a translation of his original German, *Glaube-Wahrheit-Toleranz: Das Christentum und die Weltreligionen* (Freiburg im Breisgau: Herder, 2003). The subsequent English translation is *Truth and Tolerance: Christian Belief and World Religions*, trans. Henry Taylor (San Francisco, CA: Ignatius P., 2004). (See also ZENIT, http://www.zenit.org/English/vizualizza.phtml?sid=41665, accessed September 30, 2003). As pope, he on several occasions made these specifications official. By a "multireligious format," Benedict XVI means that when diverse religions are party to joint

183

the rectangle has an opening, because all quadratures in this world refuse to close up, especially sacred ones.[4]

When steel is red hot, you can shape it into a vessel. But unless you wait for the fire to burn it red hot, you cannot mold the metal; you haven't out-waited the fire.
—"Commentary: Part 9," to *The Dharma Jewel Platform Sutra*, chapter 10[5]

". . . learn to abide attentively and wait lovingly
upon God in that state of quiet, . . ."
—St. John of the Cross[6]

In alert restfulness,
but diversely,
the Buddhists are waiting,[7] // and the Catholics are waiting.

(prayer or meditative) sessions, the spatial configurations should somehow represent the defining differences among them in regard to religious assumption and purpose. To do otherwise, in the pope's estimation, would be dishonest and furthermore could convey the impression that the diverse religions agree where in fact they fundamentally disagree.

4. Why eight Buddhist meditators and twelve Catholic meditators in this diagram? (see p. 182). The numbers are of course symbolic. Eight is a sacred number in Buddhism—The Eightfold Path, the eighth day of the fourth month (Sakyamuni Buddha's birthday in Chinese and Korean Mahayana), etc. (Note: eight "on its side," called the "lemniscate" [from Gk.], is the symbol of "infinity.") Twelve is a sacred number in the Bible, both Old Testament and New Testament—the Twelve Tribes of Israel, the Twelve Apostles, the twelve stars around the "Woman clothed with the Sun" (Mary/the Church), etc.

5. See "Commentary: Part 9" to *The Dharma Jewel Platform Sutra*, chapter 10, in *Buddhist Door* (online Buddhist magazine), Vol. 8, No. 1 (Hong Kong: Tung Ling Kok Yuen), available at http://www.buddhistdoor.com (use *Buddhist Door*'s search engine to find the reference).

6. Bk. II, ch. 12, *Ascent of Mt. Carmel*, trans. and ed. E. Allison Peers, 3rd revised edition (Garden City, NY: Image Books, Doubleday, 1958), p. 218.

7. On Buddhist "waiting," please see the very end of this monograph's Part Two.

Appendix One

Mazzocchi padre Luciano sx

ミラノ日本人カトリック教会
cappellania cattolica giapponese

La Stella del Mattino
dialogo Vangelo e Zen

27 marzo 2013

A T T E S T A T O
ai sacerdoti, religiosi e laici della Chiesa Cattolica

Il sottoscritto, p. Luciano Mazzocchi, presidente dell'Associazione "Vangelo e Zen" [1] certifica che

Robert Magliola, nato il 7 ottobre 1940

ha compiuto assiduamente la pratica dello Zazen sotto la mia direzione, per due mesi e mezzo, presso il centro Vangelo e Zen (Via Achille Grandi, 41, Desio, 20832 – Monza Brianza – Italia).

Certifico pure la sua ferma decisione di continuare la pratica dello Zazen presso questo centro "Vangelo e Zen" anche nel futuro.

Robert Magliola ha espletato un lungo cammino di formazione alla meditazione sotto la guida di riconosciuti maestri buddhisti in Asia e in America.

Certifico che Robert Magliola è qualificato a insegnare la meditazione come trasmessa nello Zen e in altre forme orientali, nella spiritualità del dialogo promosso dal Concilio Vaticano II.

Fraterni saluti nel legame della fede,

p. Luciano Mazzocchi sx

---

1 L'Associazione "Vangelo e Zen" fu fondata il 19 giugno 2008 da p. Luciano Mazzocchi, già missionario saveriano in Giappone per 19 anni e attualmente cappellano della comunità cattolica giapponese dell'arcidiocesi di Milano, e da Jiso Forzani monaco dello Zen Soto, attualmente responsabile della direzione dello Zen Soto per l'Europa, insieme con 5 laici cristiani e non, italiani e giapponesi. Nel 1999, il cardinal Joseph Ratzinger prefetto della Congregazione per la dottrina della fede, espresse per iscritto la sua approvazione e il suo incoraggiamento.
0362.300350
via Pattari 6 (20122) MILANO - Tel. 02.00502207 - cell. 338.1011101
e-mail: luciano@lastelladelmattino.org - www.lastelladelmattino.org

ENGLISH TRANSLATION: Certification granted to Robert Magliola by Rev. L. Mazzocchi, SX (St. Francis Xavier Foreign Mission Society), Association "Gospel and Zen," Italy.

March 27, 2013

CERTIFICATION

To Priests, Religious and Laity of the Catholic Church

The undersigned, Fr. Luciano Mazzocchi, president of the Association "Gospel and Zen,"*certifies that

Robert Magliola, born October 7 1940

has assiduously completed, during two and one-half months, the regimen of Zen practice under my direction, at the Center "Gospel and Zen" (#41 Via Achille Grandi, Desio, 20832, Monza Brianza, Italy).

I testify as well to his firm decision to continue the practice of Zen at this Center "Gospel and Zen" also in the future.

Robert Magliola has brought to fulfillment a long path of formation in meditation under the guidance of recognized Buddhist masters in Asia and America.

I certify that Robert Magliola is qualified to teach meditation as transmitted in Zen and in other Oriental modes, according to the spirituality of dialogue promoted by Vatican Council II.

Fraternal salutations in the union of the Faith,

Fr. Luciano Mazzocchi, SX

---

*The Association "Gospel and Zen" was founded on June 19, 2008, by Fr. Luciano Mazzocchi, Xaverian missionary formerly in Japan for nineteen years and presently chaplain of the Japanese Catholic community in the archdiocese of Milan; and by Jiso Forzani, Soto Zen monk, presently director of Soto Zen in Europe; together with five laypersons, Christian and non-Christian, Italian and Japanese. In 1999, Cardinal Joseph Ratzinger, prefect of the Congregation for the Doctrine of the Faith, expressed in writing his approval and his encouragement.

Appendix Two

My third book, *On Deconstructing Life-Worlds: Buddhism, Christianity, Culture*, was published in spring of 1997 by Scholars Press, the publishing arm—at the time—of the American Academy of Religion (it has been published since the year 2000 by Oxford UP, which had become the newly contracted publisher for the American Academy of Religion). In the early summer of 1997, I sent a copy of my new book to Jacques Derrida in France, since from 1994 onward I had been visiting him at his office during his annual spring-quarter teaching at the University of California, Irvine, and he typically welcomed what I wrote. My appointment at the (interfaith) Graduate School of Philosophy and Religions, Assumption University of Thailand (1994–1999), enabled me to return to the United States each year in late spring to tend my widowed dear mother, then in her nineties. My consultations with Jacques Derrida revolved around the topic of his own thought in relation to the ongoing philosophical and theological scenes. He knew very little about Buddhism, so my comparisons of "Derridean" thought-strategies and those of Buddhist philosophy, especially *Prāsaṅgika Mādhyamaka*, seemed to intrigue him. He had read, long before, my *Derrida on the Mend* (1984), and its treatment of Nagarjuna had whetted his interest already back then. When he received the gift copy of my new book, he generously gave of his time to read it promptly and closely: he replied with a robust affirmation of my work and its understanding of his thought. A photocopy of his letter to me appears on the following page.

Jacques Derrida
École des Hautes Études en Sciences Sociales
54, Bvd Raspail
75006 Paris

24, rue des Bergeronnettes
91130 Ris-Orangis

Ris-Orangis, 6 juillet 1997

Cher Robert ,

Quel livre magnifique ! J'y suis plongé depuis quelques jours. Je m'émerveille et j'apprends beaucoup, je joue beaucoup à vous regarder jouer si sérieusement avec toutes ces richesses (je ne parle pas de mes textes, bien sûr, mais de tous les autres, de tant et tant d'autres.)

Ce que vous faites de ma petite histoire, de El-Biar à Khôra, de mon tr jusqu'au tr d'Aurobindo, traverse tant de mondes que je dois m'accrocher et m'essouffler derrière vous pour faire semblant de savoir où je vais.

Votre profondeur, votre audace et votre indépendance m'éblouissent et m'impressionnent. Elles me rappellent aussi le souvenir de cette heureuse rencontre de Irvine.

Sachez que malgré tant de distances, et à supposer que ce mot ait encore un sens et que la chose soit désirable, je me sens très *proche* de vous, je continue de vous lire et je vous remercie du fond du coeur.

J'espère avoir la chance de vous revoir et de vous lire encore (ces jours derniers je parlais de vous avec Stephen Barker, de passage à Paris, et c'était bon.)

Avec mes voeux cordiaux et ma fidèle affection

Jacques Derrida

ENGLISH TRANSLATION: Jacques Derrida's Letter to R. Magliola,
July 6, 1997

Jacques Derrida
École des Hautes Études en Sciences Sociales
54, Bvd Raspail
75006 Paris

24, rue des Bergeronnettes
91130 Ris-Orange

Ris-Orange, July 6, 1997

Dear Robert,

What a magnificent book ! I have been diving into it for several days. I
marvel and learn much. I play much at watching you play so seriously
with all these riches (I am not speaking of my texts, surely, but of all the
others, so many many others.)
What you do with my little history, from El-Biar to Khôra,* from my
tr** through to the tr of Aurobindo, traverses so many worlds that I
must hold on and be out of breath in order to appear as if I know where
I am going.
Your profundity, your boldness, and your independence amaze and
impress me. They also revive the memory of our happy meeting at Irvine.
Please know that despite the distance, and with the supposition that the
word still has a meaning and is to be wished for, I sense myself very *near*
to you, I continue to read you and I thank you from the bottom of my
heart.

I hope to have the opportunity to see you again (in recent days, on my
way to Paris, it was good to speak with Stephen Barker about you).

With my best wishes and my faithful affection

Jacques Derrida

---

* El-Biar is the name of the Algerian village where Derrida was born. It turns out to be an anagram for the Bible's *beliar* (Gk.), called "belial" in English Bibles; and for apocalyptic literature's *Beliar* ("Belial"). My *On Deconstructing Life-Worlds: Buddhism, Christianity, Culture* (p. 157) calls this irony to Derrida's attention. Derrida in his work cites Plato's *Khôra*, but *On Deconstructing Life-Worlds* (ibid.) also interprets the word as a pun for the Bible's family/figure named "Korah."

** Derrida's **tr** is a "floating graphic trait." A graphic trait is a consonant cluster treated as an element, independent of whatever meaning-unit it happens to constitute when it joins with a vowel; thus, for example, "transfer," "intransitive," "train" (all from Lat. *trans*, "across"), but also "tree" (from ME < OE) and "tref" (from Yid. < Heb.). For Derrida, floating graphic traits act-out that which wends the way *between* meaning and non-meaning. In ODLW, I deploy them to represent the mysterious recurrences that some Catholics sense in their personal lives—recurrences that seem to signal a divine meaning, but a meaning somehow hidden from rational explanation or interpretation. I took care to design ODLW in such a way that some Buddhists, reading the "same" text, may construe the recurrences to represent the elusive and obscure unfolding of personal karma in their lives. For the Catholic, the uncanny can represent the hidden workings of divine providence. For a Buddhist, the uncanny can represent the hidden exactitudes of karma.

MINISTÈRE DE L'ÉDUCATION NATIONALE,
DE L'ENSEIGNEMENT SUPÉRIEUR
ET DE LA RECHERCHE
ÉCOLE DES HAUTES ÉTUDES EN SCIENCES SOCIALES
54, BOULEVARD RASPAIL - 75006 PARIS
Jacques Derrida

RÉPUBLIQUE FRANÇAISE
POSTES

Air mail

Robert Magliola
% F. Magliola
100 Barbados Dr. S. (H.C.B.)
Toms River
N. Jersey 08757-4024
Etats-Unis

Bibliographical Note

FOR NON-SPECIALIST but serious-minded researchers in Buddhism, a selected bibliography in Buddhist Studies can be found on pp. 50–51. Listed in it are authoritative dictionaries and encyclopedias of Buddhism, collections of Buddhist scriptures and other original Buddhist sources, and a compendium of readings in formal Buddhist philosophy. These can be supplemented, of course, by the many other scholarly Buddhist references that appear throughout this book.

For non-specialist but serious-minded researchers in Catholicism, a bibliography of authoritative sources of Magisterial documents is supplied in note 36 on p.56. A list of the several English-language translations of the Bible used in this book, accompanied by a short explanation of the norms governing their selection, is supplied in note 40 on pp. 57–58. A selected bibliography of Catholic encyclopedias, and of recommended readings in twentieth-century Catholic theology, can be found on pp. 51–52. References to many other Catholic sources are detailed throughout this book.

INDEX

Accattoli, Luigi, 142
Alexander VII, Pope, 102
alteri Christi, 101, 127
Amantes de la Croix, 115
analogia entis, 162
anātman/anattā, 67, 76–78
Angela of Foligno, Blessed, 154
anthropomorphosis, 116, 159
aporia, 124, 153
Apostolic College, 58 (defined)
apostolic constitution, 62
"appointing" of differences, 27, 29–30
arahant (P.)/*arhat* (Skt.), 39
Aristotelianism, 21, 33
Asymmetry, 155–156. *See also* dissymmetry
Atonement, Friars and Sisters of the, 87
Attachment, 77, 119. *See also* three roots of evil
Augustine, Saint, 69, 72
Awakening (*bodhi*), 23, 36, 39, 64; *sammā-saṃbodhi* ("full and perfect awakening" [P.]), 38

Balthasar, Hans Urs von, 51
Baptism, 47, 59, 63–64, 76
Barciacchi, Enzo, 5, 7
Barnes, SJ, Rev. Michael, 133
Batchelor, Stephen, 135
Bateson, Gregory, 32, 141–142
Beatific vision, 45, 72–74, 83, 120, 156; and the Blessed Virgin Mary, 74–75; not a subject-object relation, 168–169
Beatitude, supra-mundane: in Buddhism, 36, 120; in Catholicism, 36–37, 70
Benedict XVI, Pope, 21, 107, 145–150, 183–184
Bennington, Geoffrey, 157
Bernard, Saint, 74–75

Index

Husserl, Edmund, 31
Hypostases, the: Catholic doctrine, 153–156. *See also* Father, the First
Hypostasis ("Person")-, the; Son, the Second Hypostasis ("Person")-,
the; Holy Spirit, the Third Hypostasis ("Person")-, the
Hypostatic Union (Catholic doctrine), 149

images (in linguistic theory), 148
inclusivism: defined, 23–24; locus for Catholics in Buddhist doctrinal
paradigms, 85–101; locus for Buddhists in Catholic doctrinal paradigm, 101–109; whether Catholic inclusivism offends against justice
and compassion, 142 n 12
indwelling, divine, 181
infallibility: two modes of, 61–62
infinite states, the four, 94
instrumentalism, 134
intentionality, 119–122; defined, 119

Jäger, OSB, Rev. Willigis, 176
James of Milan (Giacomo da Milano), 154
Jayatilleke, K. N., 86
Jesus, the Christ (the Incarnate Word): hypostatic union, 149; universal
and unique Savior, 62–64, 115; Ven. Thich Nhat Hanh's apprehended
relationship to, 99–101; ways some Sri Lankan Buddhist monks relate
to, 126
John of the Cross, Carmelite, Saint, 184
John Paul II, Pope, 111, 142
joint-meditation, Buddhist-Catholic, 19–20, 111–122, 182–184; "locus"
where meditative foci can overlap, 131–135; proposed spiritual prepara-
tions for Catholics, leading up to joint-meditation, 132–133; "waiting,"
130–135 *passim*
Journal of Comparative Theology, 11
Journal of the Japan Society for Buddhist-Christian Studies, 87
Judgment, the (Catholic doctrine): general and individual, 81, 122

kalpa: defined, 93
kamma (P.)/*karma* (Skt.), 46–48, 78–80, 82; Ven. Thich Nhat Hanh on,
98–101.
Kamuf, Peggy, 25–27
Keating, OCSO, Rev. Thomas, 170
Kelly, CSsR, Rev. Anthony, xiv

Index

responsibility, 123–125
Resurrection, the, 45, 105, 151
Revelation (in Catholic teaching), 129, 143–156; defined, 45
Richardson, CSJP, Sr. Janet, 171
Ryan, CSP, Rev. Thomas, 87

Sacraments, the seven, 70; defined, 76, 118
Saddhatissa, Ven. Dr., 53, 79
sādhana, Tantric, 171
St. Ottilien, Abbey of, 87
St. Joseph (MA), Abbey of, 87
St. Mary (IL), Benedictine nuns of the Monastery of, 87
St. Paul ("Paulists"), congregation of, 87
Samantabhadra, Buddha, 95
"samenesses," 22, 32–33, 35–109 *passim*, 130–131
"Same-power," 44, 64–69
samsaric cycle, 46, 77
Scheuer, SJ, Rev. Jacques, 87
Scola, Angelo Cardinal, 52
Scripture (the Christian Bible in Catholic usage), sacred: *hundreds of scriptural references appear throughout this text—See* section Biblio-graphical Note at the head of this Index for a selective but extensive scriptural bibliography; allegorical *vis-à-vis* historical-critical reading of, 177; appropriation of textual/redactional/recensional criticism for Catholic *gong'an* meditation, 177–178; Magliola, sample publications in, 13 n15; New Testament "born in the bosom of the Church," 59–60; on inerrancy of, 60, 143; on a Messianic psalm, 163–164; progressive comprehension of 150; translations and ambiguity, 57–58
Second coming (Parousia), the, 59, 75, 81, 161
Self-power, 23, 36, 43, 46, 52–55, 129
Seung Sahn, Zen Master, 132
Sheng-yen, Ven. Master, 54
Shogaku Shunryu (Suzuki Roshi), Ven., 176
sin, mortal, 70
skandha (Skt.)/*khandha* (P.): defined, 77
Siddhattha Gotama (P.)/Siddhartha Gautama (Skt.), Buddha, (in Maha-yana Buddhism, also often called Śakyamuni ["the Sakyan sage"]), 38, 40–41, 184; as the Tathagata, 91
"sign of the X," the, 147–151
signifieds and signifiers (linguistics), 148

Made in the USA
Lexington, KY
30 May 2016